THE POLITICS OF
MILITARY REVOLUTION
IN KOREA

THE POLITICS
OF MILITARY REVOLUTION
IN KOREA

by Se-Jin Kim

The University of North Carolina Press
Chapel Hill

Library of Congress Catalog Card Number 71–123101
ISBN 0–8078–1168–8
Manufactured in the United States of America
Printed by Heritage Printers, Inc., Charlotte, N. C.

To my father

PREFACE

Of approximately eighty nations which have attained independence in the past quarter century, more than one-third have undergone violent political revolution. Such twentieth-century vicissitudes have also affected Korea, once a small hermit kingdom in Asia. In fact, this tiny and unfortunate land has experienced a series of cataclysmic events almost unmatched by other nations. In 1910, succumbing to the expansionism of Imperial Japan, Korea lost its independence. Not until 1945 was it liberated from colonial rule. The termination of Japanese dominance, however, was followed immediately by the military occupation of the country by the United States and Soviet Russia. When the cold war between the two powers began to loom large, the 38th parallel, the temporary demarcation line for the two occupation zones, turned into a seemingly permanent line of partition. The Northern half, under Soviet direction, became a communist police state, while the Southern half, under American tutelage, emerged as a member of the free world. Less than two years after the acquisition of separate identities as the Republic of Korea and the People's Republic of Korea, these ideologically opposed halves were caught up in a war of fratricide. Even after the cease-fire agreement in 1953, there has been an incessant and unabated threat of renewed conflict.

What resulted from this state of belligerence was the rise of a military leviathan, making massive garrison states of both halves. This sudden emergence of a modern military establishment was to have many significant political and social ramifications. Since the Confucian practice still persisted in upholding "the man of letters" and downgrading "the man of the sword," inevitable social friction arose between the young and new military officers and the old and conservative civilian elites. Also, since the military possessed the ultimate means of political power and subscribed to a more modern and pragmatic outlook, it became a new political force that no leaders could overlook.

In such an obtuse political, social, and military environment, South Korea had to undertake the exacting task of nation-building. However, those civilians who assumed the mantle of leadership during the first thirteen years of the new nation failed in their twin tasks of (1) creating an efficient political institution to articulate the public's demands and the nation's needs and (2) conjuring up a political ideology to capture and stir the imagination of the populace. Instead, they succumbed to their own inabilities and petty political desires.

In April 1960, the Student Revolution toppled Rhee's First Republic, which was guilty of a variety of political misdemeanors and economic neglect. The Second Republic (1960–1961), with John M. Chang at the helm, was unable to arrest the prevalent social and economic ills which gave rise to the political and economic crisis. This volatile situation, plus intramilitary dysfuncton, prompted the military to seize power in May 1961, thus ending the thirteen-year civil rule.

Normally, an overthrow of civilian government by the military is considered a major reversal in the development of political democracy. In a state where a strong representative heritage is lacking and where fundamental political and social changes are occurring at an unprecedented tempo, the rise of the military to power has ramifications other than a simple palace coup or a surging of militarism such as that which occurred in Japan and Germany before World War II. Military ascendance, in many cases, might portend a resurgence of a progressive authoritarian and administrative system and the simultaneous retreat from the excesses of a brief and unsuccessful parliamentary system. Indeed, the military coup in Korea was staged in the name of restoring constitutional democracy—a goal which, to some extent, has been achieved.

The baffling ambivalence of the military in politics—the overthrow of the legitimate government in defense of democracy—calls for a serious study of the military's role in nation-building. This book will attempt, first, to analyze the socioeconomic and political causes of the military revolution in 1961 in Korea; second, to discuss civil–military relations with reference to the conflict of interests between the military and civilian elites; third, to delve into the intramilitary dysfunction and the background of the leading military figures and thus show the military's reasons for staging a coup d'etat; fourth, to examine the impact of the military's involvement in civil politics as an innovating force; and, fifth, to look at the Korean military experience in the broader context of the worldwide military phenomenon today.

The original idea was conceived in 1961 when I was attending a seminar on Southeast Asia directed by Professor Lucian W. Pye of the Massachusetts Institute of Technology. Later, the idea was developed and expanded into a doctoral dissertation for the University of Massachusetts in 1966. Because of the enthusiastic encouragement from Mrs. Alice L. Hsieh of Rand Corporation (now with the Institute of Defense Analysis), who acted as my major adviser during the time she was in residence at the university as a visiting lecturer, the task of converting the dissertation to a book was undertaken. In the summer of 1966, additional research necessary for this publication was conducted in Korea while I was on sabbatical leave from Eastern Kentucky University. Time to revise and update the manuscript became available in 1968 when I received a faculty fellowship from the Cooperative Program in International Studies, conducted jointly by The University of North Carolina at Chapel Hill and Duke University with a grant from the Ford Foundation.

Acknowledgements would run, literally, into hundreds of names, so only a few persons to whom I owe particular debts can be recognized. To Professors Allen Ragen, Vernon Warren, Jr., and Kathleen M. Smith, my former colleagues at Eastern Kentucky University, and to Mrs. Francine Lerner of Durham, North Carolina, I express my thanks for their many valuable editorial suggestions; to Mr. David Steinberg of the Agency for International Development, I extend my appreciation for his effort in finding a publisher; to Professor Glenn Paige of the University of Hawaii and to Professor John P. Lovell of Indiana University, I feel deeply indebted for their many valuable critiques; to Senator Earle C. Clements, I express my gratitude for his unfailing encouragement from the very beginning of this work; to my immediate relatives and other friends, I bow my head for their untiring efforts for having located and furnished much valuable data not otherwise available in the United States; and to my school, North Carolina Central University, I express my thanks for granting a fund necessary for typing the final draft.

Finally, this study could not have been possible without the devotion and sacrifice of my wife, Heasun, who typed the entire manuscript many times over while rearing two small children. At the end, she was graceful enough to suggest that this book be dedicated to my late father, in whom my family found moral values and spiritual solace.

For the vexing problem of transliterating the Korean sounds, the McCune-Reischauer romanization system was used unless the individual has adopted a Westernized version (Syngman Rhee and John M. Chang, for example) or has done his own romanization (Park Chung-hee and Kim Jong-pil, for example).

CONTENTS

LIST OF TABLES

ABBREVIATIONS

CIA (Korea)	Central Intelligence Agency
CIC	Counter Intelligence Corps
DNP	Democratic National Party
DRP	Democratic Republican Party
JMPM	Joint Military Provost Marshal
KDP	Korean Democratic Party
KIP	Korean Independent Party
MRC	Military Revolutionary Council
NDC	National Defense Corps
NDP	National Democratic Party
OCS	Officers Candidate School
ROKA	Republic of Korea Army
SCNR	Supreme Council for National Reconstruction
UNCOK	United Nations Command in Korea
USAMGIK	United States Army Military Government in Korea

THE POLITICS OF
MILITARY REVOLUTION
IN KOREA

POLITICAL AND ECONOMIC LEGACIES OF THE PAST AND THE BIRTH OF THE REPUBLIC OF KOREA

Emergence of the military into Korean politics in 1961 was more than a historical accident. It can be postulated that the rise of the military is a reappearance of the administrative authoritarian system long ingrained in the Korean body politic. If one is to understand the basic and philosophical import of the military phenomenon today, the sociopolitical forces that undergird the Korean political foundation must be examined. Therefore, it is important to survey briefly the endemic political orientation and the major political-economic stresses that existed prior to the birth of a new republic in 1948.

Authoritarian Legacy from the Monarchical Past

The Korean monarchy which lasted until 1910 resembled early seventeenth-century British Stuart or eighteenth-century French Bourbon absolutism. With a vague notion of their divine right to rule, based upon the mythological legend of Tan-gun, Korean kings traditionally had claimed absolute authority over their subjects.[1] According to the primeval legend regarding the genesis of Korea, Tan-gun, the first ruler of the kingdom, was a semidivine being born from the mating of the Sun God (the ruling deity of heaven who descended to earth in the disguise of man) and the holy animal (she-bear) already in existence on earth. This purely mythical basis for a belief in a heaven-oriented kingdom had served throughout Korean history.[2]

Such a primitive concept of divine-oriented political authority was systematically reinforced by the arrival of Confucianism in the thirteenth century.[3] It taught that the king is "an intermediary between heaven and mankind." Hence, as "the son of heaven," the king is entrusted with a so-called "mandate of heaven" to rule in order to bring about harmony between the divine and human spheres.[4] Implicit in the teachings of Confucianism is the belief that the king is responsible only to Heaven for his performance, not to his subjects, who are only "children" of the king.[5] According to classic Confucianism, a king's "children" could overthrow the "son of heaven" if he violated the divine mandate, but in Korea this concept of the "mandate of heaven" was modified by the mythology of the divine-oriented ruler who could not be overthrown, no matter how irresponsible and tyrannical. Even the rebel leader of the

1. Cornelius Osgood, *The Koreans and Their Culture* (New York: Ronald Press, 1951), p. 246. Osgood draws a parallel between the Korean version of divine-right political authority and the Japanese Mikado.

2. Cho Ji-hoon, "Tradition of the Korean Thought," *Koreana Quarterly*, II, no. 1 (Spring 1960), 72–74. See also Kim Kyu-t'aik, "The Behavior Patterns of the Rulers and the Ruled in Korean Politics," *Korean Affairs*, I, no. 3 (1962), 320–21.

3. Confucianism, though originally introduced in 221 A.D., replaced Buddhism as the predominant religion with the coming of the Yi Dynasty in 1392. See Yang Key P. and Gregory Henderson, "An Outline of History of Korean Confucianism," *Journal of Asian Studies*, XVIII, no. 1 and no. 2 (November 1958 and February 1959), 77–101 and 259–76.

4. Franz H. Michael and George E. Taylor, *The Far East in the Modern World* (New York: Holt, Rinehart, and Winston, 1956), p. 46.

5. M. Frederick Nelson, *Korea and the Old Orders in Eastern Asia* (Baton Rouge: Louisiana State University Press, 1946), p. 8.

Tong-hak revolt in 1893–1894, a mass popular rebellion against the court, accepted the idea that the monarch was infallible. He said:

Our present king is virtuous, filial, compassionate, and loving. He is also divinely intelligent and consecratedly wise. Only if the officials were also wise and virtuous in assisting the king and seconding the brilliant one, we would have attained the days of Tao-shun and the rule of Wen-ching.[6]

Only when the monarch, out of weakness, invited regency or support from influential members of the court was there any check on absolute monarchy.[7] Even in that situation, the sanctity of the monarchy was not violated, and the royal institution was seldom challenged. Since the Silla unification of Korea in 668 A.D., there have been only two disruptions to dynastic succession; but neither resulted in any significant social or economic change.

The Korean people were also strongly influenced by the anti-materialistic philosophy of Taoism and Buddhism, which led them to suppress their acquisitive instincts and hedonistic desires by seeking refuge in the mystical doctrine of Buddhism and fatalistic quietism of Taoism.[8] In such a state, assertion of political and economic equality by the populace was not conceivable. Koreans placed trust in the ruling body to provide their guidance and protection.

After two millenniums without any basic change in political, economic, and social conditions, the first series of reform movements (Tong-hak and Kae-hyŏk) dedicated to a modernization of decadent and stagnant political institutions began to emerge. These originated during the latter part of the nineteenth century, when Korea was becoming a pawn of international politics in the wake of repeated defeats of Imperial China, the traditional guardian of Korean autonomy. However, the intransi-

6. Lee Chong-sik, *The Politics of Korean Nationalism* (Berkeley: University of California Press, 1963), p. 29.

7. Pyŏn Young-t'ai, *Korea, My Country* (Seoul: International Cultural Association of Korea, 1954), p. 109.

8. See Kang Young-hill, *The Grass Roof* (New York: Scribner, 1931). Mr. Kang made perhaps the most lucid presentation of traditional values of the Korean people ever to be offered.

gence of the declining monarch of the Yi Dynasty and the loss of Korea's independence to Japan in 1910 prevented the success of these movements.[9]

Japanese Rule and Its Legacies, 1910–1945

For the first thirty-two years of Japanese domination, 1910–1942, Korea was administered as a Japanese imperial colony under the supervision of the Overseas Ministry. The imperial representative, the Governor-General, ruled Korea with a massive network of highly disciplined Japanese military and Japanese civilian police.

After a bloody revolt in 1919, Koreans were effectively excluded from the most important political policy-making bodies and were discouraged from participating in any organized political activity.[10] Not until 1942, just three years before the end of World War II, was Korea fully incorporated as an integral part of Japan and Koreans given full Japanese citizenship.

While Korea was under Japanese administrative control, the political prerequisites to representative government—namely, organized political parties and interest groups—were effectively prevented from developing. The only organizations not under direct governmental control were business guilds, and they only served to facilitate Japanese economic exploitation.[11] Even religious organizations, particularly those connected with the Christian church, were forced to close down during World War II.[12] The net effect of the Japanese administration, as Professor George McCune aptly remarked, was "a thirty-five-year intermission on political responsibility and administration experience."[13]

9. For more information on the Tong-hak rebellion and the Kai-hyŏk movement, see Lee Chong-sik, *The Politics of Korean Nationalism*, pp. 13–33.

10. Andrew J. Grajdanzev, *Korea Looks Ahead* (New York: Institute of Pacific Relations, 1944), p. 238.

11. George M. McCune, *Korea Today* (Cambridge, Mass.: Harvard University Press, 1951), p. 278.

12. As a member of a Presbyterian church, this writer personally witnessed the conversion of the church into a military storage house in Pyong-yang, Korea, in 1943.

13. George M. McCune, *Post-War Government and Politics in Korea*

Barred from organizing political pressure groups and denied any role in the decision-making process in the formal governmental structure, the Korean populace expected the ruling body to perform every conceivable role. The inevitable result from such a situation was the continuation of paternalism and the servant-master relationship between the government and the citizenry. This is what prevailed under Korea's monarchical system, and the ruling Japanese found it to their advantage to perpetuate it.

Unlike the old Korean monarchy, Japanese rule in Korea was highly effective. It instituted a sweeping reorganization of the governmental system and replaced the old apparatus with a modern and functional Prussian model. Koreans then began to enjoy a highly efficient administrative process hitherto unknown to them.

This situation contributed to adjustment problems after World War II. While the populace continually expected the governmental machinery to function as well as before, there were only a few trained Koreans who could fill the huge vacuum in government and industry that followed in the wake of Japanese evacuation. Administrative effectiveness was further hampered by economic disruption resulting from the severance of economic ties with Japan and the exit of the Japanese, who had occupied all the important managerial positions in Korean industry.

Economic Legacy

Japanese economic policy in Korea was dictated by typical nineteenth-century imperialistic economic principles. Thus the Korean economy was to be developed so that Japan could be provided with a source of raw materials, particularly foodstuffs for its burgeoning population, and so that Korea could be a marketplace for the rapidly expanding Japanese economy.[14] Capital investments were carefully controlled

(Gainesville: University of Florida, 1947), p. 610. For a penetrating study of Japanese rule, see Morgan E. Clippinger, "Problems of the Modernization of Korea," *Asiatic Research Bulletin*, VI, no. 6 (September 1963), 1–11.

14. For more information on the Japanese economic policy, see Andrew

through collusion between the Zaibatzu and the Japanese Overseas Department. By careful manipulation of the Korean economy, the country became fully dependent upon Japan, politically as well as economically.[15] Moreover, the desperate attempt of the Japanese to mobilize all available human and material resources in Korea during the latter years of the war forced the economy almost to the breaking point and caused an unprecedented inflationary spiral which led to the depletion of many basic resources.

It was easy to predict that the evacuation of the Japanese from Korea would lead to almost total economic disintegration. Since the Korean economy had been developed as an appendage of the Japanese economy, it would be no more than a decapitated body, once ties with Japan were broken. Without the Japanese managers and technicians, such key industries as transportation, communication, electricity, and the manufacture of fertilizers could not be operated.[16]

In view of such adverse political and economic legacies, the political viability of an undivided Korea was a questionable one at best. But even before the Korean people attempted independent nation-building, an unofficial arrangement between the U.S. and the U.S.S.R. at Yalta in 1945 divided the country into two sectors of allied occupation.[17]

The Partition of Korea and the U.S. Military Government South of the 38th Parallel

What began as a temporary partition of Korea gradually took on an air of permanence. The chill of the developing cold

---

J. Grajdanzev, *Modern Korea; Her Economic and Social Development under the Japanese* (New York: Institute of Pacific Relations, 1944).

15. Ch'oi Mun-hwan, "The Path to Democracy: A Historical Review of the Korean Economy," *Koreana Quarterly*, III, no. 1 (Summer, 1961), 59–61.

16. See the excerpts from the *Conlon Report*, which appeared in the *Congressional Record*, 86th Cong., 2d sess., 1961, vol. 106, appendix, p. 1640.

17. Leonard M. Bertsch, "Korea Partition Prevents Economic Recovery," *Foreign Policy Bulletin*, XXVIII, no. 16 (January 28, 1949), 3–4. Regarding the partition of Korea, see U.S. State Department, *The Conference at Yalta and Malta: 1945* (Washington, D.C.: Government Printing Office, 1955), pp. 358–59.

war began to be felt at the conference table of the Joint U.S.–
U.S.S.R. Commission set up in Moscow in the winter of 1945
to resolve the Korean question.[18] After the complete breakdown
of negotiations on Korea between the two occupying powers
in the winter of 1947, the two Koreas were thrown into two
different tutelages: the South under the United States and the
North under the Soviet Union.

As a result, South Korea became one of those unwanted postwar problems which the U.S. had neither plans nor trained
personnel to handle. An Army officer of the day said: "When
XXIV Corps, part of the Tenth Army on Okinawa, was designated to be the occupation force for Korea, it had no directive,
no plans, no trained military government personnel, and less
than one month to prepare for the accomplishment of its
mission."[19] Thus the thankless task of restoring order and paving
the way for the institution of a new government south of the
38th parallel fell to an altogether unprepared occupation army,
dispatched to Korea from Okinawa primarily to disarm the
Japanese troops stationed in South Korea immediately after
V-J day.

The U.S. occupation forces later converted to the full-
fledged Military Government, staffed with a handful of former
missionaries who had been away from Korea for almost ten
years, and who were totally unprepared to handle the highly
chaotic postwar political situation. Generally guided by the
vague, lofty principles of American democracy, the Military
Government set out to introduce all the features of a free and
democratic system to the population. The result of this policy
was a proliferation of political parties (three hundred by August
1946) and of private armies of various ideological beliefs, rang-
ing from the extreme left to the extreme right and all vying for

---

18. Department of State Publication 5609, *The Korean Problem at the
Geneva Conference* (Washington, D.C.: Government Printing Office,
1954), p. 2. See also Shannon McCune, "The Thirty-eighth Parallel in
Korea," *World Politics*, I (1949), 223–32.

19. Carl J. Fredricks et al., *American Experience in Military Govern-
ment in World War II* (New York: Rinehart, 1948), p. 356. See also
Channing Liem, "United States Rule in Korea," *Far Eastern Survey*,
XVIII, no. 7 (April 6, 1949), p. 80.

control of the government.[20] Terrorism and assassination were commonly used by both rightist and leftist groups.[21]

When the postwar "honeymoon" between the United States and Soviet Russia ended after almost two years of vacillation, the United States Military Government belatedly initiated a "get-tough" policy toward the leftists while it condoned the terrorist activities of the rightists. In the spring of 1947 this writer personally witnessed right-wing terrorists sacking the headquarters of the South Korean Labor Party, a leading communist-front organization, while both civilian and U.S. military police merely watched. By late 1947 all the major leftist elements were forced to go underground.

More important than the elimination of the socialists and communists from the active political scene was the ensuing power struggle among the rightists. A brief exposition of the alignment after the elimination of left and center groups is necessary in order to understand the political milieu in which representative democracy was introduced in 1948. This will also provide a background for the rise of Syngman Rhee to power and the demise of Rhee's arch rival, Kim Koo. An examination of the power struggle between these two key political figures will set the stage for the discussion of the highly irregular civil-military relations in the late 1940s.

The Rise of the Right-Wing Political Parties

The Korean Democratic Party (KDP) and the Korean Independent Party (KIP) were the major ones representing the dominant rightist groups. The KDP was founded by wealthy

20. Kim Chin-hak and Han Chŏl-yŏng, *Chaehŏn Kukhoesa* [*A History of the Constituent National Assembly*] (Seoul: Shinjo Publishing Co. 1954), pp. 59–69. For a detailed analysis of political parties and social organizations immediately after the Japanese surrender, see Hugh Borton, "Occupation Politics in Japan and Korea," *Annals of the American Academy of Political and Social Science*, CCXXV (January 1948), 153.

21. Mr. Song Chin-woo, the key member of the right-wing Korean Democratic Party, became the first political leader to be assassinated on December 30, 1945. Ryŏ Wun-hyŏng, head of the People's Progressive Party, the left-wing center party, was killed on September 19, 1947, on the fifth assassination attempt. As the first victims of the purge by the Korean communists, the family of this writer underwent considerable harassments

industrialists and large landowners who in some cases had ac-
commodated themselves to the Japanese. Though it lacked a
creditable record of activities within the independence movement against the Japanese, the KDP emerged as the most
powerful political party, deriving its strength from its financial
resources and the support of the United States Military Government which favored the KDP because of its anticommunism
and its established leadership ability.

The Korean Independent Party, quite unlike KDP, was revived in 1947 by the former members of the Provisional Government, also known as the Interim Korean Government in
China, as a latter-day rival to KDP.[22] At the outset, upon their
return from Chunking the wartime capital of Nationalist China,
the leaders of the Korean Independent Movement had hoped
to take over the entire governmental machinery from the Allied
Powers. To their dismay, the Military Government barred those
repatriates from returning to Korea as official representatives
of the Provisional Government and demanded that they return
strictly as individual citizens. Disillusioned by the rejection by
the U.S. Military Government, devoid of effective political organization, and lacking strong financial backing, the leading
members of the former Provisional Government, Kim Koo and
Kim Kyu-sik, initially accepted support from the conservative
KDP in the struggle against the strong left and center groups
at the beginning of the power struggle.

In the meantime, Syngman Rhee triumphantly returned to
his native land after a thirty-three-year absence. With his impressive political record, Rhee had a large popular following

and intimidations by the left-wing elements in 1946–1947 in Seoul, Korea.
For pre-Independence Day politics, see Hugh Byas, *Government by Assassination* (New York: Knopf, 1942), p. 359.

22. Syngman Rhee was the first President of the Provisional Government, but in December, 1929, Kim Koo succeeded Syngman Rhee as the
President of the Provisional Government, and Kim Koo remained in that
position until Rhee's return to Korea. For detailed information on the cir-
cumstance in which Kim Koo succeeded Rhee, see Lee Chong-sik, *Politics
of Korean Nationalism*, pp. 165–67. The internal dissension among those
repatriated from China made this party less formidable. See National
Assembly, *The Ten-Year History of the National Assembly* (Seoul: T'ae-
sŏng Printing Co., 1959), pp. 93–95.

but no political machine with which he could bid for power. With little hesitation, he permitted himself to be drafted by the powerful KDP, which, in turn, needed a popular patriotic figure as a party leader in order for it to capture political power.[23] Hence, until the elimination of left and center groups in late 1947, Syngman Rhee and Kim Koo, the two political giants, formed an uneasy alliance based on their mutual support by the KDP.

By 1947 the common political foes in the left and middle were no longer a threat, and the inevitable personal power feud between Rhee and Kim resurfaced. Rhee was endowed with the greater political acumen and succeeded in aligning himself with the most conservative elements in the KDP and with the fanatically anticommunist North Korean refugee groups. Also, he adopted the hottest issue as his principal political slogan: opposition to any negotiated settlement for Korean reunification.

Kim Koo, on the other hand, suddenly found himself outside the mainstream of the KDP. Belatedly recognizing the fully matured collusion between the KDP and Rhee, he and his former colleagues from the defunct Provisional Government reactivated the earlier political vehicle, the Korean Independent Party (KIP), to challenge Rhee and the KDP in their bid for political power. The key platform of the KIP was the immediate independence of Korea from the Allied Powers and the reuniting of North and South. The primacy of national unification, transcending all other partisan or ideological considerations, became the basis of the KIP's political philosophy and the point by which the KIP hoped to rally popular support. Appealing to Korean nationalistic fervor, Kim Koo called for political negotiations with the North Korean communist regime.

When negotiations failed in the spring of 1948, Kim Koo not only forfeited his political position as second to Rhee but also lost popular support. The communists in the North and South had used Kim Koo merely for propaganda purposes and then betrayed the old patriot, and the anticommunist groups in South Korea bitterly condemned him for collaborating with the com-

23. Kim Chin-hak and Han Ch'ŏl-yŏng, *A History of the Constituent National Assembly*, p. 60.

munists. His image as a leader was so tarnished by the stigma of communist collaboration that he was rejected by the majority of the populace. As a result, the country's first nationwide election in May 1948 brought Syngman Rhee in as President, and an obscure octogenarian, Yi Si-young, was elected Vice-President.[24] Kim, a disillusioned and dejected life-long patriot, was murdered by one of his own countrymen on June 27, 1949. The assassin, captured at the scene of murder, was Army Lieutenant An Du-hi, an apparent henchman of Syngman Rhee.[25] Making a statement the next day on the death of Kim Koo, Rhee "inferentially disclaimed responsibility of the administration for the assassination of one of the most outstanding critics of the government."[26] Nevertheless, as shall be discussed in more detail, this murder of a leading national figure by a uniformed military officer, apparently under the direct order of President Rhee, marked the beginning of the ugly entanglement of the civil-military sectors in political process.

The death of Kim Koo not only deprived the KIP of its leader but it also robbed the nation of the services of the most powerful opposition spokesman to Syngman Rhee. The KIP soon completely disintegrated, and the followers of Kim Koo joined with their erstwhile political enemy, the KDP, to make a concerted effort to oppose Rhee, who had deserted the KDP leadership once he achieved his goal: election to the presidency in May 1948.[27] This rupture, first, marked the end of Rhee's reliance upon a political party of someone else's creation, and, second,

24. Ibid., p. 109. Rhee received 180 votes out of the total of 198, while Kim Koo was given only 13 votes; in the election of the Vice-President Kim Koo received 62, while Yi Si-young took the necessary two-thirds, 133. Rhee's personal opposition to Kim Koo's election as Vice-President was largely responsible for Kim's defeat.

25. Although Lt. An did not explicitly implicate Rhee in the assassination, he not only escaped a death penalty, but he was also to enjoy a rather comfortable military and civilian life during and after the Korean War, while Rhee was in power.

26. *New York Times*, July 1, 1949, p. 6, col. 8.

27. On February 19, 1949, a new opposition party was created and named the Democratic Nationalist Party [*Minju Kukmin Tang*], with the merging of KDP, KIP, and other opposition parties; see Han T'ae-soo, *Hanguk chŏngdansa* [*A History of Korean Political Parties*] (Seoul: Shint'aeyangsa, 1961), pp. 111–13.

marked the beginning of his independence as an unfettered one-man ruler.

The Man of the Hour: Syngman Rhee

As stated earlier, twentieth-century Korea had known unrelieved political tutelage and servility. In the Yi Dynasty, total political power was kept in the hands of the king and the court. The Japanese brought to Korea not only administrative efficiency—an unknown quality under the Yi Dynasty—but also an oppressive imperialism. The defeat of Japan in World War II resulted in the exchange, for South Korea, of arbitrary but efficient Japanese masters for a well-meaning but ineffectual American mentor. At the end of the war, Korea suffered a major economic trauma in its abrupt separation from the Japanese upon whom it had grown industrially dependent to a crippling degree. This abrupt separation was followed by the partition of Korea, an act which had economic consequences of the greatest magnitude.

In such an inhospitable political and economic milieu, representative democracy was inaugurated in August 1948. Naturally, a political superstructure based upon the most advanced democratic principles could not be expected to function easily, even though there were political leaders necessary for, and dedicated to, the success of the democratic system. Modern democracy— a most advanced, sophisticated, and demanding political system—could not be developed overnight in a traditional society without undergoing a transitional period in which the political leaders laid a foundation for succeeding generations.

Democracy is a gift, as it were, which dedicated and benevolent leaders leave to posterity. That is why the role of the power elite in newly developing nations has been carefully examined in recent years. Carlyle's national "hero" is reemerging in newly developing nations, now taking the form of a modernizing oligarchy and a charismatic leadership. It was entirely natural, then, for the Korean people to turn to the greatly revered and widely known native scholar-statesman, Syngman Rhee, because it was he who most closely epitomized the man with the "heavenly mandate" in the politically immature minds of the populace.

There is an old and shopworn cliché in political rhetoric that "the man and the hour have met." In reality this seldom happens. In the case of Korea, however, it could indeed be said that in 1948 the man and the hour met.

Rhee was not an ordinary man to the Korean people. He was the hope and symbol of the nation, for he represented the best of patriotism and the best of Eastern and Western scholarship. As a scholar, Rhee's academic achievements far surpassed any of his contemporaries in Korea. His master's degree from Harvard University and his doctoral degree from Princeton University—in addition to his mastery of Chinese classics and his cultivation of the art of calligraphy—made him the most learned man in Korea. Such academic achievements were particularly important in a Confucian-oriented country, for Confucianism considers humanistic learning per se as tantamount to the refinement of human wisdom and the cultivation of moral and ethical precepts. Even today, persons called "doctors" hold Ph.D. degrees, not only medical degrees.

Having served as the first President of the Provisional Government in Shanghai in the 1920s and having led, or claiming to have led, Korean independence movements in the United States, Rhee was revered as a founding father of an independent Korea. Even before his election, Rhee was frequently addressed as *President* Syngman Rhee. Moreover, the family name Rhee exuded a sense of nobility; for Rhee belonged to the particular clan of Rhee from which the first king of the Yi Dynasty, Yi Sŏng-ge, had come. (A Chinese character can be spelled in five or more different ways due to the absence of a uniform transliteration—e.g., Yi, Rhee, Lee, Ea, and Liegh.) Rhee was supposedly the nineteenth direct descendant of the first king of the Yi Dynasty. Though not seemingly too important in the urban areas, such noble lineage had considerable impact in the tradition-bound rural areas.

Being an astute politician, Rhee used his background most effectively to elicit maximum popularity and support from the populace. Seldom in any country had one man commanded the loyal admiration and support from such an overwhelming majority of people as Syngman Rhee did in the first days of Korean national independence. He won an "uncontested" seat in Seoul in the 1948 elections to the National Assembly, and he received 92 percent of the vote cast in the National Assembly when the election was held to choose the first president of the newly born republic.[28]

Rhee's ascendancy to the presidency had a ramification greater than the simple installation of a successful political candidate. In fact, Rhee's inauguration as First President exhibited all the dignity and pageantry of a coronation ceremony. Such was almost a natural outcome, given the endemic monarchical tradition and the vestiges of imperial Japanese rule. The Korean public was confronted with the difficult dilemma of either accepting Rhee as a new "monarch" or subscribing to a new and unfamiliar representative system. Hence, from the very inception of the new nation, there was a political dichotomy resulting from the persisting administrative and authoritarian tradition of the past and the new democratic constitution of 1948 which invested nearly all important political powers to the National Assembly.[29] This impasse was solved when Rhee elevated himself to a position of pre-eminence after systematically sapping the power of the representative Assembly. This somewhat anticipated rise of autocratic and authoritarian rule, however, was achieved only after violating the basic tenet of

28. Ch'oe Nueng-jin initially opposed Rhee in this election, but he withdrew his candidacy under strong pressure from the pro-Rhee force. Ch'oe in 1952 was executed before a firing squad for alleged collaboration with communist North Korea during its occupation of South Korea.

29. The first Constitution of 1948, which borrowed heavily from the British parliamentary system, placed the elected National Assembly in a position of predominance with such fundamental powers as constitutional amendatory power and the presidential electoral power. It was reported that Syngman Rhee strongly opposed the parliamentary system and insisted on the American system which employs a strong presidential figure. Therefore, the emergency power clause was inserted to enhance the presidential power, and the president was not to be held responsible to the National Assembly. See Kim Yong-sang, "Hŏnpŏb ŭl ssagodoneun kukhoe pungkyŏng" ["Scene of the National Assembly Regarding the Constitution"], Shinch'ŏnji, III, no. 6 (July 1948), 21–30.

governance: the respect for the "heavenly mandate" expressed through the *vox populi*. To be discussed in the following chapter is the almost cyclical nature of the rise and fall of authoritarian rule during the First Republic and the reactionary system of "enthroned legislative" rule during the short-lived Second Republic.

Chapter II

THE DEMISE OF
CIVILIAN RULE

The key to the unexpectedly easy success of the military coup d'état on May 16, 1961, lies not so much in the efficiency with which the coup was executed as in the widespread apathy of the populace. In the years since 1948, the civilian regime had failed to carry through a modernization program which might have given Koreans some faith in the intentions of their government. Instead, the opportunity for nonrevolutionary change was lost. The inability and unwillingness of the civilian leadership to meet the increasing demands made by the people gave rise to a political environment in which a military coup was condoned or reluctantly accepted as the last recourse.

The assumption of power by the military, then, can be treated as a reaction against civilian inefficiency, first under the personalized and centralized rule of Syngman Rhee, and then under the decentralized and directionless rule of John M. Chang. The desire for a return to the functionally efficient administrative system of an earlier period was another important factor.

The criteria for assessing Rhee's First Republic (1948–1960) and Chang's Second Republic (1960–1961) will be (1) their commitment to the creating of an honest and functional political system (organization) capable of utilizing available resources in the interest of public welfare, and (2) their ability to fashion a political ideology that outlines national purpose and promises good life for its citizens.[1] Creating an effective organization means, first, the construction of a political basis to win and maintain political power and, second, the institutionalization[2] of an efficient administrative machinery to carry out political goals in the interest of the people as a whole.

Syngman Rhee as a Political Organizer

Syngman Rhee, during the twelve years of his rule, demonstrated masterful political genius in building a political basis, but he built his political organizaton at the expense of representative government. The legislative assembly, the locus of political sovereignty according to the 1948 Constitution, was gradually emasculated;[3] the judiciary branch, the guardian of the principle of "due process" and fundamental civil liberties,

1. For an extended study on theories of political organization and ideology as prerequisites to political development and modernization, see Franz Schurmann, *Ideology and Organization of Communist China* (Berkeley: University of California Press, 1966); Fred W. Riggs, *Administration in Developing Countries: The Theory of Prismatic Society* (Boston: Houghton Mifflin Co., 1964); Samuel P. Huntington, "Political Development and Political Decay," *World Politics*, XVII, no. 3 (1965), 386–430.

2. Institutionalization is defined as the establishment and continuity of basic political and legal frameworks—of common symbols of political-national identification, of organs of legislation, administration, and political parties. The natural outcome of institutionalization is then to have highly functional and stable administrative machinery in order to process political and economic needs. See A. N. Eisenstadt, "Initial Institutional Patterns of Political Modernization," *Civilizations* (Brussels: International Institute of Differing Civilizations), XII, no. 4 (1962), 461–72.

3. On the methods and tactics of imposing executive supremacy, see this author's "Military Revolution in Korea, 1960–63" (Ph.D dissertation, University of Massachusetts, 1966), pp. 43–59; Richard C. Allen, *Syngman Rhee: Unauthorized Biography* (Rutland, Vt.: Charles Tuttle Co., 1960), pp. 141–51; Ma Han, *Hanguk chongch'i ui ch'ong pip'an* [*A Critique of Korean Politics*] (Seoul: Hanguk chŏngch'i yŏnguwon, 1959) pp. 96–192; Suh Byŏng-cho, *Jukwonja ui chŭngŏn: Hanguk daeui chŏngch'isa* [*A Testimony by a Sovereign: A History of a Representative Government*] (Seoul: Moumsa, 1964), pp. 130–41.

was relegated to the auxiliary position of punishing the enemies and rewarding the friends of the chief executive;[4] the administrative branch, particularly the National Police, became the political tool of the President; and political organizations outside the government—labor unions and professional associations —turned into subsidiaries of the ruling party and became useful agents of the government.[5] In addition, a new political party, the Liberal Party, was formed to oversee and coordinate the entire political enterprise.[6] What Korea witnessed was a reassertion of traditional executive supremacy, achieved at the expense of the legislature and the judiciary which lost its stature as an autonomous body. Indeed, political power in every sense was concentrated in the hands of the Chief Executive.

This concentration of power, or reappearance of administrative tradition, might have greatly facilitated the modernizing process. Often, dynamic political leadership can best come from a charismatic figure, particularly in newly emerging nations where political immobility is a by-product of the decentralization of decision-making power. Regrettably, the fusion of power under the personal aegis of Rhee occurred not as a prelude to a vigorous nation-building effort, but for the imposition of what one scholar called "personalized rule."[7]

Considering personal loyalty to be the key element to the organizational cohesion, Rhee constantly relied on those who professed their personal allegiance to him rather than on those who demonstrated administrative competence or personal in-

---

4. In 1959, Cho Bong-am, a former member of Rhee's cabinet and Rhee's perennial opposition candidate, was sentenced to death by the civilian court on a flimsy and fabricated charge of "international communist conspiracy." See Kim, "Military Revolution in Korea, 1960–63," pp. 51–55.

5. Shin Sang-ch'o, "Interest Articulation: Pressure Groups," in C. I. Eugene Kim, *A Pattern of Political Development* (Kalamazoo, Mich.: Korean Research and Publications, 1964), p. 43.

6. See Han T'ae-soo, "A Review of Political Party Activities in Korea, 1953–54," *Korean Affairs*, I, no. 4 (1962), 413–27. This study was originally presented in a full-length book under the title, *A History of Korean Political Parties.*

7. For a detailed study on "the ceasaritic rule" of Syngman Rhee, see John K. C. Oh, *Democracy on Trial* (Ithaca: Cornell University Press, 1968).

tegrity. Rhee failed, therefore, to establish the permanent administrative machinery that was prerequisite to an efficient modernization program.[8] Fearful of the erosion of his personal authority, he undertook periodic cabinet shakeups to prevent the entrenchment of ministers in the executive branch. As a result, more than two hundred individuals held cabinet positions during the twelve years of Rhee's reign—an average of slightly less than eleven months in office for each minister.

All this had an inhibitory effect on the institutionalization of administrative machinery. First, the virtual monopoly of decision-making power in the hands of the President prohibited the administrative departments from assuming the power and autonomy necessary to function effectively. Second, periodic cabinet shake-ups deprived the administrative agencies of stability and consistency and, at the same time, engendered the temptation for the ministers to amass a fortune and pay off political debts while in office. This latter practice further undermined the stability and morale of public servants, already concerned about the wholesale turnover of low ranking administrators in conjunction with ministerial changes. Third, the emasculation of legislative and judicial power deprived the country of any check on the administration and had the "effect of inoculating the bureaucracy against criticism and change."[9]

The outcome of these developments was the further weakening of the already fragile administrative machinery (only a little over ten percent of the high ranking civil servants under Japanese rule were Koreans). In short, under Rhee administrative decay rather than institutionalization began to occur. As the political organization became increasingly dysfunctional, the whole system weakened. When Rhee was overthrown in 1960,

---

8. The appointment of Yim Young-shin, a totally inexperienced woman, to the key position of Minister of Commerce and Industry in 1948; the continuous reliance upon rightists with rather undistinguished records for cabinet posts throughout the Rhee reign; the selection of the physically unsound and mentally weak, but singularly loyal, Lee Ki-poong, to the second highest spot in Rhee's organization—all these testify to what has been observed in Rhee's handling of personnel.

9. Gregory Henderson, *Korea: The Politics of Vortex* (Cambridge, Mass.: Harvard University Press, 1968), p. 298.

the entire political organization was shattered and the once predominant Liberal Party simply vanished from the political scene altogether.

Ideology

The importance of political ideology in developing nations cannot be overstressed. Political ideology in its diverse forms—nationalism, socialism, democracy, and communism—performs various and vital roles. It provides political direction and national purpose; it works as a catalyst and unleashes the energy of the populace, which is stimulated by promises of a good life and hope for the future; it supplies citizens with a feeling of solidarity in the community; and it gives the individual a conscious view of the world and of himself in his relations with the world. When ideology complements political organization, it is possible to mollify a revolutionary rise of expectation and thus buy time for modernization.

With the exception of the communist bloc nations, political ideology in developed nations is synthesized from the process of harmonizing the conflicting interests of various politically active groups. The legislative chamber, as the representative body, has traditionally played the key role in this synthesis. However, in the country where political decision-making power is centralized and controlled by the administrative chief, political ideology must emanate from him. The political ruler, therefore, must perform the dual role of constructing an effective political organization and fashioning a political ideology with which he can brunt the demand for immediate results. Unfortunately, Rhee failed to conjure up a meaningful political ideology. Political ideology in the First Republic was, by and large, of a negative nature, centered around one dominant theme—anticommunism.

By constantly repeating and reminding the public of the evils and dangers of communism, Rhee hoped to achieve the role of a guardian father as well as to receive the needed political support from strongly anticommunist and politically influential North Korean refugees. Unsurprisingly, Rhee's public statements called for the unification of the country by crushing the communists and preparing for the inevitable encounter with the external enemy. Rhee never crystallized his political philosophy beyond these slogans.[10] Neither a "red book" nor biography containing Rhee's political thought ever existed. Public appearances were infrequent and usually occurred as rough, rare speeches before radio audiences. In these speeches Rhee never attempted to relate his political ideology to popular needs. Even at the irregular and prearranged news conferences, reporters were barred from asking Rhee any ideological questions.

The absence of political ideology deprived his regime of any long-term goals and the country of any forward political direction. During the twelve years of Rhee's rule, no developmental program was conceived and no meaningful reform measures were enacted other than the draconian legislation in the name of national security, a euphemism for anticommunism.[11] The only exception was the development and modernization of the armed forces under the direct supervision of the United States Military Advisory Group. The lack of political direction and the existence of a corrupt political organization led to poor utilization of human and material resources and simultaneous retreat from responsible actions at both public and private levels.

In the economic sector during the eight-year period of reconstruction from 1952 to 1960, the rate of growth stagnated at 4.5 percent per annum in spite of the massive infusions of economic aid from the United States and the United Nations in excess of two billion dollars.[12] The per capita income remained a pitiful

10. In both major works on Syngman Rhee, Rhee's political philosophy was not discussed in any meaningful way; only Rhee's political activities are examined. See Richard Allen, *Syngman Rhee,* and Lee Won-soon, *Ingan Syngman Rhee* [*A Human: Syngman Rhee*] (Seoul-Shintaiyang-sa, 1965).

11. In 1958, the so-called National Security Law was enacted. This law empowered the police, the most faithful and efficient instrument of the Rhee regime, with almost unlimited authority to arrest and imprison anyone for vaguely defined antistate activities. For further information on this draconian law, see Moon In-kyu, *Shin gukka boanpŏb gaeron* [*The National Security Law and Its Interpretation*] (Seoul: Sinhung Publishing Co., 1959).

12. *United Nations Statistical Year-Book, 1961,* p. 488; *Korea Annual, 1970,* p. 132.

low of $80 per annum during that period. At the same time, the lack of planning was reflected in the rise of an unhealthy economic phenomenon: proliferation of consumer industries of no immediate value in the developing nation. Also emerging anew in this period was a large class of the nouveau riche.[13] Vast fortunes were easily made through collusion with the government which dispensed the foreign exchange (Rhee at one time personally approved any amount in excess of $500). A disparity of 3:1 in the official and black market exchange rate could have made anyone instantly rich if he was given access to the foreign exchange.[14]

The absence of political ideology, together with an ineffective political organization, also caused a rapid dissipation of public confidence. To compensate for diminishing public support, Rhee increased his reliance upon arbitrary tactics, which in turn caused a further decline of popular support, thus requiring added dependence upon even more unsavory political conduct.[15] Indeed, in the latter days the Rhee regime had most of the characteristics of Plato's corrupt state in which "private ambitions are rarely restrained by a sense of public authority and the role of power (force) is maximized," and in which public laws (effective legislation), authority (acceptance of rule by the public), cohesion and discipline (or the organization), and consensus (ideology) are lacking.[16]

By the spring of 1960, the accumulated burden had so overladen the system that it could not be saved even with a full use of the National Police. As a consequence, in April 1960 the

13. *The Conlon Report*, issued by the U.S. Senate in 1959, cites the emergence of numerous millionaires in Korea through the manipulation of aid funds from the United States. See U.S. Senate, *Asia* (Washington, D.C.: Government Printing Office, 1959), pp. 109–288.

14. For the most comprehensive socioeconomic data, see *Urinun irŏkke sara watda, 8.15 esŏ 5.16 kachi, Haebang 17 nyŏn ilchi [This Is The Way We Lived, from National Independence to the May Revolution, 17-Year Diary]* (Seoul: Kwanghwamun ch'ulp'an sa, 1962).

15. For a detailed account of the elimination of political opponents by Rhee, see Kim, "Military Revolution in Korea, 1960–63," pp. 51–59. Also see Gregory Henderson, *Korea*, pp. 162–82.

16. *The Republic* (Fornford trans.), Book VIII, pp. 29–93.

military had to be called in to restore order in the wake of the nationwide student uprising against the massive and uninhibited election irregularities in the preceding month (Rhee and his running mate won the election by an incredible margin of 9 to 1).[17] This attempt to restore order and to protect the regime with the deployment of military troops represented the last stage of civilian politics.[18] Indeed, when the military, the ultimate source of political power, failed to respond to the order to suppress demonstrating students, the regime had no other choice but to retire. Rhee officially resigned from the presidency on April 27.

After nearly forty years of foreign domination, the critical moment of nation-building occurred, and Rhee rejected the mantle of leadership in order to consolidate his personal power. At this crucial time the Korean people experienced the vices of authoritarian rule—monopoly of power, governmental inefficiency, and public and private corruption at all levels. The bitter memories associated with "democratic politics" carry serious ramifications for the future of Korean national life.

The shattered trust in Rhee reenforced popular skepticism toward all forms of public authority, even if exercised by indigenous leaders. Public corruption, particularly the extensive

17. Election irregularities of the 1960 presidential election were discussed in detail in Suh Byŏng-cho, *A Testimony by a Sovereign*, pp. 297–344; David W. Reeves, *The Republic of Korea* (London: Oxford University Press, 1963), pp. 48–49.
18. Mobilization of the military for political purposes clearly signifies the inadequacy of the police and other terrorist groups organized by Rhee to protect the regime. The violation of the political neutrality of the military historically precedes the downfall of the other undemocratic and ineffectual civilian regimes. In the 1960 election, Menderes' government in Turkey tried to use the military for electoral and constabulary purposes when the police were not able to cope with a deteriorating situation. In September 1958 U Nu of Burma invited General Ne Win to take over the government when he was unable to deal with the mounting political turbulence. In both cases, once the principle of military aloofness was violated, the civilian governments became the victims of military coups. See Walter F. Weiker, *The Turkish Revolution 1960–61: Aspects of Military Politics* (Washington, D.C.: Brookings Institution, 1963); and John F. Cady, "Burma's Military Regime," *Current History*, XXXVIII, no. 22 (February 1960), 75–81.

use of various vote-buying practices, led to a general corruption of political morality among the inexperienced electorate. As a result, even today election outcomes are largely determined by the size of the campaign chest, not by a candidate's past record or his personal merits. Personalized rule also led to a strong aversion to the centralized system; and the subsequent reactionary demand for a differentiated and decentralized political system during the Second Republic had a crippling effect on the institutionalization of political organization.

In the final analysis, Rhee was neither the builder of a republic nor an ideological leader. At best he was a traditional "monarch," and his personal failure was a national tragedy. Had Syngman Rhee, *the man of the hour*, generated benevolent and dedicated leadership, his tutelage would have been not only accepted, but also would have greatly compensated for the unpreparedness on the part of the populace for a nation-building endeavor. Unfortunately, he bequeathed to Korean politics many bitter legacies that impede nation-building.

The Rise and Fall of the Second Republic, 1960–1961

In direct response to the one-man dictatorship of the First Republic, the initial action that the Interim Government of Huh Chung undertook was the revamping of the Constitution in order to redress the imbalance between the executive and legislative power.[19] The most significant amendments to come from the revision were the replacement of the nonresponsible presidential system with a cabinet system of government responsible to the national legislature.

The President of the Republic became a figurehead devoid of real political power. According to Articles 50 and 53, the President was to be simply "the head of the state"; further, he could neither affiliate "with a political party, nor engage in a public or private profession nor practice any business."[20] Moreover, the President was once again to be elected for a five-year

---

19. The entire text of the 1960 Constitution is found in the Secretariat of the Supreme Council for National Reconstruction, *Military Revolution in Korea* (Seoul: Dong-A Publishing Co., 1961), pp. 115–48.
20. Ibid., p. 127.

term by a two-thirds vote of a joint session of both houses of the National Assembly. The real executive power of the Second Republic was vested in a State Council headed by the Prime Minister. The State Council, the cabinet, was to be "collectively responsible to the House of Representatives" and was subject to a nonconfidence vote by the House of Representatives.[21]

The return to a legislature-centered government system had a debilitating effect on the political process during the Second Republic. It is axiomatic that the responsible cabinet form of government can function effectively only when the executive leadership can command and receive the undivided support and loyalty of the majority in the legislature. Such was not the case during the Second Republic. Since coming into power after the general election on June 29, 1960 (the March 15 election was declared void), the new John M. Chang government was greatly hampered by the scrambling for spoils and by the factional division of the newly consolidated ruling party, the Democratic Party.[22] This new party, originally organized for the purpose of opposing Rhee during the First Republic, was a conglomeration of disgruntled opposition forces which never achieved power. As such, this party was incapable of demonstrating party discipline or exercising political integrity when it came to sharing the political spoils.[23] The younger members, content to represent the spirit of the Student Revolution which toppled the Rhee regime, openly challenged the older and basically conservative leadership of the party and formed a new faction.[24] There was also the customary reappearance

21. Ibid., p. 130.
22. Suh Byŏng-cho, *A Testimony by a Sovereign*, pp. 368–84.
23. A major scandal, the so-called "Tungsten Case," rocked the country in February 1961. Ranking Democratic members in the National Assembly were charged with taking a three million dollar bribe for arranging a consignment sale contract for 4,000 tons of tungsten between a Japanese company and the Korean Tungsten Company, the semigovernment monopoly company. Instead of cleaning out the massive and widespread corruption inherited from the First Republic, the once "incorruptible" Democratic Party let corruption flourish, and they themselves were involved in many cases of financial irregularities.
24. Suh Byŏng-cho, *A Testimony by a Sovereign*, pp. 380–84. See also Henderson, *Korea*, pp. 299–303. See also John M. Barr, "The Second Re-

of factional groupings around the several dominant political personalities.[25]

Without organizational cohesion within the ruling party, the legislature became a divided and directionless body. This political immobility in the newly "enthroned legislature"[26] virtually precluded any serious action by the administrative branch, which had been politically emasculated as well as tarnished by its behavior under the Rhee regime. In this difficult situation, Chang assumed the dual task of (1) creating a new political organization by revitalizing the administrative machinery and consolidating the feuding factions, and (2) shaping a new political ideology representative of, and responsive to, the aspirations of the populace.

Unfortunately, Chang lacked those necessary qualities that the situation demanded—political acumen, ideological vision, dogged determination, and charisma. Indeed, as a former high school principal and as a defrocked political opponent during the First Republic, Chang was incapable of performing his dual task. Lacking political organization and ideology, the Chang government was unable to offer either short-term relief or long-term hope to the populace. In fact, as a result of Chang's weakness, socioeconomic conditions deteriorated from bad to worse.[27]

From December 1960 (Chang was inaugurated in November) to the beginning of April 1961, crippling inflation beset the already hard-pressed families of fixed incomes—particularly the public officials—and industrial production showed continuous

_____

public of Korea," *Far Eastern Survey*, XXIX, no. 9 (September 1960), 129–32.

25. Ibid.

26. Ernest Barker used this term in describing post-revolutionary politics in France in the 1790s. See Ernest Barker, *Reflection on Government* (New York: Oxford University Press, 1958), pp. 98–99.

27. According to an editorial in the independent newspaper *Hanguk Ilbo* on May 3, 1961, less than two weeks before the coup, ". . . The streets are filled with the unemployed and the beggars, while the farmers and laborers are suffering from starvation and privation. The price of goods is on the rise, while production is on the decline to the point of shutdown. Robbery and thievery run rampant everywhere, while the efficiency of law enforcement is vitiated. . . . Everyone—farmers, laborers, teachers, civil servants, soldiers, merchants, artists, and industrialists—is complaining and bewailing. Life has certainly become more unbearable than before."

decline. During that period the price of such an essential item as rice went up 60 percent, while other items such as coal and oil jumped more than 23 percent.[28] Also, production from November 1960 to the end of February 1961 dipped more than 12 percent.[29] Furthermore, in the months of March and April the severe "spring hunger" of the peasants further compounded the grim economic situation.[30]

The worsening economic picture and the ineffective Chang leadership begot two related problems: a rising crime rate and an abuse of freedom. The rate of crime was more than doubled since the downfall of the Rhee regime, while the arrest rate dropped from 90 percent to 68 percent under the Chang administration.[31] The National Police was so discredited for its pernicious role during the Spring Revolution of 1960 that it became overly timid in performing its normal functions.

Taking advantage of the lax and lethargic political atmosphere after the removal of Rhee's caesaristic rule, numerous periodicals and newspapers sprang up overnight. This journalistic saturation, a threefold increase in less than a year, created a problem of great magnitude. The majority of the reporters were, in fact, nothing more than high-class extortionists and blackmailers, whose targets were wealthy profiteers, corrupt bureaucrats, and high-ranking military officers suspected of financial irregularities under the Rhee regime.[32] Uneasiness from impending exposure engendered an atmosphere of personal crisis to many, thus further undermining stability both in and out of the government and military. In addition, during this

28. *United Nations Economic Bulletin for Asia and the Far East,* XI, no. 3 (1960–61), 67.

29. *The Bank of Korea Monthly Report, March 1961;* appeared in *Hanguk Ilbo,* April 23, 1961, p. 1.

30. So many marginal farmers are normally hard hit during each spring when the winter crops are consumed and the summer crops are not yet available.

31. *Haptong Yongam, 1961* (Seoul: Haptong Tongshin Sa, 1962), pp. 152–53.

32. Republic of Korea, Office of Public Information, *Hyŏngmyŏng chŏnpu ch'ilgaewolganui ŏpjŏk* [Accomplishments of the Revolutionary Government in the First Seven Months] (Seoul: Samwha Printing Co., 1962), p. 34.

volatile period the communist-oriented Socialist Party appeared, and a left-wing paper, *Minjok Ilbo* (*People's Daily*), began publication in February 1961.[33]

These developments contributed to the air of national crisis, particularly among those North Korean refugees and military officers who were strongly anticommunist. Fear of communist penetration in the South, as will be seen later, provided a major justification for the revolutionary forces in May 1961.

Another major political development that further aggravated the political situation was the rise of the students as the "fourth branch" of the government. As the heroes of the Student Revolution in April 1960 which toppled the Rhee regime, the students regarded themselves as the only genuine and unadulterated political force qualified to protect and promote national interest and political purity. As the self-appointed caretakers of the political process, the students participated in politics in various and often in highly disruptive fashion. They invaded the legislative chamber when they considered it was not enacting the kind of legislation which they deemed necessary or proper.[34] Mostly they resorted to street demonstrations to demand and get what they wanted. During the period between the downfall of Rhee in April 1960 and the overthrow of Chang in May 1961, 51 major demonstrations were staged by university students and 117 by students of high and middle school level.[35] The negative effect of student demonstrations on the political process during the Second Republic needs no further elaboration.

What was even more significant than the physical presence of the students in politics was the role that the students assumed as harbingers of political ideology. First, they challenged the

33. It was reported that *Minjok Ilbo* (*People's Daily*) received its financial backing from a communist-front organization, the League of Korean People's Association, in Japan. Cho Yong-su, the publisher, and two others associated with the press were tried and sentenced in 1961. See *Hanguk Ilbo*, August 13 and 29, 1961.

34. On October 11, 1960, several hundred students, enraged by the relatively light sentences given to those who masterminded the election fraud and to those who were charged with killing students in March and April, took over the National Assembly, demanding a stiffer legislation. See *Hanguk Ilbo*, October 12 and 15, 1960.

35. *Korea Annual, 1962*, p. 113.

wisdom of the older generations and censured them for having created and failed to resolve all the ills in the society. They also blamed their elders for the seemingly permanent partition of the country and for its recent tragic war between the divided halves. For a solution, the students advocated a new nationalism.

This was a double-edged program, first, to revitalize and uplift the sagging public morale and morality, and, second, to offer a remedy to the basic national problems. For the former, the students initiated what is known as the "Movement for New Life," which called for economic austerity and a boycott of all foreign goods.[36] For the latter, the students espoused political neutralism.[37]

Many students viewed the neutralization of the entire country as the only course that the nation could take if it was to solve basic problems. First, the adoption of a nonalignment policy would free Korea from the grips of cold war and, at the same time, would facilitate the political unification of the country. (Indeed, partitioning of Korea was the work of the two major international antagonists, and the ensuing power struggle between the two has prolonged the painful division of the country.) Second, political reunification, which was to follow the neutralization of the country, would restore economic balance;

36. For an empirical study on the motivations behind the student uprising, see Kim Sŏng-t'ai, "Sawol sipkuil Seoul haksaing ui hyŏngmyŏng dongki" ["A Study of the Motivating Factors of the April 19 Student Upheaval in Seoul"], *Sŏngkyungwan taehakkyo nonmunjip* [*Collected Essays of Sŏngkyungwan University*], no. 5 (1960), pp. 80–106. This survey study is based upon interviews with a sample population of 570 students selected from five universities and one high school in Seoul. Some of the major factors given for participating in the demonstrations were: (1) dissatisfaction with the lawless and corrupt Rhee regime, 72%; dissatisfaction with the arrogance of the privileged class, 64%; and attempt at supporting organizations defending democracy, 53%. See also C. I. Eugene Kim and Kim Ke-soo, "The April 1960 Korean Student Movement," *Western Political Quarterly*, XVII, no. 1 (March 1964), 83–92. This study also cites corruption in government, economic depression, and rigging as the three primary factors in the student uprisings.

37. Senator Mike Mansfield, the United States Senate majority leader, speaking before that body, recommended a study of the feasibility of Korean reunification in a manner similar to the Austrian settlement of 1955. His argument was widely used by the students to buttress their proposal. See *New York Times*, October 2, 1960.

the agricultural South would complement the industrial North and the labor-abundant South would furnish labor to the manpower-hungry North. Third, political neutralism in the fashion of Austria would remove the need for having a large standing army to claim nearly half the nation's budget. Fourth, as a politically unified and economically strong neutral nation in the manner of Nasser's Egypt, Korea could command attention and respect from both sides of the international community. Stimulated by these plausible ideas, the students resorted to direct political action.

The first resolution adopted by the League of National Unification, the organization founded by Seoul National University, the citadel of higher learning in Korea, clearly attests to the political sentiment and moral outlook of the young intellectuals. The resolution strongly recommended the following points:

1. The older generation must take full moral responsibility for the nation's division, and must recognize the right of the younger generation to speak out on the unification issue.
2. In preparation for the forthcoming nationwide elections, all the political parties in the South must band together to challenge the Communist Party.
3. The government must streamline its foreign policy in preparation for national unification, and should be ready to consult with representatives of both the United States and Soviet Russia.
4. Negotiations must begin for the immediate inauguration of communications between the North and South.[38]

What complicated this demonstration of a noble intent by the students was the opportunistic reaction from North Korea. The communist North immediately responded to the call from the South by announcing a seven-point message via Radio P'yŏngyang.[39] Among other proposals, the message proclaimed (1) "free election" throughout all parts of the country without United Nations supervision and (2) the immediate reduction of the military to 100,000.[40] The Chang government rejected the

38. *Dong-A Ilbo*, November 2, 1960.
39. Hanguk Hyŏngmyŏng Chaep'an Sa P'yŏnch'an Wiwonhee, *Hanguk hyŏngmyŏng chaep'ansa [Records of the Korean Revolutionary Tribunal]* (Seoul: Dong-A Sŏjŏk Co., 1963), I, 218. Hereafter cited as *Records of the Korean Revolutionary Tribunal.*
40. Ham Sŏk-hŏn et al., *Hanguk hyŏngmyŏng ui panhyang [Direction*

proposals as a transparent scheme to impose communist rule and, at the same time, it reaffirmed the competence of the United Nations to act as the sole channel for unification.[41]

In reaction to the nonconciliatory policy of the Chang government, some elements among the students advocated national reunification without either the United Nations or governmental participation. On May 13, 1961, just three days before the military coup, the student leadership—with the backing of several members of the National Assembly—staged a public rally to arouse and gain support for the immediate beginning of negotiations between the North and South as the first step toward national unification. The following resolutions were proclaimed:

1. We are prepared to undertake, at the earliest possible moment, negotiations for the peaceful unification of North and South Korea by the political parties of both sides in a manner consistent with complete national self-determination.
2. We wholeheartedly support such a conference, and those who oppose the objectives of the meeting must acknowledge their mistakes and join in this noble endeavor.[42]

The determination and impatience with which the students demanded negotiations for national unification with the North engendered both ideological crisis and political insecurity.[43] Also, implicit in the student movements was the rejection of a long-standing principle of South Korea's foreign and domestic policy: uncompromising anticommunism. The acceptance of a more conciliatory attitude toward communism represented such a radical departure that considerable political uneasiness began to appear among the older citizens and particularly among the military officers. Anticommunism, an outgrowth of personal suf-

---

of the Korean Revolution] (Seoul: Choong-ang Kongronsa, 1961), pp. 290–95. See also "Background of the Unification Plan Designed by North Korean Puppet Regime," *Korean Report*, III, no. 7 (October/November 1963), 22–24.

41. *Hanguk Ilbo*, November 10, 1962.

42. *Records of the Korean Revolutionary Tribunal*, I, 224–25.

43. For an excellent discussion on the psychological frustration which the Korean people have with regard to political division, see Hahm Pyŏngch'oon, "Korea's Mendicant Mentality: A Critique of United States Policy," *Foreign Affairs*, XLIII, no. 1 (October 1964), 165–74.

fering at the hands of communists during the dark days of the Korean War in the 1950s, is like a sacred god of wrath. It is best served by continuing adulation, not by disapprobation. The compromising attitude of the students was destined to arouse reactionary forces.

What made this ideological challenge from the youth so deleterious was the way in which the Chang government handled the situation. In the first place, the Chang administration totally failed to channel the enormous emission of youthful energy, nor was it able to provide psychological security to the old, either by reaffirming unflinching anticommunism or by offering an ideological alternative. In the second place, the lack of a definite policy regarding the extent to which the students could engage in political activities directed toward achieving an immediate commencement of political negotiaton with the North had the effect of leading the communist North to interpret the situation as being ripe for a major political offensive. Indeed, since the inception of the Second Republic, political propaganda from the North had intensified and the infiltration of agents markedly increased. The mounting pressure from the North plus the ideological vacuum and the absence of an effective political organization in the South gave rise to a feeling that South Korea had reached a point of national crisis.

As a result, what had started out as a noble task only further aggravated the already abstruse political situation and, at the end, helped create a political atmosphere which would even condone the assumption of power by the most reactionary force, the military. In other words, the intrusion of well-meaning students into the political arena provided the revolutionary forces with their most defensible justification for overthrowing the ineffectual civilian government—that of saving the country from the communist threat. Indeed, the first of the six public pledges by the military junta on the day of revolution on May 16, 1961, reads: "Positive, uncompromising opposition to communism is the basis of our policy."[44] The leader of the military revolution, General Park Chung-hee, has continuously expounded on the

44. Secretariat, the Supreme Council for National Reconstruction, *Military Revolution in Korea*, p. 11.

danger of communism and the threat of neutralism. The following excerpts from his first book epitomize uncompromising anticommunism:

> Compromise with the Communist Party is the beginning of defeat. It must be remembered that the advocacy of territorial unification with the society in a state of chaos, as it was under the Chang regime, is the way to national suicide. Theories about unifying the country under neutralism, such as those loudly proposed by the students, provide the opportunity for a bloodless Communist coup d'état. We must defend to the last the democracy and freedom that we now enjoy.[45]

In the final analysis, the Chang regime was a victim of the public mood and political system which favored a moderate and structurally diffused political power structure. This political proclivity, the emergence of undisciplined political forces such as the students, and a spurious press virtually denied Chang an opportunity to construct an effective political organization. Indeed, Korea under Chang resembled Kornhauser's unstable mass society where, in the absence of an effective political institution, elites are too accessible to masses and masses are available for political activities by the leadership elements.[46]

As the political pendulum swung to the left during the period of the "legislative enthronement," a greater political decay occurred. The movement in the other direction became almost inevitable if the country was to gain the balance necessary for the development of a lasting political organization. Into this situation intruded the hitherto untested institution having the highest administrative cohesion—the military.

45. Park Chung-hee, *Our Nation's Path: Ideology of Social Reconstruction* (Seoul: Dong-A Publishing Co. 1962), p. 192.
46. William Kornhauser, *The Politics of Mass Society* (Glencoe, Ill.: The Free Press, 1959).

Chapter III

THE BIRTH AND GROWTH
OF AN ARMY: A STUDY OF
INTRAMILITARY STRUCTURE

The environmental factors leading to the downfall of the civilian government do not fully explain the revolutionary conduct of the military officers. This chapter discusses the factors within the military establishment which led some military officers to risk their lives in staging a coup d'état. These factors can be divided into institutional and personal. Personal factors, such as the individual motives of those who engineered the coup, account for the immediate reasons the coup was carried out. A full understanding, however, requires the examination of institutional factors with reference to (1) recruitment of officers, (2) intraservice factionalism, (3) civil-military relations, and (4) friction between low-ranking and high-ranking officers. The significance of institutional factors cannot be overemphasized, because there is convincing evidence that the military revolution of May 16, 1961, was as much against the inept and corrupt civilian politicians as against the incompetent and corrupt high-ranking officers, who compromised themselves both politically and financially along with the ruling regimes in order to advance their personal ambitions.

Formation and Growth of the Korean Military Forces: The Recruitment of Officers and the Beginning of Factionalism

Under Ordinance No. 28, issued on November 13, 1945, by the United States Army Military Government in Korea (USAMGIK), a National Defense Command (NDC) was created within the USAMGIK. Its purpose was, first, to undertake the task of establishing a Korean defense force capable of performing constabulary functions when the U.S. occupation ceased and, second, to pave the way for elimination of de facto military and paramilitary groups which sprang up immediately after the Japanese surrender.[1] Brigadier General Lawrence E. Shick of the U.S. Army, the first Director of the National Defense Command, embarked upon this colossal task of creating a new defense force without the benefit of any established tradition of military experience in Korea.

The first task of the NDC was the creation of the Military English Language School. This school would teach those Koreans who had some previous military experience enough English so that a proper liaison could be established between the NDC and the projected Korean constabulary forces, which were to number 25,000 at their full strength.[2] For this purpose, in November 1945 invitations were sent out to the various de facto private armies. The plan of creating a defense force was also announced in the press and radio, calling for those who had had prior military experience to join as officer candidates. The first instruction in military English began with sixty candidates on December 5, 1945, at the newly created Military English School, which was set up in the deserted and dilapidated Methodist Seminary in Seoul.[3] This unimpressive beginning

1. Robert K. Sawyer, *Military Advisors in Korea: KMAG in Peace and War* (Washington, D.C.: Government Printing Office, Office of the Chief of Military History, Department of the Army, 1962), p. 13.
2. Ibid.
3. These sixty original candidates—twenty each—came from three

for the instruction of potential military officers was to have a very significant effect upon the future of the Korean Army, for these officers were destined to become its generals.

In the meantime, the political situation in South Korea in the latter part of December 1945 rapidly deteriorated, not only because of the bloody political struggle between the extreme leftist and rightist elements within Korean politics, but also because of paramilitary groups' opposition to the decision of the U.S. and the U.S.S.R. to put the country under joint Soviet-American trusteeship for a period of up to five years. Gravely disturbed by the mounting political disorder—which was rapidly becoming a crisis—the Military Government disbanded all existing private armies on January 15, 1946, and on the same day the South Korean National Constabulary was formally established.[4] This marked the birth of a Korean defense force, and immediately thereafter the various army units were formed.

The first major jurisdictional change was made September 12, 1946, when General Ryu Dong-yŏl, a former independent fighter, took command of the Korean Constabulary, replacing Lt. Col. John T. Marshall of the U.S. Army, the first commander of the South Korean National Constabulary forces. The U.S. military personnel were to function strictly in an advisory capacity.[5]

---

groups: former Korean Independence fighters from China; former Korean student draftees in the Japanese Army; and former police officers nominated by Cho Byŏng-ok, the Chief of Police. The number of this class swelled later to two hundred as a result of the special admission of many young candidates by Major Reese, the head of the school, and by Col. Won Yong-dŏk, the associate head of the school. For additional information on the creation of the Korean Army, see Chŏnsa P'yŏnch'an Wihonhoe, *Hanguk Chŏnjaengsa: Haebang kwa Kŏngun* [*History of the Korean War: Liberation and Creation of an Army*] (Seoul: Bochinje, 1967), Vol. I, pp. 247–436. Hereafter cited as *History of the Korean War*. See also A. Wigfall Green, *The Epic of Korea* (Washington, D.C.: Public Affairs Press, 1950), pp. 62–63.

4. *Korea: Its Land, People and Culture of All Ages* (Seoul: Hagwon Sa, 1961), pp. 199–200.

5. Republic of Korea, Department of National Defense, *Kukpangbusa* [*The History of the Department of National Defense*] (Seoul: Songkwang sa, 1956). Hereafter cited as *History of the Department of National Defense*. See also U.S. Department of State, *Korea: 1945–48*, Far Eastern Series 28 (Washington, D.C.: Government Printing Office, 1948). On

In the meantime, with the graduates of the Military English School as the nucleus, an extensive recruitment of enlisted men began in the spring of 1946. On May 1, 1946, as a replacement for the Military English Language School, the South Korean Constabulary Officers Candidate School was established to produce an officer corps for the rapidly expanding army.[6]

In November 1946, less than a year after the military program had begun operation, the Korean Constabulary numbered 6,000 men. By December 1947, there were three fully equipped brigades, each having over 7,000 combat-ready soldiers in addition to complementary units comprising 10,000 men. By the summer of 1948, just before the birth of the Republic of Korea, the total of the South Korean Constabulary exceeded 50,000 men, including a small contingent of Coast Guard.[7]

Following the birth of the Republic of Korea on August 15, 1948, the military build-up gained additional momentum. On November 30, 1948, the Armed Forces Organization Act came into effect.[8] The act provided for the creation of the office of the Joint Chiefs of Staff, comprising the Army Chief of Staff and Navy Chief of Staff. The act also created fourteen other complementary service branches. At the same time, the Army moved a step further and promoted each of its existing seven brigades to divisions. Appointed at the time were five new generals to the renamed Republic of Korea Army (ROKA).[9]

At the outbreak of the Korean conflict in June 1950, the total strength of the South Korean Army exceeded 100,000 men. Even with such impressive strength, however, the ROK Army was inferior to the North Korean People's Army in terms of both weapons and manpower.[10] With the outbreak of hostilities,

September 11, 1946, Koreans were placed in government administration in South Korea and American personnel were to assume advisory status.

6. Shin Won-shik, *Taehan kukkun paldalsa* [*The History of the Development of the Republic of Korea Army*] (Seoul: Tongwon munwha sa, 1959), p. 184. See also *History of the Korean War*, pp. 247–373.

7. Sawyer, *Military Advisors*, pp. 36–37.

8. *History of the Department of National Defense*, pp. 16–18.

9. Ibid., p. 20.

10. See Sawyer, *Military Advisors*, p. 105; see also Office of Public Information, Headquarters, ROK Army, *Republic of Korea Army* (Seoul: ROK Army, 1956), II, 163, and *History of the Korean War*, pp. 263–333.

South Korea underwent a total mobilization of all eligible men from 17 to 40. By 1952, ROKA manpower had reached 250,000 in spite of the loss of 80,000 soldiers and officers in the first two years of fighting. By 1954, ROKA strength reached its peak of 650,000 men, organized into twenty full-combat divisions and ten reserve divisions. Since 1954, South Korea has maintained an army of no less than 600,000.[11]

Background of Senior Officers

The breakneck speed at which the military was increased in eight short years, 1946–1954, from virtually nothing to 650,000 men, had created a new breed of young colonels and generals.[12] To fill the ever-expanding high command posts, generals and colonels had to be produced from young and often inexperienced officers whose sole qualifications were a greater number of "bowls of rice," which symbolized their seniority. As of 1960, the list of field-grade officers was distributed in this manner:

General	Lt. General (Active)	Major Gen. and Brig. General	Maj., Lt. Col., and Full Colonel
5	20	145	7,000*

*The highest ranks attained by those who entered the service after the outbreak of war are Major in the Army, and Lt. Col. in the Marines and Air Force, as of 1961.

Those graduates of the Military English School and the first six classes of the South Korean Constabulary Officers Candidate School, all of whom were the products of preindependence Korean military forces, constituted the new group of full colonels and generals. Commissions up to the rank of full colonel generally were made on the basis of seniority.

As shown in table 2, the training periods for the officer candidates were one-and-a-half to three months at the beginning, and six months from 1947 to the outbreak of war. Such shallow and inadequate military training for future generals and colonels was matched by the minimal entrance requirements of the training program. A prospective entrant had to be a Korean

11. See the *Congressional Record,* 83rd Cong., 1st sess., 1953, vol. II, pt. 1, p. 137; see also *Republic of Korea Army,* II, 167.
12. See table 1 for the format of the ROK Army.

TABLE 1. *Organizational Structure of the ROK Army*

Army Headquarters

Army Chief of Staff
(Lt. Gen. or General)

The First Field Army	The Second Rear Army	Six Administrative
Lt. General	Lt. General	Departments
		Maj. Gen. to
Six Corps	Five Military Districts	Brig. General
Major Generals	Major Generals	
19 Combat Divisions	10 Reserve Divisions	
Brig. or Maj.	in the different	
Generals	Training Schools	
70 Regiments	Brig. or Maj.	
Full Colonels	Generals	

Complementary Units Directly under
the Army Chief of Staff

Engineering	
Medical	
Logistics	
Armament	
Chemical	Brigadier Generals
Transportation	
Communication	
Intelligence	
Information and Education	
Counter-Intelligence	

Military Academy	Maj. Gen. or Lt. Gen.
Army War College	Maj. Gen. or Lt. Gen.

SOURCE: *Republic of Korea Army*, II, 161–70.

male at least 21 years of age, with no criminal record and with middle school or more education (American equivalent of eleventh grade). Once admitted to the program, 90 percent of the candidates were commissioned.

During the postwar confusion from 1946 to 1948, many young men with falsified academic records and birth certificates also entered the program. The division of the country made it im-

TABLE 2. Graduates of the Constabulary Officers Candidate School

Class	Month and Year Commissioned	Length of Training	Rank as of 1960
1st	August 1946	Six weeks	Major Gen. to General
2nd	December 1946	Three months	Major Gen. to General
3rd	March 1947	Three months	Brig. Gen. to Major Gen.
4th	July 1947	Three months	Full Colonel to Major Gen.
5th	January 1948	Six months	Full Colonel to Major Gen.
6th	June 1948	Six months	Full Colonel to Brig. Gen.
7th	January 1949	Six months	Full Colonel to Brig. Gen.
8th	June 1949	Six months	Lt. Colonel to Full Colonel
9th		Six months	Major to Lt. Colonel

Entered with the ninth class was the first class of the four-year regular Military Academy. Candidates were commissioned at the outbreak of war in June 1950, after one year of training.

10th	First class of the regular one-year Military Academy		Lt. Colonel to Full Col.

NOTE: The Constabulary Officers Candidate School was renamed Republic of Korea Army Officers Candidate School in August 1948.

possible to verify such records if the candidates were born in North Korea and/or claimed to have been educated there. Two major questions, then, can be asked. What were the military backgrounds and qualifications of these high-ranking officers to justify such rapid *ascendancy* in the military hierarchy? Through what channels were these officers advanced in rank? The answers to these questions make clear the origins of factionalism within the military, for promotions were based not on merit necessarily, but on arbitrary factors such as geographical background, preliberation military background, and the decisions of the President of the government, who had direct power to promote and assign the key high-ranking officers.

As has been indicated, the graduates of the Military English School and of the first three classes of the Constabulary Officers Candidate School attained different grades of generalship. This study will look into the backgrounds of high-ranking officers who have commanded and are commanding in the Korean Army. They fall into four major categories: (1) Korean officers and patriotic fighters who battled the Japanese in China and Manchuria, either with the regular Chinese Army or as independent guerrilla forces after the annexation of Korea to Japan in 1910; (2) Koreans who were former officers and noncommissioned officers in the Japanese Imperial Army; (3) former Korean officers from the Manchurian Defense Force created by the Japanese in Manchuria; (4) North Korean refugees who came down to South Korea after being purged by the North Korean communists.

Such well-known military figures as Kim Sŏk-wŏn, Colonel of the Japanese Army, Kim Hong-il, Maj. General of the regular Chinese Army, and Yi Pŏm-sŏk and Yi Ch'ŏng-ch'ŏn, self-proclaimed generals of Korean independence forces in China, did not join the lackluster constabulary forces of 1946–1948. Those who did join were either young men with limited military experience or old independence fighters with only guerrilla experience.

The officers who held command positions at the initial stage of the formation of the Korean Army were those with service background in China, but they were the first to be eliminated from the intramilitary power struggle. After brief domination of the constabulary forces, which was made possible because of the favored treatment given to them as an acknowledgment of their lifelong struggle for the cause of Korean independence, those with backgrounds of service in China had to give in to young officers who had either Japanese or Manchurian service backgrounds. Handicapped by old age and the lack of formal education and modern technical training in military science, these old fighters for Korean independence were ill-equipped to meet the demands of the American military advisors, who looked for young, progressive officers knowledgeable in Western ways—particularly those who had a working knowledge of English.[13]

The plight of the aged Korean independence fighters who had engaged in guerrilla warfare against the Japanese in China was particularly regrettable. They had undergone ceaseless hardship due not only to the lack of funds, supplies, and leadership, but also to internal dissension, betrayal by fellow members, and constant harassment by Japanese troops. Under such prolonged harsh conditions, the achievement of any degree of sophistication in political art or military science could not be expected.[14] Also, since China itself suffered from corrupt, internal, warlord regimes, intermittent civil war, and ravaging external war with Japan, it did not provide Korean soldiers with an environment conducive to the cultivation of the political sophistication necessary for the building of an army in the democratic framework.[15]

In spite of these weaknesses, the real reason for the eclipse of this group lies in the power struggle between Kim Koo and Syngman Rhee. Immediately after his election as president, Syngman Rhee—fully aware of the potential role of the military in politics—sought to assure himself of the loyalty of the officer corps by installing young and more malleable officers in the key posts. Deliberately passing over Ryu Dong-yŏl and Song O-sŏng, the first and second commanding officers of the Constabulary, both of whom had Chinese military experience, Rhee installed Col. Yi Ŭng-jun, an officer of Japanese experience, as the first Army Chief of Staff in November 1948.[16] At the same time, Ch'ae Pyŏng-dŏk, a young man who has an ordnance officer

13. Personal interview with Lt. General Ch'oi Kyŏng-rok (retired), ROK Army, in summer of 1964.

14. Ch'ae Kun-sik, *Mujang toknip undong p'isa* [*A Hidden History of the Military Independence Movements*] (Seoul: Office of Public Information, 1954). The ordeal to which the Korean independence fighters were subjected is fully discussed in this work.

15. For a detailed study of the birth and growth of the modern Chinese Army, see F. F. Liu, *A Military History of Modern China: 1924–1949* (Princeton: Princeton University Press, 1955).

16. Gen. Song O-sŏng defected to North Korea at the outbreak of the Korean War in June 1950.

TABLE 3. *Major Military Leaders to Come from China, 1963 (Korean Independence Fighters)*

Partisan Political Involvement	Yi Pŏm-sŏk[a]
	Yi Ch'ŏng-ch'ŏn[b]
	Ch'oi Yŏng-dŏk[c]
	Ch'oi Sŏng-dong
Constabulary Service	Ryu Dong-yŏl[d]
	Song O-sŏng[e]
ROK Military Service	Kim Hong-il (retired in 1955, became ambassador to China and, in 1960, a member of the Upper House)[f]
	Ch'oi Tŏk-shin (retired in 1956, became delegate to U.N.)
	Park Yŏng-jon (became delegate to U.N.)
	Kim Wun-cho (retired in 1955, became delegate to U.N.)
	Song Ju-bŏm (retired in 1953, entered Foreign Service)
	Ch'oi Yŏng-dŏk (retired in 1954, entered Foreign Service)
	Kim Shin (retired in 1961, entered Foreign Service)

a. Concurrently the first Prime Minister and Defense Minister of the Republic of Korea. After 1951, Yi broke away from Rhee.

b. A graduate of the Japanese Military Academy, but he later defected from the Japanese Army and was actively engaged in the independence movement in China. He was a rival of Yi Pŏm-sŏk and was never tolerated by Rhee. He died in 1957.

c. The former Vice-Minister of the Defense Department in 1948.

d. The first head of the Korean Constabulary Forces.

e. The second commander of the Constabulary Forces, but later he defected to North Korea during the Korean War in 1950. He was deliberately passed over after Rhee came into power in 1948.

f. The most respected general to come from the Chinese Regular Army. He was a Maj. General in the Chinese Army, but he never held key positions while serving the Korean Army. He was the President of the Korean Military Academy.

There were other minor military figures such as Ch'ae Won-ki, O Kwang-son, and Yi Jun-sik. Most of the officers from China were special appointees.

under the Japanese and who had had no previous combat experience, was appointed first Chief of General Staff.[17] Moreover, there was a plot which provided that the officers with service

17. *Republic of Korea Army,* I, 14.

TABLE 4. Commanders of the Constabulary and the Army
Chief of Staff of the ROK Army: Their Service
Background and Years in Command

Chinese Background	Korean Independent Fighters Song O-sŏng (1947) Regular Chinese Army Ryu Dong-yŏl (1946)
Manchurian Background Graduates of the Manchurian Military Institute	Northeast Faction (NE) Chung Il-gwon (1950) (NE) Chung Il-gwon (1954) (NE) Chung Il-gwon (1955) Northwest Faction (NW) Paik Sŏn-yŏp (1953) (SE) Paik Sŏn-yŏp (1957) (SE) Paik Sŏn-yŏp (1958)
Japanese Background Graduates of the Japanese Military Academy	(CS) Yi Ung-jun (1948) (NW) Ch'ae Pyŏng-dŏk (1948) (CS) Shin T'ae-young (1949) (NW) Ch'ae Pyŏng-dŏk (1950) (CS) Yi Chong-ch'an (1951–52) (CS) Yi Hyŏng-gŭn (1956)
Japanese Officers Candidate School	(SE) Ch'oi Kyŏng-rok
Student Draftees	(NW) Chang Do-young (1960)[a]
Noncommissioned Officers	(SE) Song Yo-ch'an (1959)

NOTE: (NE) Northeast; (NW) Northwest; (CS) Central South; (SE) Southeast.
a. Generally aligned with the Northeast faction.

backgrounds in China were to be eased out of the military altogether or relegated to minor posts after the assassination of Kim Koo, the powerful opposition leader against Rhee. What made the death of Kim Koo almost fatal to the China faction was the compromising testimony given by the captured assassin.[18] The assassin, an Army officer, justified his action on the grounds that Kim Koo had planned a coup to overthrow the Rhee government with the help of those officers with China backgrounds. Kim Koo, as the leader of the Korean independence struggle in

18. See pp. 12–13.

TABLE 5. Major Military Leaders to Come from the Japanese Army, 1961

Graduates of 4-year Military Academy		Graduates of 2½-year Officers Training School	College Draftees	Noncommissioned Officers
Four-Star General	Yi Chong-ch'an[a] (Retired)	Min Ki-shik[a]	Kim Chong-o[a]	
Four-Star General	Yi Hyŏng-gŭn[a]			
Lt. Gen.	Kim Chŏng-yŏl[a]	Ch'oi Kyŏng-rok[a] (Retired)	Chang Do-young	Song Yo-ch'an
Lt. Gen.	Shin T'ae-young[e] (Retired)		Kang Young-hun	Ch'oi Young-hee
Lt. Gen.	Kim Ch'ang-gyu[a]			
Lt. Gen.	Shin Ŭng-gyun			
Lt. Gen.	Yu Che-hŭng			
Maj. Gen.	Chung Rai-hŏk		Kim Ŭng-su	Kim Chin-hi
Maj. Gen.	Kim Sŏk-wŏn[e] (Retired)		So Yu-jun	Kim Ch'ang-yong
Maj. Gen.	Yi Ŭng-jung (Retired)		Kim Sŏng-ŭn[a]	
Col.	Ahn Kwang-su[b] (Retired)			

a. Graduates of the English Language School.
b. First Class of the Constabulary Officers Candidates School.
c. Second Class of the Constabulary Officers Candidates School.
d. Third Class of the Constabulary Officers Candidates School.
e. Special appointment because of previous military experience.

China, commanded overwhelming loyalty from these officers. In fact, many officers were the products of the military training center which Kim Koo himself had operated in China.[19]

The fact that such a grave allegation of an attempted coup was never fully investigated either by the military or by the civilian authority leads one to believe that it was a fabrication concocted by Rhee supporters to vindicate the assassination of Kim Koo and to eliminate the China faction from key posts.[20]

19. Lee Chong-sik, *Politics of Korean Nationalism*, pp. 186–87. See also Ch'ae Kun-sik, *A Hidden History of Military Independence Movements*, pp. 192–93.
20. The convicted assassin, An Du-hi, was released during the war and

Regardless of what was behind this intrigue, the death of Kim Koo further weakened the positions of the officers of Chinese background, and Japanese- and Manchurian-oriented officers took pre-eminent positions in the Army.

Most important to the formation and development of the Korean Army were those officers with a Japanese background. There were altogether about 50,000 Koreans who served in the Japanese Army, but most of these were draftees inducted during the last days of World War II. Of these 50,000 only several hundred Koreans attained officer rank, but the majority of them were products of the Officers Candidate School established during the war. About twenty Koreans were graduates of the regular four-year Japanese Military Academy. There were also a few Koreans who graduated from the 2½-year and 1½-year Preparatory Officers Training School.

Those who solidified their positions after the gradual phase-out of the majority of the China faction were the graduates of the Japanese Military Academy and the Preparatory Officers Training School. Rhee relied on these officers for two reasons: superficially to project a better image of the infant Korean Army, and to dislodge some of the members of the well-entrenched Chinese faction at the highest levels of the Army.[21] As respected members of the regular Japanese Army, these officers were seasoned professionals with considerable military experience. The Korean people, while violently resenting all political vestiges of the Japanese rule, retained a great respect for the military tradition of the Japanese Army. Upon a personal appeal from Rhee, the enlistment of former colonels in the Japanese Army—Kim Sŏk-won, Shin T'ae-young, Yi Ŭng-jun, and Paik Hong-sŏk—and the announcement of the military reorganization in 1948 not only added great prestige to the Korean Army, but also skillfully served the political purpose of rendering the Chinese faction inadequate.[22]

---

fully reinstated in the Army. Since 1961, however, An has been in a series of trouble with the government and with the former followers of Kim Koo.

21. See p. 57 for the changes of Army Chief of Staff.

22. They are the highest-ranking former Japanese officers still alive. Lt. Gen. Hong Jwa-ik, the highest-ranking Korean general in the Japanese

Considering the military crisis and recognizing the capability of these officers, Rhee depended upon them fully during the critical period of the Korean War. While they were in the key posts, the Korean Army maintained its political neutrality; but with the passing of the military crisis when the armistice talks got under way, Rhee began to meddle in military affairs for political purposes. When these professional soldiers proved to be firm-willed, they were gradually replaced with young and often inexperienced officers with Manchurian backgrounds. A brief sketch of the following three highest-ranking military officers from the Japanese Army shows why and how their stars faded into obscurity during the Rhee regime.

Yi Ŭng-jun, a 52-year-old former colonel in the Japanese Army and a graduate of the Japanese Military Academy, had been acting as an advisor to the American Military Advisory Group since the inception of the military training program in Korea. In 1948 Yi was appointed the first Army Chief of Staff of the reorganized Republic of Korea Army. This, as has been mentioned before, was a political move directed against the officers of Chinese background who had been sympathetic with Kim Koo, leader of the anti-Rhee forces. General Yi served as the Army Chief of Staff for only five months, from December 15, 1948, to May 9, 1949. He was never to assume a major command post again. When he retired at 59 in 1955 with the rank of Lt. General, he was still a vigorous man but was given a consolation job as the powerless Minister of Communication in the Rhee government for a brief period.

The most decorated and perhaps the most flamboyant soldier ever to come out of the Japanese Army was a tough professional named Kim Sŏk-won. An honor graduate of the Japanese Military Academy and a full colonel who affected a Kaiser Wilhelm mustache, Kim Sŏk-won was a symbol of the old military school in which bravery and loyalty were the two cardinal virtues. As a Battalion Commander of the Japanese Army, he accumulated a brilliant war record in the China theater. During the latter

---

Army, was executed after World War II. He was in charge of the prison camp in the Philippines during the war.

phase of the war, the Japanese, hoping to encourage more Koreans to serve in the Japanese Army, dramatized his military career, making him a greater hero than perhaps he really was.[23]

In the fall of 1948, both to solidify his position in the military against the Chinese faction and to bolster the anticommunist front against North Korea, Rhee made a personal request to Kim Sŏk-won to join the ROK Army. Kim accepted and was given a post as division commander. A refugee from North Korea after 1945 who strongly believed in national unification at any cost, this old soldier acted as Rhee's spokesman on the issue of national reunification.

Kim Sŏk-won's famous remark, "Give me the ROK Army, I will take P'yong-yang by lunchtime, and I will eat my supper in Sinuiju," was effectively exploited by the North Koreans when they launched an all-out attack in June 1950. They contended that it was the South Koreans, not they, who had been belligerent; that the South Koreans, not they, had violated the 38th parallel on June 25, 1950. Therefore, they argued, the general attack on the South was only a defense measure of the North Koreans to repulse South Korean aggression.[24] Although Colonel Kim was a highly capable professional, he was completely helpless before the swarming, Russian-made, heavy tanks and superior long-range artillery of the North Korean troops. After the military debacle during the early phase of the war, he fell out of Rhee's favor and was never promoted or assigned to any higher position than that of division commander until his retirement in 1955 at the age of 62.

Given the fact that these two former senior officers of the Japanese Army were handicapped by their old age and perhaps by their outdated military tactics, the creation of conditions

23. In the early stage of the war, the Japanese sought Korean volunteers; in the later stage, the Japanese drafted them.

24. See the speech by Andrei A. Gromyko, Soviet Deputy Foreign Minister, charging the United States and Korea for initiating the aggression, in Donald G. Tewksbury, comp., *Source Materials on Korean Politics and Ideologies* (New York: Institute of Pacific Relations, 1950), pp. 163–73. See also "The North Korean Protest to the United Nations" in the same book, pages 163–67. (General Kim was reappointed shortly after the outbreak of the war; he got out of the army because of a disagreement with young General Ch'ae Pyŏng-dŏk.)

miserable enough to force their retirement could possibly be justified. Even more difficult to justify, however, was the sudden elimination of Lt. General Yi Chong-ch'an as Army Chief of Staff during the war in 1952. General Yi was a graduate of the Japanese Military Academy, a former Major in the Japanese Army, and a highly respected professional soldier. At the age of 42, he was old enough and experienced enough to command the rapidly growing army of 300,000; yet he was still young enough to adapt himself to the modern system of warfare. His extraordinary good looks contributed to his popularity.

General Yi Chong-ch'an's case graphically demonstrates the dilemma with which many capable and respected military generals were faced—dilemmas created, of course, by Rhee. During the spring of 1952 Rhee was trying to assure his reelection by amending the electoral process.[25] To put pressure on the recalcitrant opposition—National Assemblymen and the highly critical newspapers—Rhee attempted to pull two combat divisions from the frontline to the Pusan area, the wartime capital. Knowing the implications of such a military move, General Yi, as the Army Chief of Staff, had to choose one of two harsh alternatives: to obey Rhee and destroy the political neutrality of the military, or to disobey Rhee and jeopardize his future military career. General Yi courageously chose the latter course, strongly supported by the U.S. Commander, General Mark W. Clark.[26] For this valiant but politically unwise defiance, General Yi was immediately removed as Army Chief of Staff and was sent to the United States in "exile." Several army officers whom this writer interviewed said that General Yi's life was in such danger from the extreme pro-Rhee elements in the Army that he had to seek sanctuary within the U.S. Eighth Army Compound during the critical moments.[27]

The removal of General Yi from the post of Army Chief of

25. See pp. 70–71.
26. Mark W. Clark, *From the Danube to the Yalu* (New York: Harper, 1954), p. 154.
27. The U.S. Army compound was used by many other political opponents when they were threatened. Mr. John M. Chang during the 1962 crisis stayed in the compound for several months. See also Suh Byŏng-cho, *A Testimony by a Sovereign*, p. 144.

Staff marked a turning point for the Korean Army in terms of its relations with Syngman Rhee. Those whom Rhee could not control completely were never again appointed to any of the key military positions. This meant that those highly respected military professionals from Japan—the ones from China were already in eclipse—were to be eased out of the key positions and subsequently from the military service itself. There emerged at this juncture a third group, the young and generally inexperienced officers of Manchurian background.[28] They were to monopolize Rhee's trust and favor from 1952 until 1958.

It is important to understand the origins of this military group if one is to see why Rhee gave them his support. Surely they seemed an unlikely choice for a number of reasons. These officers had been deeply involved in political scandals, factional power struggles within the military, and financial irregularities. Furthermore it has been persuasively asserted that the May 16, 1961, military coup d'état against Chang was the work of some of these same officers, who had harbored revolutionary sentiments since their days in Manchuria. What, then, did they have to offer to Rhee in 1952?

The Manchurian army was created when Japan's Kwantung Army combined recruits from Manchuria, Korea, and Japan to support the Japanese puppet regime in Manchuria—the Manchukuo government of Henry P'u Yi in 1932.[29] The Manchukuo Military Institute was formed at the same time to provide an officers training school for the new Manchurian Army.[30] Many Koreans attended this school, and those who completed the

28. See p. 62 for the background study of the commanders of combat units of the ROK Army. General Yi Hyŏng-gŭn, a graduate of the Japanese Military Academy, was occasionally involved in a power shuffle with generals Paik Sŏn-yŏp and Chung Il-gwon.

29. Sadako N. Ogata, *Defiance in Manchuria: The Making of Japanese Foreign Policy, 1931–1932* (Berkeley: University of California Press, 1964), pp. 118–23. The Kwantung Army was the regular Japanese Army unit stationed in Manchuria in the 1920s.

30. *Manchukuo Yearbook, 1942* (Hsingking, Manchukuo, 1942), p. 338. The Academy was established in 1929 under the terms of the Japan-Manchukuo protocol of September 15, 1932; the defense of Manchurian territory was entrusted jointly to the National Army of Manchukuo and the Imperial Japanese Forces.

course were commissioned as second lieutenants after they had completed a three month's training course, followed by an additional eighteen months of course work. The educational requirement for entrance to the school was the middle school education, or the American equivalent of an eleventh grade education.[31]

Created as an auxiliary to the Kwantung Army, these officers were not trained to engage in large-scale comprehensive war games but were trained in counterinsurgency tactics so that they could be best utilized in suppressing the roaming bandits and remnants of Korean nationalist units, which had continually engaged in guerilla warfare throughout Manchuria since the 1920s. (The Manchurian forces under Chang Hsueh-liang, war lord after the death of his father Chang Tso-lin at the hands of the Japanese, also opposed the Japanese presence).[32]

The most important consequence of the presence of Korean officers in the Manchurian Army was the political conditioning these officers experienced within and without the military compounds. First, the young Korean officers must have come in contact with Korean communists who were operating in Manchuria as a part of the nationalist revolutionary movement.[33] Moreover, there were several hundred thousand Koreans living in Manchuria who were invariably sympathetic to the Korean independence movements. In most cases, they looked to the Russians as potential allies to the Korean cause.[34] Second, the physical setting of Manchuria also had an important political impact. In the vast, thinly populated and frontier-like area, the nomadic inhabitants had fiercely resisted many would-be con-

---

31. This information was furnished by Lt. General Kang Moon-bong, a graduate of the Manchurian Military Institute.

32. Akira Iriye, "Chang Hsueh-liang and the Japanese," *Journal of Asian Studies*, XX, no. 1 (November 1960), 33–43.

33. Ch'ae Kun-sik, *A Hidden History of the Military Independence Movements*, pp. 47–50. See also Robert A. Scalapino and Lee Chong-sik, "The Origin of the Korean Communist Movement, I," *Journal of Asian Studies*, XX, no. 1 (November 1960), 12. There is no concrete evidence to substantiate this observation, but the circumstances and political conduct of the Manchurian-oriented officers in 1948–49 make this a safe assumption.

34. Lee Chong-sik, *Politics of Korean Nationalism*, p. 259.

querors who had sought to bring reason and discipline to their politics.[35] In fact, there is no nation-state, as such, in the modern term. Hence, banditry was an endemic and permanent phenomenon.[36]

Throughout its history Manchuria had remained outside the Chinese national experience, and the Chinese aim regarding Manchuria was only to control the border territories, not to occupy them permanently.[37] Even in the days of the Manchu Dynasty, Manchuria was not fully incorporated as an integral part of the dynasty, although Chinese suzerainty was recognized over Manchuria. Serious colonization of Manchuria by the Chinese was not attempted until the 1890s.[38] In such a primitive, almost predatory political environment, the Japanese trainers of the Manchurian Army had, unsurprisingly, no respect for civilian authority. Indeed, since the Meiji Restoration in 1866, the Japanese military had maintained its independence from both the civilian sector and the government.

Commenting on the anticivilian attitude of the Japanese military in Manchuria, Mrs. Sadako N. Ogata wrote, "To the Kwantung Army, the Foreign Office was the symbol of the policy vacillation caused by too much deference to the pressures of the League of Nations and of the great powers."[39] Thus the Kwantung Army, without either the authorization or the consent of its government, proceeded with the North Manchuria campaign in 1931, which marked the unofficial beginning of the long military conflict between Japan and China. As products of such a political environment and of the military training program, the Korean officers could not help acquiring political values and tactics quite contrary to democratic ideas. With such an orientation, many officers with Manchurian back-

35. The total population in 1930 was estimated at about 30,000,000 in the vast territory of 512,000 square miles. This population figure is double that of 1910, when the population was estimated at 15,000,000. See Owen Lattimore, *Manchuria: Cradle of Conflict* (New York: Macmillan, 1953), p. 21.

36. Ibid., pp. 224–35.

37. K. K. Kawakami, *Manchukuo: Child of Conflict* (New York: Macmillan, 1933), pp. 98–99.

38. Lattimore, *Manchuria*, p. 31.

39. Ogata, *Defiance in Manchuria*, p. 114.

grounds became the source of the factionalism and intrigues within the Korean Army.

Mutinies and Defections during the Formative Period

The infiltration of the communist elements into the military compounded the complex and difficult task of building a new army within the context of democratic principles. During the chaotic period following the liberation from Japan many young persons who were discontent with the social inequity under the traditional and ascriptive system in the rural South were recruited into the South Korean Labor Party, the forefront of the communist movement in South Korea. Either in cooperation with or under the direction of the North Korean Workers' Party, a large number of the South Korean Labor Party members were systematically placed in the army to start "a war of national liberation."[40] As a result, from 1947 to 1949, the new army was caught up in the throes of rebellions and defections. The Yŏsu-Sunch'ŏn incident, the largest communist-led uprising in 1948, claimed no less than 5,000 lives before the major part of the rebellion was suppressed.[41] The Cheju Island incident in 1947 and the Taegu incident in 1948, though much smaller in scale, resulted in several hundred casualties in civilian and military personnels. In May 1949 two frontier battalions under the separate commands of Major Kang T'ae-mu and Major P'yo Mu-jŏng defected to North Korea.[42]

In response to these ignominious developments, the army undertook a massive purge—the shake-up actually began after the Yŏsu incident in 1948—which ended with the liquidation of some 4,750 commissioned and noncommissioned officers.[43] Affected by this purge was more than 10 percent of the entire army personnel. Upheaval of such a magnitude within a barely three-

40. For additional information on communist infiltration into the military, see *History of the Department of National Defense* and *History of the Korean War.*

41. Sawyer, *Military Advisors,* pp. 39–40.

42. These two defections are fully discussed in *History of the Korean War,* pp. 415–23.

43. Sawyer, *Military Advisors,* p. 40. See also *History of the Korean War,* pp. 494–98.

year-old military establishment inevitably left some indelible marks on the hierarchy and personnel of the organization. First, this liquidation uprooted the communist organizations and impelled other officers with revolutionary leanings into hibernation. Second, many officers who were closely acquainted with the purged officers were to come under continuous suspicion and were prejudiced against in their assignments and promotions. Included in this group were many officers of Southeastern origin.[44] Third, to utilize the mood of purge and liquidation for petty personal and factional reasons numerous conspiratorial allegations were made against loyal but potentially rivalrous officers.[45] These traumatic aftereffects following such sanguinary incidents were destined to have far-reaching reverberations.

The Feud within the Army

Another important result of the purge of the disloyal elements from the army was the rise of the officers with North Korean backgrounds. These officers were the victims of the communist purge in the North and constituted the most militantly anticommunist elements in the Army; they were also most willing to serve the right-wing cause. They pledged, therefore, a blind and unswerving loyalty to the rightist President Syngman Rhee from the very outset of their enlistments. Syngman Rhee, however, knew the political implications of this military support and lost no time in taking advantage of this opportunity.

With support from the young officers of North Korean birth as the foundation, Rhee built his personal power within the military and gradually eased out those elderly senior officers of Chinese and Japanese background who proved to be less manageable. (For eight of the ten years from 1948 to 1958, the post of the Army Chief of Staff was held by officers of North Korean birth and Manchurian Army backgrounds. The average

44. President Park Chung-hee might have been a case in point, given that defected majors P'yo and Kang and President Park are products of this region.

45. Even colonels Chung Il-gwon and Paik Sŏn-yŏp were charged with disloyalty by some officers. See *History of the Korean War*, p. 497.

age of the Army Chief of Staff, except for two five-month periods, was 34.5—incredibly young by most military standards.)[46]

Those most likely to be looked upon favorably by Rhee were youths who were born in North Korea, had marginal military experience, and, most preferably, had seen service in the less dogmatic and less orthodox Manchurian Army. Generals Chung Il-gwon from the Northeastern area and Paik Sŏn-yŏp from the Northwestern area were the two most important to have this magic combination of factors. Carefully guarding against the domination of the Army by one man or by one group, Rhee skillfully and deliberately abetted factional struggles between these two generals by manipulating both promotion and assignments.

The following chronology for the promotion and assignments for Generals Chung and Paik clearly testifies what has been postulated:

Year	General Paik Sŏn yŏp	General Chung Il-gwon
1948	Colonel (28)	Brig. General (31)
1949	Brig. General (29)	
1950		*Major General (32)
1951	Major General (31)	*Lt. General (33)
1952	*Lt. General (32)	
1953	*General (33)	
1954		*General (36)
1955		*General (39)
1956		*General (39)

* Asterisks denote the position of Army Chief of Staff. Figures in parentheses signify the ages of the generals.

General Chung became the first Lt. General as well as the Army Chief of Staff at the age of 33 in 1951, but it was General Paik who first attained the rank of general at the age of 33 in 1953. These two generals alternated in commanding the vastly expanded army of almost 600,000 until 1956.

To make the relationship between these two generals even more competitive, Rhee deliberately nurtured feelings of mutual

46. For a background study of high-ranking generals, see table 6, p. 61.

suspicion and distrust between them. Rhee's system was most effective. He would call in one general and treat him with paternal affection, praising him for his well-performed service to the country and to the Rhee government. Then just before leaving the presidential mansion, the overwhelmed general would be given a grandfatherly admonition to get along with his rival. Immediately this would be construed as a threat from the other general, and defensive measures would then be planned. To make the cycle complete, the clever Rhee would resort to similar tactics with the other general.[47]

As a result of this Machiavellian maneuvering by Rhee, the two rival generals became the leaders of opposing factions. General Chung represented the Northeastern faction, while General Paik became the head of the Northwestern faction.[48] The ensuing power struggle between the two came to an abrupt end in 1956 when General Chung was sent to Turkey as the Korean ambassador, a reprimand for his alleged involvement in the assassination of Major General Kim Ch'ang-yong, the Chief of the Counter-Intelligence Corps (CIC), who had been Rhee's hatchet man.[49]

The case of Major General Kim Ch'ang-yong and subsequent events were to have a far-reaching significance both to the Rhee power apparatus and to the entire Northeastern faction. Rhee

47. Often included in the creation and manipulation of factionalism was General Yi Hyŏng-gŭn. For further information on the intramilitary power struggle, see *Hanguk Ilbo Weekly*, beginning May 7, 1966. A lengthy serialization on this matter is presented by Ko Chŏng-hun, a former army officer.

48. With a long history of factionalism stemming from different dialects and sharply distinct temperaments in the different provinces, the Korean people can easily be provoked into a deadly factional struggle. Four major groupings can be seen: a Northeastern Hamykyŏng faction; a Northwestern Pyŏng-an faction; a Southeastern Kyŏng-sang faction; and a Southwestern Cholla faction. Of course, there were some exceptions—Lt. General Chang Do-young, Northwesterner, was more closely associated with General Chung while some Southeasterners and Southwesterners were aligned with General Paik.

49. The death of Major General Kim Ch'ang-yong in January 1956 turned out to be a big blow both to the Liberal Party and to Rhee in the election of 1956, when Rhee only polled 52 percent of the total votes and Rhee's running mate lost out to the opposition, John M. Chang. See Kim Rin-sŏh, *In Defense of Syngman Rhee*, pp. 122–23.

lost his most trusted and powerful servant, Kim Ch'ang-yong, and at the same time forfeited his support from the Northeastern faction, thereby losing a major pillar in his power structure.

Commenting on the significance of this case, staunch Rhee defender, Kim Rin-sŏh, wrote in 1963: "Had the Major General Kim lived, John M. Chang would not have been elected to the Vice-presidency in 1956, and the April 19, 1960, Student Revolution would not have been successful."[50] He also said that the loss of support from the Northeastern faction marked the beginning of Rhee's decline, because in 1960 the Northeastern faction failed to support Rhee.[51]

What must be remembered is that Rhee was a victim of his own schemes. The supposedly tight control he exercised over the military and the carefully constructed system of checks and balances with the Army failed to work when the officers were too personally involved in the power struggle. It was later revealed to this author by a high-ranking officer who wishes to remain anonymous that General Kim was eliminated because he planned to enhance his position by investigating the leading generals who were presumed to have engaged in unsavory conduct. Apparently included in his list was General Chung Il-gwon, the leader of the Northeastern faction.

Following these events, the Northeastern faction lost leaders who had been links in Rhee's power chain, and consequently this faction fell out of Rhee's favor. As shall be shown later, the Military Revolution of May 16, 1961, could not have been successful without the active and/or tacit support of several high-ranking generals—specifically, those generals of Northeastern background.

From this study of the backgrounds of high-ranking officers and of their relations with Rhee we can conclude that the only officers who enjoyed Rhee's confidence and favor were those young and often inexperienced officers who demonstrated their personal loyalty to him. But even these officers, when it came to choosing between their own plans for the future and the obvi-

50. Kim Rin-sŏh, *In Defense of Syngman Rhee*, p. 121.
51. Ibid., p. 122.

ously uncertain future of frail Syngman Rhee, became reluctant to support their 85-year-old benefactor.

Indeed, the more mature and politically astute young generals stayed aloof from Rhee during the student uprising in April 1960, thereby leaving him without the support of the military upon which his regime ultimately depended. It was even reported later that some of the frontier officers had threatened in the presence of General Song Yo-ch'an, the martial law commander during the crucial days of the Student Revolution, that they would frustrate any military action against the demonstrating students and college professors.[52]

In conclusion, during its formative period the Korean military establishment was subjected to many undue internal and external stresses and strains. There was a highly competitive factional struggle on the basis of common military backgrounds and geographical ties. There were also communist conspiracies that took a heavy toll before the left-wing revolutionaries were purged from the military. A catastrophic war only four years after the founding of a new army necessitated the regrouping and reorganizing of the entire military establishment, which was undergoing expansion at breakneck speed. These difficulties, plus Rhee's deliberate manipulations to abet factionalism, seriously undermined the budding military professionalism.

To compound the intramilitary tensions and frictions and the civil-military dysfunctions, additional disruptive factors surfaced after the downfall of Rhee: the challenge of the politically comprised and financially unclean *senior* officers by the reform-minded *junior* officers; open censure of the high-ranking generals by the members of the newly elected National Assembly; and the Chang regime's reinstatement of the practice of raising political funds from the military. These new problems will be discussed in succeeding chapters.

52. Lt. General Yu Che-hŭng, commander of the First Army, was singularly responsible for preventing the use of arms against the students during the April 1960 uprising.

TABLE 6. *Background of Generals and Lieutenant Generals (Late 1960)*

Rank	Number	Average Age	Rural Origin	Geog. Origin N.W.	Geog. Origin N.E.	Geog. Origin Cent.
General	3	36	3	1	1	1
Lt. General Active	12	34.5	9	3	3	3
Lt. General Reserve	7	53	4	2	0	3

Rank	Military Background Manch.	Jap.	Chin.	Educational Background Grammar School	Middle School	College (no degree)	College Grad.
General	2	1	0	0	2	1	0
Lt. General Active	3	6[a]	0	2	4	3	3[b]
Lt. General Reserve	1	2	3	1	1	0	6

NOTE: Generals: Chung Il-gwon, Paik-Sŏn-yŏp, and Yi Hyŏng-gŭn; Lt. Generals in active service: Chang Do-yong, Choi Young-hee, Ham Byong-sŏn, Kim Chong-o, Kang Moon-bong, Paik In-yŏb, Shin Wung-gyun, Song Yo-ch'an, Won Yong-dŏk, Yi Chong-ch'an, and Yu Che-hŭng; Lt. Generals in Reserves: Ch'oi Tŏk-shin, Ch'oi Young-dŏk, Kim Hong-il, Kim Il-hwan, Shin T'ae-yŏng, Shon Won-il, and Yi Wung-jun.

a. Only three are graduates of the Japanese Military Academy; the rest are noncoms or student draftees.

b. The graduates of a four-year military academy are considered college graduates.

TABLE 7.   Commanders of Combat Units of the ROK Army, 1956

Army Chief of Staff	General Chung Il-gwon, 37, former Manchurian Army officer
Commander of the First Field Army	General Paik Sŏn-yŏp, 35, former Manchurian Army officer
Commander of the First Corps	Lt. General Ch'oi Tŏk-shin,* 42, former Chinese Army officer
Commander of the Second Corps	Lt. General Han Byŏng-sŏn, 36 former sergeant in the Japanese Army
Commander of the Third Corps	Lt. General Song Yŏ-ch'an, 37, former sergeant in the Japanese Army
Commander of the Fifth Corps	Lt. General Ch'oi Young-hee, 34, former (student draftee) officer in the Japanese Army
Commander of the Sixth Corps	Lt. General Yi Han-rim, 34, former Manchurian Army officer
Commander of the Second Army	Lt. General Kang Moon-bong, 34, former Manchurian Army officer

NOTE: *Lt. General Ch'oi was retired in 1956 and was sent to Vietnam as the Korean ambassador. From the list it can be seen that there is not a single product of the Japanese Military Academy or Officers Preparatory School in Japan.

TABLE 8. *Major Military Leaders to Come from the Manchurian Army (According to Their Geographical Origin)*

Northwest	South or Central South, thus Non-Aligned in Factional Struggle	Northeast
Gen. Paik Sŏn-yŏp[a]*	Gen. Park Chung-hee[c]	Gen. Chung Il-gwon[a]
Lt. Gen. Yang Kug-jin[a]	Lt. Gen. Shin Hŭn-jun[d]	Lt. Gen. Kang Moon-bong[a]
Maj. Gen. Kim Sŏk-bŏm[b]	Maj. Gen. Song Sŏk-ha[d]	Lt. Gen. Yi Han-rim[a]
		Lt. Gen. Yun T'ai-il[b]
		Lt. Gen. Park Im-hang[a]
		Maj. Gen. Ch'oi Ch'ang-ŭn[b]
		Maj. Gen. Park Ki-yŏng[b]
		Brig. Gen. Yi Chu-il[b]
Maj. Gen. Kim Ch'ang-nam (Navy)		Maj. Gen. Kim Dong-ha[c] (Marines)

*General Paik was supported by other generals from the Northwest, but they are not the products of the regular Manchurian Army.

a. Graduate of the English Language School.

b. First Class of Constabulary Officers Candidate School.

c. Second Class of Constabulary Officers Candidate School.

d. Not clear.

Chapter IV

CIVIL-MILITARY RELATIONS

The entrance of the military into the political arena is usually precipitated by a breakdown of mutual respect for the distinctive spheres of civil and military authority. Often this occurs when one or both violate the basic rules which delineate their separate functions and responsibilities. This chapter discusses the factors responsible for an exclusiveness and, to some extent, a hostility between the civil-military elites, and it discusses steps leading to the adulteration of civil-military relations and the disruption of intramilitary cohesion.

Traditional Civil-Military Relations

Long influenced by nonviolent and ascetic Buddhism, as well as aesthetic and quiescent Confucianism, the Korean people encouraged mental and spiritual development rather than physical prowess. The ultimate objective of life was the cultivation of an ability to appreciate aesthetic beauty. Intellectual wisdom as the foundation of metaphysics was considered infinitely superior to physical development. In such a context, the man of arms, the symbol of physical violence, was considered inferior to the man of letters; therefore, the former must be subservient to the latter.[1]

Both the neglect of physical development and the relegation of the man of arms to a lower social stratum persisted throughout the history of Korea, even in the face of repeated national disasters. Korea has been invaded and conquered many times, but never once in its history has it attempted a military conquest of another nation; Korea has never had either the proclivity or the military strength with which to make such a bid. Moreover, unlike many other emerging nations, Korea did not earn her political independence through military struggle; it was arranged by the Allied Powers after the defeat of the Japanese in World War II. The most recent nationalistic military hero to appear in Korean history is Admiral Yi Sun-shin, who successfully stymied a Japanese invasion of Korea in the fifteenth century. Hence, prior to the outbreak of the war in 1950, a career in the military was seldom sought by young men with established family background and/or university education. The majority of the officer corps and the recruits during the initial period of the formation of the Korean army were North Korean refugees and those who came from rural and indigent families.[2]

In view of the foregoing reasons, both military and civilian leadership had problems of adjustment when the military sud-

1. In 1170 occurred what is known as the "Revolt of the Military Leaders." The direct cause was the discrimination of the military officers by civil officials of the state. The state examination system paved the way to the state offices only for civil servants, and the path of a government career for the military man was blocked. After the fifty years of domination by the military, the previous system of "man of letters" was revived and persisted throughout history. See Chang Do-bin, *Kuksa Kangyi [A Lecture on National History]* (Seoul: Kuksa won, 1955), pp. 250–59.

2. For an excellent study on the recruitment pattern of the Korean Army, consult John P. Lovell *et al.*, "Recruitment Pattern in the Republic of Korea: Military Establishment," *Journal of Comparative Administration*, I, no. 4 (January 1970), 428–54, and the companion article by the same authors, "Professional Orientation and Policy Perspective of Military Professionals in the Republic of Korea," *Midwest Journal of Political Science*, XIII no. 3 (August 1969), 415–38. Their empirical findings on the background of the officer corps clearly substantiate my observations regarding the rural, North Korean origin of these leaders.

denly emerged as an entirely new political, social, and economic force in the 1950s. On the one hand, the tradition-bound and more class-conscious South Koreans found it difficult to accept the new military as the most advanced sector in society. What the civilian elite failed to recognize was that the military had rectified much of its past inadequacies by undergoing new and advanced education and training at home and abroad. Indeed, thanks to two billion dollars in American aid for the expansion of the armed forces, the military has become the most technically and scientifically advanced sector in Korean society. (More than 4,270 officers and a small number of noncommissioned officers had received training in the United States and other countries as of January 1963).[3] On the other hand, the military establishment itself was faced with much trouble in working out the myriad problems which normally accompany a sudden growth of any organization. (The Korean Army in 1950 was demoralized, defeated, and ill-prepared; it grew to an army of 600,000 in less than six years.)

In the 1950s the demand for high-ranking officers to fill newly created positions often led to the promotion of inexperienced and ill-qualified young officers to the ranks of colonel and general. This sudden thrust into positions of authority and material abundance—as regimental or division commanders—inevitably resulted in overindulgence and other aberrant behavior among many senior officers. Some attempted to erase their undistinguished backgrounds by illegally acquiring and displaying their new affluence; other tried to improve their social status by divorcing their original wives and marrying more sophisticated urban girls and by patronizing the most exclusive nightclubs.[4] It was common among high-ranking officers to use a number of enlisted men as cooks, tutors, errand boys, and even dancing instructors. The natural reaction to this sort of

3. Hanguk Kunsa Hyŏngmyŏngsa P'yŏngch'an Wiwonhoe, *Hanguk kunsa hyŏngmyŏngsa* [*Records of the Korean Military Revolution*] (Seoul: Dong-A Sojok Co., 1963), I, 743. Hereafter cited as *Records of the Korean Military Revolution*.

4. One of the first actions the military junta undertook in 1961 was to abolish such practices. Ibid., pp. 752–53.

living was righteous indignation as well as jealousy on the part of the less audacious civilian elites. Frequent incidents involving undisciplined behavior by enlisted men on leave from front-line duty and the impotence of the civilian police to control them further aggravated civil-military relations.

At the heart of the matter is the fundamental difference in outlook between the civilian and military sectors. While the civilian world has changed little in recent years, the military has undergone a vast transformation. The Korean Army, like other modern armies today, is a microcosm of the state; it possesses its own separate and self-contained systems of supply, communication, engineering, and education. Also, having developed in line with modern military systems, the Army possesses highly sophisticated military weapons, such as 280 mm. atomic cannons and F-5 supersonic jet fighters. In addition, the extensive mechanization of the troop transport system made the Army highly mobile.[5]

Army training, geared to the use of scientific rationale to produce the most efficient group actions, results in a major change in problem-solving techniques. Simple power equations control the conduct of military officers on the battlefields, while a clear-cut hierarchy and discipline govern the relationship between the lower and higher officers. The reliance on the utilitarian value of discipline and rank on esprit de corps as the foundation of group action, and on mechanized intercommunication and transportation, has made the military much more efficient and functional than its civilian equivalent. As a result, military men tend to see any problem as amenable to direct and concerted scientific action and they therefore pay little attention to due process.

This functional outlook is in conflict with the civilian mentality of the old order, which is shackled by "greater inertia, inefficiency, skepticism, and greed in products of modern

5. For a good discussion of the indirect role of the military for development under the name of "military civic action," see John Lovell, "The Military as an Instrument for Political Development in South Korea," *Studies in the Developmental Aspects of Korea* (Kalamazoo: Western Michigan University, 1969), pp. 13–29.

science."[6] The military is easily repulsed by "indirect solution and the willingness of political leaders to temporize as a way of solving problems."[7] It must be remembered that as products of the old school—which placed primary emphasis on the importance of philosophy and history in the educational process—60- and 70-year-old men of the civilian elite clearly lacked the notion of human and social engineering that the military learned to develop. However, they had social grace and literary sophistication that the military elite lacked. (As shall be seen later, the anti-intellectual and pro-technical temperament of the military threaded the fabric of the Park leadership.) The emphasis on physical science and technical training and the simultaneous deemphasis on social studies;[8] the adoption and utilization of an administrative system similar to that of the military hierarchy and the relegation of the legislative body to a secondary position; the supreme concern for economic growth and only moderate regard for due process; the bold implementation of urban renewal with little attention to human cost; the currency reform in 1963; and above all, the precision and exactness with which the military coup was executed—all these clearly represented the soldier mentality which the civilian elite failed to demonstrate while in power.

The conflict between military and civilian value systems became increasingly pronounced as the economic situation deteriorated and the political situation became more acute, particularly after the downfall of Rhee. As a consequence, the military began to consider itself as the only remaining cohesive, disciplined organization to supplant a politically corrupt and scientifically backward civilian rule.[9] The high-ranking senior officers, however, remained aloof from these considerations.

6. Manfred Halpern, *The Politics of Social Change in the Middle East and North Africa* (Princeton: Princeton University Press, 1963), p. 258.

7. Morris Janowitz, *The Military in the Political Development of New Nations* (Chicago: University of Chicago Press, 1964), p. 66.

8. As late as December 1969 the government continued the reorganization of public and private institutions, increasing the training of students in the natural sciences at the expense of students in the humanities.

9. Yi Ok-sŏp, "Chisŏng ŭl gatch'un kumini dŏeja" ["Let's be a Soldier of Intelligence"], *Uriuihim*, 196 (1961), 39–40. See also Hugh Byas, *Government by Assassination* (New York: Alfred A. Knopf, 1942), pp.

Their political involvement in the system precluded any re-formist tendency.[10] Those who demanded reform within and without the military were the junior officers, who had puritani-cal and self-righteous attitudes and who became increasingly bold, particularly after the success of the Student Revolution.

Civil-Military Relations during the Rhee Regime

"When the Chairman is unable to execute his office for any reason, the Vice-Chairman acts in his stead, and if both the Chairman and the Vice-Chairman are unable to perform their duties, the *youngest* member acts in their stead."[11] This is from Article Six of the Emergency Law proclaimed by the junta government, the Supreme Council for National Recon-struction (SCNR).[12] This astonishing, perhaps unprecedented, provision regarding the order of succession clearly epitomizes the psychological undercurrent of the military revolution. It also provides a convincing verification to what has been pos-tulated earlier with regard to the one major cause of the revolution—namely, the conflict between those politically and financially tainted senior officers of higher rank and the self-righteous junior officers. The extent to which the senior officers were financially corrupt and politically involved in the ma-chinations of the Rhee regime is pertinent to the build-up of tension within these groups in the military.

As has been discussed in the preceding chapter, it was Syng-man Rhee, not the military, who initiated the political involve-ment of the military. The turning point of civil-military relations occurred in 1952, for prior to that time Rhee's handling of the military was primarily aimed at consolidation of his control so

---

37–39. Byas discusses the similar mentality of the Japanese Army prior to the rise of the military in Japan.

10. For a theoretical treatment of social malfunction as the cause of violent revolution, see Chalmers A. Johnson, "Revolution and the Social System," paper presented to the 59th Annual Meeting of the American Political Science Association in New York, September 1963.

11. Secretariat, The Supreme Council of National Reconstruction, *Military Revolution in Korea* (Seoul: Dong-A Publishing Co., 1961), p. 23.

12. The Emergency Law was promulgated under the name, Law Re-garding Extraordinary Measures for National Reconstruction. For more discussion of this law, see pp. 103–6.

that he could forestall any future threat from the generals. In May of that year the President proclaimed martial law in order to impose his will on the recalcitrant legislative branch and to circumvent the still-independent judicial branch.[13] By bringing the country under martial law, Rhee planned not only to push through the National Assembly a constitutional amendment on presidential succession,[14] but also to crush one of his powerful opponents in the National Assembly, Suh Min-ho. Mr. Suh was on trial in connection with the killing of an Army officer in an altercation at a drinking establishment in the city of Masan a month earlier. Rhee, unsure of a conviction in the still-refractory civilian courts, had reason to be confident of a verdict of guilty in a military court.

The declaration of martial law produced positive results for Rhee. The presence of military police in the chamber of the National Assembly guaranteed the passage of the constitutional amendment. Mr. Suh, who had been released by the civilian court after an investigation, was rearrested and sentenced to death by the military court-martial. The case of Assemblyman Suh shows how the military could be used for political purposes; it also reveals the political unscrupulousness of Rhee.

After the constitutional amendment was introduced in January 1952, rumors circulated that the key opposition figures in the National Assembly were marked for assassination by the extremist elements of the military. Mr. Suh was the special target of the military officers because of his role in instigating a legislative investigation of the notorious scandal concerning the National Defense Corps.[15] Incidentally, the investigation resulted in a death sentence for the Corps Commander and the resignation of the Defense Minister.

Feeling uneasy under such harassing circumstances, Mr. Suh

13. See p. 51.

14. See pp. 51–52. The extent to which Rhee exerted coercion during the 1952 political crisis was fully discussed there. See also Kim, "The Military Revolution in Korea, 1961–63," pp. 43–47.

15. For a discussion of this case, see Suh Byŏng-cho, *A Testimony by a Sovereign*, pp. 112–20. According to Mr. Suh, over 90,000 recruits died of starvation and other related causes. See also *Records of the Korean Revolutionary Tribunal*, I, 16–19.

left Pusan secretly, seeking a momentary sanctuary in the city of Masan. On the evening of April 24, Mr. Suh and his entourage were having dinner at a nightclub-restaurant in the company of several kisang girls. Late in the evening, a drunken Army captain was rampaging through the place, trying to find his favorite girl. On that particular evening, she was entertaining the Suh party. When the captain cornered Mr. Suh, he threatened to shoot Suh for "stealing" his girl; and during the ensuing struggle several shots were fired by both the captain and Mr. Suh. The captain was killed; Mr. Suh was unharmed.[16] During the trial at the civilian court, the National Assembly appointed a special investigating committee to probe the case. When the committee ruled that the shooting was justifiable homicide, Mr. Suh was instantly released by court order.

In conjunction with the declaration of martial law on May 25, Mr. Suh was rearrested, this time by the military police. He was immediately turned over to a military court for the alleged murder, even though it had been committed prior to the proclamation of martial law. On July 2, after a month of secret judicial maneuvering, the General Army Court-Martial announced the verdict: "guilty of the willful murder of an ROK Army officer."[17] The sentence was death.[18]

This writer interviewed Lt. General Ch'oi Kyŏng-rok, the Chief of Military Police and the Presiding Judge of the First Army General Court, who said that Rhee gave an explicit order to each member of the court to render the maximum punishment to Mr. Suh. When the first judges of the military court failed to deliver a guilty verdict, General Ch'oi and several others were immediately replaced by more loyal members of the military.[19] Soon after, the verdict of guilty was announced.

16. Suh Byŏng-cho, *A Testimony by a Sovereign*, pp. 144–46.
17. *New York Times*, July 2, 1952, p. 4, col. 4.
18. The announcement of this sobering news served as a chilling warning to those National Assemblymen who still might contemplate opposition to Rhee. But, on the following day, 130 assemblymen courageously signed the petition reaffirming the earlier finding that Mr. Suh killed the Army captain in self-defense.
19. Personal interview with Lt. General Ch'oi Kyŏng-rok in Washington, D.C., in the summer of 1964.

Rhee, recognizing the futility of further antagonizing the embittered National Assembly and the concerned public, and seeing an opportunity to demonstrate his compassion, issued a personal order on July 9 for a new trial for Mr. Suh. This order came five days after the passage of the constitutional amendment which paved the way for his reelection. On August 2, at the second military courtmartial, Mr. Suh was sentenced to eight years in prison.[20]

Quite apart from demonstrating the imposition of executive supremacy over the legislative branch and the debilitation of the civilian court system, the foregoing events marked the beginning of new civil-military relations. First, politically uncooperative high-ranking officers, such as General Yi Chongch'an and General Ch'oi Kyŏng-rok, were replaced with more malleable and personally loyal officers in the key military positions. Second, and more important, a new military police unit was established within the Department of National Defense, not within the Army, in order to scrutinize the entire military establishment.[21] This was an obvious move to circumvent the Taejŏn Agreement between General Douglas MacArthur and Syngman Rhee on July 14, 1950, in which Rhee turned over the entire Korean Army to the United Nations Command.[22] Rhee no doubt intended this move as a guarantee against the recurrence of a situation such as had presented itself when he attempted to pull out two combat divisions from the front lines during the 1952 political crisis. (Indeed, Lt. General Yi Chongch'an was dismissed as Army Chief of Staff during this period for his refusal to heed Rhee's demand to release combat units for political purposes.)

Organized outside the Army, which was under United Nations jurisdiction, the military police unit was responsible only to the civilian Minister, who was, in turn, accountable only to

20. *New York Times*, August 2, 1952.
21. *History of the Department of National Defense* (Seoul: Sungkwang sa, 1956), p. 373.
22. Ibid., pp. 422–23. The entire text of the agreement can be found there. The English version of this agreement can be found in Mark W. Clark, *From the Danube to the Yalu* (New York: Harper & Brothers, 1954), p. 169.

the President himself. In March 1953, the commander of the unit was designated Joint Military Provost Marshal (JMPM), having jurisdiction over all military branches and civilians.[23] The first to become the chief of this hypermilitary unit was Lt. General Won Yong-dŏk, who had carried out the orders of Rhee faithfully during the political crisis in 1952 as the Commander of the Martial Law Administration. This unbelievably loyal individual was later characterized by General Mark W. Clark, the Commander of the U.N. Command in Korea (UNCOK), as the man who "did such yeoman service for Rhee."[24]

While General Won's military police unit was emerging as a formidable political tool, Maj. General Kim Ch'ang-yong's Counter-Intelligence Corps (CIC) was in the offing as a rival to the JMPM. Here again, Rhee was careful to promote rivalry and not let one general monopolize the military police jurisdiction. The deadly rivalry between the two units was graphically demonstrated when Maj. General Kim Ch'ang-yong was assassinated in January 1956. Not yet fully aware of the power struggle at the highest level of the military hierarchy—in the form of the private war between Generals Paik and Chung which was discussed in the previous chapter—the first person the CIC arrested was the commander of General Won's Seoul Unit. The CIC suspected General Won to be the perpetrator. The fact that both Generals Won and Kim had enjoyed the confidence of Rhee leads one to infer that the rivalry between the two was a result of Rhee's manipulation.

Throughout the Rhee regime, these two highly *sub rosa* units continually engaged in extralegal and violent tactics, not excluding the outright murder of politically undesirable people. Although the cases were never fully disclosed, more than a few minor political figures vanished permanently behind the doors of these units. During the post-Revolution trials, one major case was reinvestigated at the insistence of the victim's determined family, Kim Sŏng-ju, a young and outspoken po-

---

23. *History of the Department of National Defense*, p. 391. See also Clark, *From the Danube to the Yalu*, p. 170.
24. Clark, *From the Danube to the Yalu*, p. 152.

litical aspirant, was noted for his anticommunist radio series transmitted to North Korean audiences. Upon the fall of the North Korean capital, P'yŏng-yang, in October 1950, he was appointed governor of the northwestern province of P'yŏng-an Do, occupied by the U.N. forces.

A disagreement with Rhee regarding the controversial release of prisoners of war during the armistice talks led to Kim Sŏng-ju's arrest in the spring of 1953 by the civilian police. He was accused of vague antistate activities. After his trial in a civilian court where he was sentenced to seven years in prison, he was, for some unknown reason, transferred to General Won's JMPM. Within a few days, it was announced that Kim had been found guilty in a court-martial and that he had been sentenced to death and executed. Some foul play was suspected, but the unseen yet deadly hand of the JMPM silenced the clamor.

In July 1960, soon after the downfall of the Rhee regime, this whole case was reopened and the appalling truth was finally revealed. According to the testimony by General Won Yong-dŏk, the former Chief of the JMPM, Kim Sŏng-ju was "accidentally" shot to death while undergoing an interrogation in the basement of General Won's residence. On the following day, a special military court-martial was held to hand down a death sentence to the already dead Kim Sŏng-ju. Two days later, General Won testified that the JMPM had announced Kim's execution before the firing squad. What made the case particularly reprehensible was General Won's subsequent revelation that he had acted upon Rhee's written request for Kim's "severe punishment."[25] The Kim case, and many other cases of a similar nature, are a shocking indication of the nature of the Rhee autocracy. General Won ultimately was sentenced by the military court of the junta government to fifteen years imprisonment for his part in the Kim case.

Emerging parallel with the extramilitary units JMPM and CIC was the new office of Chief of Staff Conference. This

25. David M. Earle, "Korea: The Meaning of the Second Republic," *Far Eastern Survey*, XXIX, no. 11 (November 1960), 172. See also the entire series on the Kim Sŏng-ju case which appeared in *Hanguk Ilbo* in 1961.

office was created on August 23, 1952, under the order of the Defense Minister (No. 193, 1952).[26] This supreme military body, encompassing all three chiefs of the three service branches, was designed to give the President direct access to all military units. On March 30, 1954, the headquarters of this temporary organization were moved, most strategically, to the rear quarters of the Kyŏngmu Dae, the presidential mansion. On May 3, under executive order (No. 895, 1954), this body gained permanent status as the office of Joint Chiefs of Staff,[27] to which the President had all-encompassing power of appointment. In addition, he could call meetings at his discretion.[28]

All such moves indicated one thing: Rhee's growing personal domination over the military. The intensity with which Rhee interfered with the military gained momentum in direct proportion to the attrition of his popularity in the civilian arena. Rhee asked more than mere loyalty from the favored officers— he asked for financial contributions that were used to shore up the sagging political popularity of the President.[29] The military, which dispensed over 40 percent of the national budget and roughly 400 million dollars of annual aid from the U.S. in arms and other commercially valuable goods, became the major supplier of political funds for Rhee's vast political machine.

Among many unlawful plans to raise money, the most frequently used method was the outright marketing of such commercially valuable war materials as petroleum, automobiles and their parts, and most vital foodstuffs. A more ingenious method —and one which yielded a tremendous amount of money—involved the diverting of monetary allowances designated for the purchase of secondary foodstuffs for 600,000 soldiers. Also, kickbacks were openly demanded, not only for granting a contract, but also for allowing goods of inferior quality to pass inspection.

26. *Records of the Korean Military Revolution*, I, 736.
27. *History of the Department of National Defense*, p. 397.
28. Ibid., pp. 445–56. The entire text of Executive Order 895 is found there.
29. Although documented evidence on this subject never became public, it is a widely known fact that a large portion of political funds was extracted from the military.

The gravitation of the senior officers into the world of politics and financial irregularities led them to increasingly shady operations. In order to be protected from the often harassing National Assembly, from the Government Auditing Office—the watchdog of government expenditures—and from the JMPM, the high-ranking generals had to make increasingly greater financial concessions to Rhee and his party, further compromising their personal integrity and political neutrality. The financial and material misappropriation rapidly spread at all levels of the military; low-ranking officers began to imitate their superiors.[30] Indeed, the corruption within the military was rampant.

In the final analysis, corruption and graft, the decline of morale and the compromise of leadership, and the friction between the junior and senior officers were largely the results of violating political neutrality by the military and the abetting of factional struggles by Rhee. Given these considerations, the military establishment was destined to undergo an internal disruption and to become subject to external censure following the demise of Rhee. Many vindictive members of the new National Assembly (1960–1961) openly chastized top military officers for their collusion with Rhee, further aggravating the hostility of the groups for each other. Given these intramilitary and civil-military tensions, flourishing in the midst of a rapidly deteriorating political and social situation, the eruption of reform spirit within the military was almost predestined.

30. The ridiculously low pay scale for the ROK Army in the early 1950s was the reason for the military personnel's itchy fingers. In 1952, privates received only the dollar equivalent of fifty cents a month, and captains received the equivalent of six dollars a month. In 1963 this situation was considerably rectified. According to the latest income scale of the military officers, the combined annual income in salary and allowances averages $1,500 for generals and $650 for junior officers.

Chapter V

THE CRESCENDO
OF THE MILITARY

Scarcely a week after the official resignation of Rhee in the wake of the student uprising on April 19, 1960, the pent-up tension existing between the tainted high-ranking generals and the junior officers began to manifest itself in a serious challenge to the ranking military hierarchy. On the eighth of May, eight lieutenant colonels from the eighth class of the Officers Candidate School began to contemplate the elimination of corrupt generals by means of a "purification campaign."[1] The five slogans that they adopted for their potentially rebellious action were these:

1. Investigate and punish those high-ranking generals who took a part in the March 15 presidential election rigging.
2. Investigate and punish those officers who have amassed an illicit fortune.

1. Kunsa Hyŏngmyŏng Sa P'yŏnch'an Wiwonhoe, *May 16 Kunsa hyŏngmyŏng ui chonmo* [*A Complete Study of the May 16 Military Revolution*] (Seoul: Moonkwangsa, 1964), pp. 62–63. Hereafter cited as *A Complete Study of the May 16 Military Revolution.*

3. Eliminate all incompetent and impudent officers serving in commanding positions.

4. Preserve and uphold the political neutrality of the military and remove all elements which cause factionalism.

5. Ameliorate the treatment of military personnel.[2]

The slogans indicate the intramilitary nature of the movement. On May 9 and 10, the move was detected and the key figures were put under arrest, charged with "plotting to overthrow the government."[3] There were, indeed, indications that the internecine struggle might become a revolutionary action against the state. All eight officers were released, however, with the announcement that Lt. General Song Yo-ch'an, the Army Chief of Staff and Martial Law Commander under Rhee, had resigned. Evidently he was fearful of even greater repercussions should these officers be punished. Because of his active involvement in the March election fraud, he himself felt particularly vulnerable. His resignation on May 20 resulted in his transfer to the reserves.[4]

Following Song's example, General Paik Sŏn-yŏp, Chairman of the Joint Chiefs of Staff and the highest-ranking officer in the Korean Army, tendered his resignation on June 1 and was also placed on the reserve list. Both generals were immediately sent abroad. General Paik became the Korean ambassador to the Philippines, while General Song came to the United States to attend George Washington University in Washington, D.C.

General Carter B. Magruder, the United Nations Commander in Korea was gravely disturbed by the intramilitary developments since the downfall of Rhee. In a speech at the ceremony marking the departure of Lt. General Song, he warned junior officers to refrain from denouncing their senior officers of "irregularities committed in the past." General Magruder gently adjured them to be "a force for stability" in the highly fluid political situation since the overthrow of the Rhee regime.[5]

In the meantime, Lt. General Yi Chong-ch'an was appointed Minister of Defense in the caretaker government of Huh

---

2. *Records of the Korean Military Tribunal*, I, 916.
3. Ibid., p. 64.
4. Inmulge Sa, "On a Revolutionary Leader: Park Chung-hee," p. 89.
5. *New York Times*, May 27, 1960, p. 6.

Chung, replacing Rhee's appointee Kim Chŏng-yŏl.[6] As has been noted earlier, General Yi was a highly respected soldier who was almost banished by Rhee for his defiance during the political crisis in 1952.[7] With General Yi as the Defense Minister and with the resignation of the two top generals, the tension within the Army was considerably abated. Moreover, Lt. General Ch'oi Young-hee, the new Army Chief of Staff, took a stronger position in regard to the recalcitrant junior officers. His hard line had strong backing from Minister Yi, who was greatly concerned about the possible disruption of the chain of command by the rash and drastic demands made by the junior officers.

Movements similar to the Army's "purification campaign" were also looming in the other service branches. In the Marines, Brig. General Kim Dong-ha, the Commander of the First Marine Division, petitioned the Defense Minister for the immediate dismissal of his superior, Lt. General Kim T'ai-sik, the Commandant of the Korean Marine Corps. He charged Lt. General Kim T'ai-sik with financial irregularities and involvement in rigging the Marine votes in the Presidential election of March 15.[8] In the ensuing squabble between the two, both generals were transferred to reserve status in June 1960. Kim Dong-ha was promoted to Major General in the process. As will be seen, Major General Kim played a key role during the May 16 military coup the following year. Lt. General Kim Ch'ang-kyu, Air Force Chief of Staff appointed by Rhee, was dismissed on July 16, and the man appointed to replace him was none other than Lt. General Kim Shin, a son of Kim Koo, the ill-fated opponent of Syngman Rhee.[9]

Corresponding shake-ups occurred in the Navy. Both Lt. General Yi Woon-yong, the Navy Chief of Staff, and Major General Kim Ch'ang-nam, Deputy Chief of Staff, were replaced in June and July respectively. In spite of this complete change in

6. The caretaker government of Huh Chung functioned until the birth of the Second Republic in August 1960. See *Haptong Yŏngam,* 1961.

7. See pp. 51–52.

8. Personal interview with Lt. General Ch'oi Kyŏng-rok in Washington, D.C., in 1964.

9. *Hanguk Ilbo,* July 16, 1960, p. 1.

the top commands of all three branches of the armed forces, however, the dissatisfaction within the service branches had not been alleviated.

On July 17, 1960, at the occasion commemorating Constitution Day, all three new Chiefs of Staff, together with the Marine Corps commandant, pledged that "the military keep out of politics in order to maintain political neutrality of the armed forces."[10] Strongly implied in the pledge was the warning that the civilian politicians must also keep hands off the military and that the peevish junior officers must restrain themselves from any unsanctioned movement against senior officers.

Such a well-intentioned pledge evaporated in the face of political realities and unabated intramilitary pressure. On August 23, with the formation of the new government, Defense Minister Yi Chong-ch'an was replaced by a civilian, Hyŏn Sŏk-ho. This change considerably weakened the already shaky position of Lt. General Ch'oi Young-hee, the newly promoted Chairman of the Joint Chief of Staff. Lt. General Ch'oi had been a target of the "purification campaign" from the beginning for his alleged financial irregularities.

On September 10, eleven colonels, including Kim Jong-pil, Kim Hyŏng-wook, Kil Chae-ho, Oh Ch'i-sŏng, and others— eight of whom were previously involved in the May "purification campaign"—submitted a formal petition to the civilian Defense Minister, Hyŏn Sŏk-ho, asking that he undertake an immediate "purification" throughout the entire military service. Minister Hyŏn expressed sympathy for the petition and promised to carry out the necessary cleanup.[11]

Two days later, the first shake-up of the new cabinet took place. Minister Hyŏn was replaced by another civilian, Kwŏn Chung-don, and all eleven colonels who had signed the petition were placed in the custody of the military police for interrogation regarding an alleged charge of insubordination. Upon the release of these officers, Minister Kwŏn announced that as the first step toward a cleanup in the military, a screening committee would be established to investigate, first, the commanders

10. Ibid., July 18, 1960, p. 1.
11. *Haptong Almanac, 1961*, p. 163.

who were involved in the rigging of the March presidential election and, second, those officers who were alleged to have amassed an illicit fortune. As the cleanup gained momentum, the junior officers became further emboldened, while the senior officers became more uneasy.

At this juncture, on September 18, U.S. General Williston B. Palmer, Director of Military Assistance in the Defense Department, arrived in Seoul, apparently at the personal invitation of Lt. General Ch'oi Young-hee. Two days later, on the day of his departure, General Palmer, expressing a serious concern for the internal stability of the Korean Army, stated that he was adversely impressed by a "great deal of uneasiness among the top Korean military officers" and by "the retirement of the top generals."[12] He also questioned the wisdom of the policy planned by the new Chang government to reduce military manpower.

Palmer's remarks touched off a series of emotional outbursts. Minister Hyŏn called them "interference with internal affairs."[13] Lt. General Ch'oi Kyŏng-rok, the new Army Chief of Staff, asserted that "the statement by General Palmer is a clear violation of Korean sovereignty."[14]

Responding to such unexpected and vociferous reactions, General Carter M. Magruder appealed to the two men to take the statement by General Palmer as "constructive advice" rather than as an interference with national sovereignty.[15] On the morning of September 24, a delegation of sixteen officers representing the seventh, ninth, and tenth classes of the Officers Candidate School, *demanded* that Lt. General Ch'oi Young-hee resign from his post. These men claimed that General Ch'oi had invited General Palmer in order to seek Palmer's support to enhance his shaky position as Chairman of the Joint Chiefs of Staff.[16]

This open challenge to the highest military authority posed

12. *New York Times,* September 21, 1960, p. 18, col. 8.
13. *Hanguk Ilbo,* September 22, 1960, p. 1.
14. *Haptong Yŏngam, 1961,* p. 162.
15. Ibid., p. 163.
16. *A Complete Study of the May 16 Military Revolution,* p. 64.

a direct threat to the military hierarchy. All sixteen officers were charged with rebellious conduct and were turned over to the military court-martial. On December 12, after a month-long trial, the results were announced: Colonel Kim Dong-bok, the highest-ranking officer involved, was sentenced to three months in prison; the others were reprimanded and acquitted. This case is known as the Ha Kŭk Sang incident—literally, "the challenge of the seniors by the junior." The major events related to the May 16, 1961, military coup developed from this case.[17]

One of the first repercussions was the removal of Lt. General Ch'oi Young-hee from his post as Chairman of the Joint Chiefs of Staff on October 15; he was immediately transferred to the reserves.[18] The junior officers interpreted this as a moral victory for their "purification campaign." Now bigger group actions might be undertaken.

The following February the Ha Kŭk Sang case was reopened. Colonel Kim Dong-bok, resenting the prison sentence which he alone received, exposed those who were really responsible. Arrested at this time were three Lt. Colonels who were to play a key role in the May 16 coup: Kim Jong-pil, Kim Hyŏng-wook, and Sŏk Chŏng-sŏn. On February 12, all three officers opted for "voluntary resignation" from the service rather than face the court-martial. Their action marked the end of the first stage of the "purification campaign" but signaled the beginning of a serious plot to overthrow the Chang government. These officers felt that they had been eased out of the government for an action which they deemed just. The Chang government naively believed that the discharge of these officers meant the end of the rebellion. On February 21, Army Chief of Staff Lt. General Ch'oi Kyŏng-rok, a respected officer, was replaced by Lt. Gen-

17. Ibid., pp. 62–65.
18. At the farewell party for Lt. General Ch'oi Young-hee, General Carter M. Magruder, the United Nations Commander in Korea, urged an end to the dispute in the military forces and admonished Koreans to maintain "the confidence of her allies and her own people in the armed forces." He also strongly hinted in his speech that General Ch'oi, like many other top generals, was victim of forced retirement. See the *Korea Times*, October 14, 1960. p. 1, and the *New York Times*, October 15, 1960, p. 5, col. 1.

eral Chang Do-young, an abrupt change of command which was to prove ill-advised.

Lt. General Ch'oi Kyŏng-rok had been appointed Army Chief of Staff in August 1960, five months earlier, by the Chang government as a reward for his judicious maintenance of political neutrality during the Rhee period. He and Lt. General Yi Chong-ch'an, the ROK Defense Minister, were the two major military officers who defied President Rhee in the 1952 political crisis. General Ch'oi was, therefore, one of a few senior officers free from the stigma of once having been "Rhee's boy," and he was considered the best potential stabilizer in the highly volatile intramilitary situation. Unfortunately his tenure in office was brief.

On February 17, 1961, Lt. General Ch'oi Kyŏng-rok resigned.[19] The reason he gave several years later was the Chang government's revival of one of Rhee's favorite political devices, the solicitation of financial contributions from the military. He claimed he was requested to divert 1,700,000,000 whan (about 2.5 million American dollars) from the Army fund to the Chang government.[20] His rejection of this request, he said, cost him his position.

Judging from the sharp reaction of the National Assembly when the resignation of Lt. General Ch'oi Kyŏng-rok was announced, there is little doubt as to the veracity of what Lt. General Ch'oi confided to this writer.[21] On February 25 and 26, sensing some kind of political chicanery, the National Assembly demanded a full inquiry into the circumstances surrounding the ousting of Lt. General Ch'oi. Premier Chang then asserted that General Ch'oi's continuing service as Army Chief of Staff would have jeopardized future relations with the United States in

19. Lt. General Ch'oi is a graduate of a two-and-half year Preparatory Officers Candidate School in Japan. In 1945 he was discharged by the Japanese with the rank of First Lieutenant, and in December 1945 he entered the Military English School. As a product of South-central South Korea, he was not involved in the factional struggle.

20. From an interview with Lt. General Ch'oi Kyŏng-rok in 1964 in Washington, D.C.

21. See *Hanguk Ilbo*, February 19, 1961, p. 1. A serious concern for the frequent changes of the Army Chief of Staff is expressed in the editorial of this issue.

view of his demonstrated hostility toward that country. He referred, of course, to the incident which had taken place four months earlier during General Williston Palmer's visit.

General Ch'oi was succeeded by Lt. General Chang Do-young. It was he who became the first head of the military junta (regardless of whether or not he was forced into this). Because he held the most important position when the revolution occurred, his personal involvement and background deserves to be scrutinized.

Lt. General Chang Do-young, born in 1923, was reared in the Northwestern province of North P'yŏng-an Do. Like many ambitious young men, he went to Japan to study. In 1944 while he was attending Doyo College, a mediocre Japanese institution, he was inducted into the Japanese Army where he served until the end of World War II. Upon his return to Korea in December 1945, he entered the newly created Military English School and graduated from it the following spring.[22] This gave him seniority in the Korean Army, and he rose steadily despite his youth. In 1953, at the age of thirty, he became the Commander of the Second Army Corps with the rank of Major General and was again promoted in 1959.

During these years, Chang gained a reputation as a dashing and enterprising young officer. His close association with Mr. and Mrs. Lee Ki-poong, the most powerful family next to Rhee himself, during the 1950s made him one of the few persons who had direct access to Rhee. Also, his geographical ties with the Northwestern faction which dominated the Chang government made him a very powerful man both in the Army and in civilian politics during the Second Republic, 1960–1961.

Because of his earlier political ties with Rhee, Lt. General Chang would seem the least likely person to succeed Lt. General Ch'oi Kyŏng-rok, particularly since the Chang government's promised clean-up had not been completed. One might conclude that the only basis for the general's appointment was his Northwestern background. Premier Chang's cabinet members, many of whom were Northwestern products, no doubt

22. John Cravan, "Members of ROK's Ruling Junta and Their Associates," typescript, SAIS, Johns Hopkins University, 1963.

counted on General Chang's geographical ties to guarantee his unswerving loyalty. For this very reason the appointment of Lt. General Chang was immediately interpreted as another case of civil-military collusion, and it caused an uproar in the National Assembly.[23] This new appointment was considered the prelude to total domination of both military and civilian politics by the Northwesterners.

Neither the military nor the members of the National Assembly outside the inner circle were pleased by this new source of tension. The predominance of the Northwestern faction in the military inevitably invited resistance from the rival Northeastern faction, which later played the decisive role in actual execution of the coup d'état. In the National Assembly, Lt. General Chang became the favorite target of the junior members, who formed a new faction, Shin Pung Hoe—literally, the "fresh wind club"—to oppose the senior members of the Democratic Party, many of whom were Northeastern products.

To complicate matters further, the all-important Armed Forces Committee in the National Assembly was led by Yi Ch'ŏl-sŭng, the youthful and outspoken leader of Shin Pung Hoe. With Assemblymen Yi Ch'ŏl-sŭng as the nucleus, the members of Shin Pung Hoe undertook several important projects, one of which was the creation of the Council of the Investigation of National Defense.[24] The Council, already at odds with Premier Chang's faction over the distribution of cabinet posts, wasted little sympathy on General Chang, Premier Chang's appointee. Moreover, the split of the senior members of the Democratic Party into two factions—the Northeastern-oriented "new faction" and the South- and South-central-oriented "old faction"—failed to insure the legislative protection which high-ranking officers had received under the Rhee regime.[25]

The antipathy which the assemblymen and others expressed toward the high-ranking officers, particularly toward Lt. General Chang Do-young, and the inability of the Chang govern-

23. *Dong-A Ilbo*, February 18, 1961, p. 1.
24. *History of the Korean Military Revolution*, I, 198.
25. The "new faction" was led by Premier John M. Chang while the "old faction" was dominated by President Yun Po-sŏn.

ment to provide necessary legislative protection must have been the military officers' key sources of resentment toward the civilian politicians. This hostile relationship between the military services and the legislative branch, according to one news commentator, was the compelling reason for General Chang's betrayal of the Chang government, which had repeatedly failed to protect him from the abuse of civilian politicians.[26]

Parenthetically, the military-baiting Assemblyman Yi, who was on a tour to the U.S. at the moment of the military coup in May, dared not return to Korea for fear of reprisal by the avenging military government. He remained in exile in the U.S. for two years and did not return to Korea until 1963, after the "termination of military rule." By this time most of the black lists for politicians were lifted.

The confusion resulting from the unabated conflict between the senior and junior officers, the hostility between the legislature and the military services, the change in the Army Chief of Staff, and the rapidly deteriorating social and economic conditions in the spring of 1961 led to a climate extremely suitable for plotting a military coup.

The Planning and Execution of the Military Coup

Capitalizing on such a highly chaotic and vulnerable political and military situation were those who had been associated with agitation in the military throughout the years: Park Chung-hee, Kim Dong-ha, and Kim Jong-pil. Kim Jong-pil, the youngest of the three, has been much-publicized. The leader of the junior officers in their "purification campaign" and the man behind the Ha Kŭk Sang case, Kim had been a controversial figure ever since the downfall of Rhee. As one of the rare college graduates who became a military officer, he was known for his political ambition.

He was born in the rural district of the South Ch'oong-ch'ŏng Province in 1926. Upon the completion of primary and secondary school there, he entered the College of Education of Seoul

26. Stated by Mr. Bong Ju-ahn, a Washington correspondent of *Hanguk Ilbo*, in summer, 1964.

National University, which in itself was quite an accomplishment for a student with a rural background. Bored by teaching high school, he entered the Officers Candidate School in January 1949 and was commissioned in June 1949 as a member of the eighth class. He was immediately assigned to the intelligence section of the Korean Army. In 1952 he rose to the head of the North Korean Section in the Korean Army Intelligence Bureau with the rank of Major.

Kim's experience in intelligence meant that, unlike other infantry officers with front-line duty, he was much less restricted in terms of time and movement. This gave him the opportunity to maintain a close contact with many of his OCS class members. He also had access to the personnel files of the high-ranking officers, and this made him fully aware of the personal life and military qualifications of the senior officers. As a counterintelligence officer, he had been required to master the art of espionage and counterespionage.

Equipped with confidential information concerning the senior officers and armed with the technique of conspiracy, Kim Jong-pil became the first to instigate the "purification campaign" after the overthrow of Rhee, and later he organized the Ha Kŭk Sang case. The rebellious conduct which he displayed could be explained by looking into the sources of his complaints and resentment against the military.

Kim Jong-pil had been dissatisfied with his rank and position ever since he graduated from OCS. As an officer with a college education in the intellectually barren Korean Army, he could not help resenting the higher-ranking senior officers who seldom had more than a middle school education—and occasionally even less. Moreover, the members of the eighth class of OCS did not receive special advancement, as had earlier graduates who had benefited from the expansion of the Korean Army. In terms of rank, the members of the eighth class rose no higher that Lt. Colonel, while earlier-commissioned but less-educated graduates became generals. Also, this class felt that they were the only bona fide officers of the ROK Army, because their class was the first to enter and graduate from OCS since the inception of the Republic of Korea Army in December 1948. As has been noted, prior to that time the military establishment functioned under the name of the National Constabulary Forces.

The slow promotion pattern became the primary grievance of this class, and Kim Jong-pil as its de facto leader conceived the "purification campaign" and the *Ha Kŭk Sang* case as much to make room at the top of the military hierarchy for junior officers as to improve the quality of the military by eliminating the incompetent and politically tainted high-ranking officers. For his role in fomenting this rebellious action, he was forced to resign and was placed on reserve status on February 17, 1961.

The civilian society, which was already burdened with a severe unemployment problem, had little sympathy for an ex-intelligence officer. Also it was infinitely difficult—after 12 years of service and a fairly high living standard as an intelligence officer—to readjust to civilian life. While his frustration mounted, his resentment against the Army and the government from which he had been discharged intensified. He and his colleagues viewed themselves as "martyrs" for a just and righteous cause—the "purification campaign." At the same time, being unemployed civilians, they had at their disposal two elements essential for revolutionary activity: time and mobility. The third element, money, was reported to have been secured by selling Kim Jong-pil's home. Having contributed his organizational skill, money, and support from the eighth class, Kim Jong-pil later felt entitled to claim: "I was the father of the Revolution."

Fully assured of support from his discontented classmates from OCS, Kim Jong-pil searched out those who shared his revolutionary penchant. The first one to whom he turned was Major General Park Chung-hee, who had been long known to represent the dissident elements among the high-ranking officers. Since the two men were related through marriage, there was a further basis for mutual trust.

"Who inspired the revolution?" is the inevitable question after the fact. It soon became apparent that it was not Lt. General Chang Do-young, the first chairman of the Military Revolutionary Council, who could take the credit, but Maj. General

Park Chung-hee.[27] After the elimination of General Chang in July, General Park formally took over the chairmanship of the Supreme Council of National Reconstruction.

Park was born in a small village in the rural North Kyŏng-sang province in 1917.[28] Son of an indigent farmer who had seven other children, he attended Taegue Normal School. In those days the government paid all the expenses for the Normal School students; therefore, many bright students attended. After graduation in 1940, Park entered the Manchukuo Military Institute. Upon his graduation in 1942, he applied to the regular four-year Japanese Military Academy for additional training. A year later he was assigned to the Manchuria-based regular Kwantung Army as a Second Lieutenant, and by the end of World War II he had risen to First Lieutenant. It seems that his experience in Manchuria was to remain a dominant factor in his political thinking as he never quite divorced himself from the revolutionary propensities to which he had been exposed.

He returned to Korea after the war, spent a year unemployed, and then entered Officers Candidate School in September 1946. Later in that same year he achieved the rank of Captain.

After a brief legal entanglement with the Army for his alleged association with rebellious elements in 1948, Park returned to Army Headquarters where he remained as a civilian intelligence officer until the outbreak of war on June 25, 1950.[29] In July, a few days after the fall of Seoul, he was reinstated, given his former rank of Captain, and was assigned as Chief of the First Section of the Army Intelligence Bureau. It was reported that Park's reappointment was prompted by the masterful and imperturbable leadership which he demonstrated during the chaotic period of withdrawal on June 28, 1950. He was

27. *Hanguk Ilbo*, May 20, 1961.

28. For additional information on General Park, consult Inmulge Sa, "On a Revolutionary Leader: Park Chung-hee" and Kim Chong-shin, *Seven Years with Korea's Park Chung-hee.*

29. Rebellions and defections and the subsequent mass purge within the military are fully discussed in *History of the Korean War*, pp. 437–505. See also the *New York Herald Tribune*, July 4, 1961; Glenn D. Paige, "Korea," in Cyril E. Black and Thomas P. Thornton, eds., *Communism and Revolution* (Princeton: Princeton University Press, 1964), pp. 236–37.

credited with leading to safety the trapped members of the Army Headquarters in Seoul.

After his three months at the Intelligence Bureau, he was to be transferred approximately twenty-five times in the next eleven years, from 1950 to 1961.[30] This does not include two interruptions of service so he could attend the advanced course of the U.S. Army Artillery School, Fort Sill, Oklahoma, in 1955 and later the Command and General Staff School of the ROK Army in 1957. At the time of the revolution he held the rank of Major General as Deputy Commander of the Second Army. An important observation to be made here is that General Park remained outside of the main political traffic in the Army. A product of the Southeastern region, he was never aligned with either one of the two four-star generals who had North Korean and Manchurian backgrounds. As a result, he was not favored either in assignment or in promotion, a fact which may explain twenty-five transfers in eleven years. Inevitable resentment against the faction- and favoritism-ridden Army must have played a part in his decision to participate in the revolution, but his motive seems to have been much deeper. First, his decision can be seen as a revival of the long-harbored revolutionary sentiment which almost ended his life in 1948. His dogged determination and unswerving dedication for a cause at the risk of his life indicates more than personal ambition; it represents an ideological commitment to social and political revolution.

Park was also a strongly anti-urban reformer. "Rotten" and "filthy" are two words he frequently uses to describe urban life. The long neglect of rural interests by civilian politicians, except for occasional bribes (or harassment) to induce votes, resulted in a greater privation in agriculture than in any other major sector. The massive grants and loans to agriculture during the initial period and the emphasis placed on constructing fertilizer plants by the junta government reflect Park's rural interests. Park is still basically a farmer, or country gentleman at best. Even today he is at his best in the rice paddies, working with the farmers. He does not, or cannot, seem to separate him-

---

30. Inmulge Sa, "On a Revolutionary Leader: Park Chung-hee," p. 17.

self from rural life and values. His love of native folk music rather than Western music further demonstrates his unbreakable attachment to that which is endemically Korean.

On the other hand, Park represents the new breed of scientifically oriented officers. As an artillery expert—he was the Commandant of the Artillery School upon his return to Korea because of his training in the U.S.—he seems to be thoroughly aware of the supremacy of technology in the modern world. His Five-Year Plan, unsurprisingly, is based upon the two goals of technological advancement and agricultural improvement. The plan excludes such matters as education and social welfare.

As a political leader, Park is more closely tied to the traditional system of administrative government than to representative democracy.[31] He belongs to the old and almost Prussian school of thought, which values administrative efficiency above individual freedom or popular representation. A revulsion for the bungling legislature of the Second Republic appears to have played a part in his decision to undertake the coup. The immediate dissolution of the National Assembly and the replacement of civilians with military officers in all the key executive and administrative positions bears out his distrust of representative government. General Park presented a sharp and enigmatic contrast to his predecessors, Syngman Rhee and John M. Chang. He was a soldier of rural background, a cultural chauvinist who embraced the new science, a revolutionist with a predilection for rule by administration, and a thoroughly modern man who nevertheless retained the traditional Confucian faith.

Park's decision to undertake the revolution would seem to be as much a reflection of genuine nationalism as personal resentment. His role in the coup is particularly important for several reasons. As the highest-ranking and oldest active-duty officer, he provided a central unifying element to more than 250 activists. His reputation as an uncorrupted officer projected a better

31. Park's political philosophy is well illustrated in two books which bear his name as the author: Park Chung-hee, *Our Nation's Path: Ideology of Social Reconstruction* (Seoul: Dong-A Publishing House, 1962), and *Kukka wa Hyŏngmyŏng kwa na [Nation, Revolution and I]* (Seoul: Hyang mun sa, 1963).

image for the revolutionary group, even though his loyalty was questioned at the outset of the revolution. Above all, his unflinching determination to push through the highly risky coup at a time of uncertainty made the revolution a success.

Park Chung-hee and Kim Jong-pil form the first two sides of the triangle. The third is Kim Dong-ha. A retired Marine Major General, Kim Dong-ha played a vital role in the coup by providing most of the troops actually used for the takeover of the capital city, Seoul.

Born in 1920 in the northern tip of the North Hamkyŏng Province contiguous to Manchuria and Soviet Russia, he was educated in Manchuria. Upon his graduation from the Yong Jeng Middle School in Kanto, Manchuria, he entered the Singkiang Military Institute in Singkiang, Manchuria, and graduated in 1942. After serving in the Kwantung Army as an officer until 1945, he returned to Hamkyŏng Province, which was now under communist rule. Defecting from North Korea, he came south in 1946 and immediately enlisted in the newly created South Korean Coast Guard. Because he was trained as an infantry officer, he was shifted to the Marine Corps when the war broke out, and he commanded various combat units until his retirement in 1960.

A product of the mountain region of rural Hamkyŏng Province and a career military man, he lacked urban manners and was known for his uncouth Northeastern mountain dialect. His brusqueness and stubbornness hindered his career in the Marines, and he never advanced beyond Brigadier General, the lowest rank among his contemporaries. Nonetheless, he was known for his military capability and for his relatively clean living. These qualities earned him the respect of his fellow officers, and he developed a self-righteous attitude.

As has been noted,[32] immediately after the downfall of the Rhee regime, Kim Dong-ha, as a Brigadier General commanding the Field Marine Division, clashed directly with Lt. General Kim T'ai-sik, the Rhee-appointed Marine Corps Commandant. For this insubordination, he was forced either to resign or to

32. See p. 79.

face a court-martial. Confronting the same situation as Kim Jong-pil, Kim Dong-ha developed a strong feeling of resentment both for the Marine leadership and for the government. Also, being an ardent anticommunist from North Korea, he was easily attracted by the revolutionary group, whose chief article of faith was anticommunism. Moreover, he, like most other *Northeastern*-oriented officers, resented the Northwestern prejudice of the Chang government and of the Army Chief of Staff, Lt. General Chang Do-young; and his revolutionary orientation received in Manchuria must have given him the final push for his decision to take part in the military coup.[33] With these three men—Kim Jong-pil, Park Chung-hee, and Kim Dong-ha —as the engine, hull, and fuel, the ship of revolution was launched.

May 16, 1961

During the predawn hours of May 16, 1961, the revolutionary forces—spearheaded by the First Marine Brigade, which dispersed the token resistance of about one hundred military police hastily deployed at the north of the Han River bridge— rolled into the capital city, Seoul. The predetermined key targets—radio stations, power plants, key government buildings, and police stations—were easily secured within three hours.

At exactly 5:00 A.M., the military takeover of the government was announced in the name of the Army Chief of Staff, Lt. General Chang Do-young, and this was immediately followed by the dropping of 350,000 leaflets of this same announcement. The announcement read as follows: "Our beloved patriotic brethren! The military authorities, having shown forbearance and self-restraint, at last launch all-out action this dawn, taking over the executive, legislative and judicial branches of the state and organizing a Military Revolutionary Council (MRC)."

The MRC then made six pledges:

1. Anti-communism will be the cardinal point of national policy and the nation's anti-communist alignment, which has thus far been no more than a matter of convention and a mere slogan, will be rearranged and strengthened.

33. See pp. 53–54.

2. The United Nations Charter will be observed and international agreements will be faithfully carried out. The friendly ties with the United States and other Free World nations will be further strengthened.

3. All corruption and past evil practice in this country will be wiped out and fresh and clean morality will be pursued in order to redress the degenerated national morality and spirit.

4. The condition of national life which is on the brink of despair and starvation will be quickly ameliorated and all-out efforts will be made for the reconstruction of a self-reliant national economy.

5. In order to implement the long-cherished national desire to reunify the divided land, all-out efforts will be directed towards making the nation capable of coping with communism.

6. As soon as such tasks are accomplished, we will ready ourselves to turn over the reigns of power to new and conscientious politicians and return to our original duties.

Next they appealed for the trust and support of the citizenry:

Beloved brethren!

We hope that the people will completely trust the Military Revolutionary Council and go about their daily tasks as usual.

Our nation from this moment is entering a new and glorious historical era with high hopes.

Our nation commands us to have patience and courage.

Long live Korea! Long live the revolutionary forces![34]

At 9:00 A.M., once again in the name of General Chang Do-young, nationwide martial law was proclaimed. The Army unit commanders consented to be responsible for the martial law administration. Months of arduous conspiracy, preparation, precision, and coordination by Kim Jong-pil had borne the first fruit. But the capture of Seoul was only one step; the real tests lay ahead.

The first test was making General Chang Do-young assume the leadership of the military revolution. As the Army Chief of Staff, General Chang held the highest command post of all Army units. His association with the conspiracy, therefore, would establish uninterrupted hierarchical authority over the Army units. At 4:30 P.M. on May 16,[35] after twelve hours of in-

34. *Hanguk Ilbo*, May 16, 1961, p. 1. The translated version of the first six pledges is from Park Chung-hee, "What Has Made the Military Revolution Successful?" *Koreana Quarterly*, III, no. 1 (Summer 1961), 18–19.

35. *A Complete Study of the May 16 Military Revolution*, p. 178. This book is the most complete coverage on the actual planning and execution

decision, General Chang became the Chairman of the Military Revolutionary Council. Although the circumstances in which he agreed to assume the leadership of the coup are still controversial, his action was the major turning point. Without his participation, the coup forces could have been crushed by the frontier units at the 'insistence' of General Carter M. Magruder, commander of the U.N. forces in Korea.

The second, and more important, test was to gain the support of the ROK First Field Army, for any one of those twenty combat-ready divisions could have destroyed the revolutionary forces, which numbered only 3,600.[36] The fate of the coup rested with the Army's Commander, Lt. General Yi Han-rim. General Yi had grave misgivings about the military revolution, not because he was opposed to the military coup as such, but because of his doubts about the leader of the movement, General Park. He gave four reasons for his denunciation of the coup:

1. The revolution cannot be supported because it ignored the Commander of the First Field Army.

2. The revolution cannot be supported because it was started by Park Chung-hee.

3. The revolution cannot be supported because it could be wiped out by deploying one tank company.

4. The revolution cannot be supported because many central figures of the revolution were known to be communist.[37]

Yet after issuing such a serious statement, General Yi did not take any decisive action to break up the coup during the first two critical days. On the third day, the revolutionaries placed him under arrest. His reluctance to act no doubt reflected his

---

of the military coup d'état yet to be published. The reader should be cautioned on the pro-junta interpretation of the military revolution.

36. The total revolutionary forces on May 16 were comprised of the following units: 1,000 Marines from the First Brigade under the direct command of Brig. Gen. Kim Yun-kun and Maj. Gen. Kim Dong-ha, retired; 1,000 members of the 30th Division under the command of Lt. Col. Yi Paek-il; 1,000 members of the Artillery unit in the Sixth Corps under the direction of Col. Moon Chae-jun and Lt. Col. Shin Yŏn-ch'ang; 500 members from the Paratrooper regiment under the leadership of Col. Park Ch'i-ok; 40 members from the Communication unit of the Sixth Army District Headquarters. All together 3,600 men were commanded by Maj. Gen. Park Chung-hee. For the detailed assignments each unit played, see *Records of the Korean Military Revolution*, p. 933.

37. *A Complete Study of the May 16 Military Revolution*, p. 182.

immediate concern for his own safety and the thousands of lives which would be lost. He was not asked to send in forces by any of the higher authorities, that is, the Chairman of the Joint Chiefs of Staff, the Army Chief of Staff, the President, or the Premier of the Republic. Moreover, there were several known active supporters of the coup under General Yi's command.[38] It also seemed that although General Yi condemned the unconstitutional aspect of the military revolution, he did not have such loyalty to the Chang government that he would risk his life for the protection of it. Possible communist takeover seemed somewhat remote.

General Yi, who was a product of the Northeastern region and the Manchurian Military Institute, in the final analysis let the revolution succeed by maintaining a neutral position. Unlike those who openly opposed the coup, he now enjoys considerable government favor under the present Park regime. He became the Minister of Construction after heading a government corporation for some years.

The third critical barrier to be overcome by the revolutionaries was the unequivocal opposition that would undoubtedly come from General Carter M. Magruder, the Commander of the United Nations Command in Korea, and from Minister Marshall Green, chargé d'affaires of the U.S. Embassy. As expected, at 11:00 A.M. on May 16 the following denunciation of the coup was announced by the U.N. Command:

General Magruder, in his capacity as Commander-in-Chief of the United Nations Command, calls upon all military personnel in his command to support the duly recognized Government of the Republic of Korea headed by Prime Minister Chang Myun (John M. Chang).

General Magruder expects that the chiefs of the Korean Armed Forces will use their authority and influence to see that control is immediately returned to governmental authorities and that order is restored in the armed forces.

Green then added:

The position taken by the Commander-in-Chief of the United Nations Command in supporting the freely elected and constitutionally

38. Ibid., pp. 180–85.

established Government of the Republic of Korea is one in which I fully concur.

I wish to make it emphatically clear that the United States supports the constitutional Government of the Republic of Korea as elected by the People of the Republic last July and as constituted by election last August of the Prime Minister.[39]

Such unequivocal words—released without reference to Washington—were terrific blows to the cause of the revolutionaries.

President Yun Po-sŏn, having heard a broadcast over the Voice of the United Nations Command (VUNC) of the Magruder and Green statements at about 11:00 A.M., requested that the two Americans come to the Blue House.[40] At the same time, General Magruder prepared a plan to mobilize a part of the U.S. troops in Korea and a contingent of the ROK First Army to crush the revolutionary forces in Seoul. This plan had to be abandoned at the insistence of President Yun Po-sŏn, who categorically opposed it. He considered it unwise to defend the Chang government, which had lost popular confidence, when to do so assuredly meant a blood bath in the capital city.[41]

President Yun's opposition to General Magruder's plan became even more decisive on the following morning. He dispatched his personal letters by air to the frontier commanders, pleading with them not to resort to any military action against the revolutionary force lest it cause destruction of life and property. Excerpts of the letter stated the following points:

. . . Our nation's fate is dependent upon how well we handle this sudden and grave situation which has already caused domestic and international reverberations.

There must be no human sacrifice in controlling this grave situa-

39. Walter Briggs, "The Military Revolution in Korea and Its Leader and Achievement," *Koreana Quarterly,* V, no. 2 (Summer 1963), 30.

40. There are two widely accepted views regarding the actions of the United States during the critical moments of the revolution. The first represents the American view that the United Nations Command in Seoul was helpless in the face of an implacable objection raised by the President against the deployment of U.S. and loyal Korean troops to put down the revolutionary forces. The other represents the speculative view of the Korean intelligentsia that the coup had been supported either directly or indirectly by some agency of the United States, because the revolution could not have been successful without American sanction.

41. Briggs, "Military Revolution in Korea," pp. 31–33.

tion. Mindful of the well-being of the citizens, the military must meet
this situation with equanimity, must be vigilant in defense of the
38th parallel, and must display its loyalty and strength for the best
interest of the country.

In closing, I am emphasizing again that there must be no bloodshed in bringing the situation under control.[42]

This personal message from President Yun, the head of state,
must have had a decisive effect on the frontier officers, because
they were not about to take the responsibility for unavoidable
bloodshed. To have acted without the sanction of higher authorities would have placed them in rebellion too. It was later
speculated that the revolutionary forces had made a prior agreement with President Yun with regard to his role during the
coup. Judging from his conduct immediately after the coup,
such a deal does not seem unlikely. How else would one explain
his insistence that the cabinet members, including Premier
Chang, who had gone into hiding, present themselves? Yun
stayed on as President for the first ten months of military rule.
His stay in office provided a sense of legitimacy and continuity;
most important, it did not require new diplomatic recognition
of the military regime.

In the light of these developments, Premier Chang, the political chief of the Second Republic, had little choice but to officially
"resign" from the premiership. On the afternoon of May 18, after
55 hours in hiding, he turned over the government to the Military Revolutionary Council—headed by General Chang Do-
young, one of his own appointees.[43] Chang's capitulation marked
the consummation of the long-brewing revolution. More im-
portantly, it ushered in a new epoch in which the "administrative" government supplanted the less than one-year-old Second Republic which placed the legislature in the position of
predominance.

Several immediate observations can be made concerning the
May 16 Military Revolution. First, a clear-cut manifestation of
factional elements can be observed both within and without the
Army. Three of the four major military figures who supported

42. *Records of the Korean Military Revolution*, I, 260.
43. *Hanguk Ilbo*, May 18, 1961, p. 1.

the coup were Northeastern products of Manchurian background,[44] and the fourth, of South-central origin, also had a Manchurian background.[45] General Yi Han-rim, the commander of the First Field Army, whose vacillation gave almost tacit permission for the coup, also was a Northeasterner of Manchurian persuasion. Without the support of these men—not to mention Kim Dong-ha and Kim Yun-kun, the two Marine Generals of Northeastern origin who provided a Marine Brigade for the coup—the outcome of the revolution would have been uncertain.

In the civilian arena, a similar manifestation of factionalism can be seen. The fact that President Yun opposed any counter-coup in defense of the Chang government seems to imply that he may have secretly welcomed the coup as a means of avenging himself upon his political rivals. Chang and Yun were members of the Democratic Party until their split after the election of July 29, 1960.

The popular reaction to the military takeover during the critical days was neither one of enthusiastic welcome nor of violent rejection. Rather, the people showed indifference to the coup as if the inevitable had finally occurred. After the coup, the prevailing mood was one of uncertainty as to the future.

The revolution effectively demonstrated what a small number of determined officers could accomplish under proper direction and coordination. A dozen or so original conspirators among 250 activists, which is an infinitely small number in an army of 600,000, staged a successful coup. Effective neutralization of many potential foes within the officer corps was the artful work of Kim Jong-pil, the director and coordinator of the coup. Once the act was committed, the reluctant and indecisive officers were caught up in the whirlwind of the initial thrust. This seemingly easy accomplishment was to become the alluring example for sixteen subsequent abortive countercoups attempted since May 16, 1961.

44. Lt. General Park Im-hang, Commander of the Fifth Corps, who replaced Lt. General Yi Han-rim on May 18; Maj. General Yi Chu-il was Chief of Staff of the Second Army; and Brig. General Yun T'ai-il was assigned to Army Headquarters.

45. Lt. General Min Ki-shik, Commander of the Second Corps.

The majority of the revolutionary activists were recruited from a group of outcasts—the malcontent and rural-oriented officers from the eighth and the second classes of OCS.[46] Personal dissatisfactions, however, were only partly responsible. These officers were also deeply aware of social injustice and seized power in the name of, and for the sake of, the masses—but without the active participation of the masses.[47]

The military revolution of May 16 can be viewed as the culmination of the nationalistic revolution started by the students a year earlier. Although the military's concept of nationalism was at some variance with that of the students, the two groups shared the desire to see a reassertion of Korean values and the adoption of a "Korea-first" policy. Foreign products and values were denounced by the students in the "New Life Movement"[48] and by the military in its demand for the "elimination of the old evils."[49] The students simply demanded the elders not to smoke foreign cigarettes and not to drink foreign coffee; the military used the cruder but more effective method of burning such products before the eyes of the public. The students advocated neutralism as the solution for all political and economic problems; the military made an avowed reaffirmation of anti-communism as the ideological facade. In the Korean context, neutralism and anticommunism were two sides of the same coin —nationalism. Neutralism must not be interpreted as capitulation to the communist threat, nor anticommunism as simple acquiescence to American demands. They are similar manifestations of the "Korea first" notion.[50]

46. For further information on the socioeconomic backgrounds of the revolutionary activists, see C. I. Eugene Kim, "The South Korean Military Coup of May 1961," in Jacques Van Dooran, ed., *Armed Forces and Society* (The Hague: Mouton, 1968), pp. 298–316.

47. Johnson, "Revolution and Social System," p. 22.

48. See p. 31.

49. Several other frequently used mottoes by the military were "recreation of man," "the change of generations," "national unification through the destruction of communism."

50. Kim Jong-pil, the spokesman of the junta government, espoused the highly chauvinistic new principle of "nationalistic democracy." See Hong Sǔng-myǒn, "Park chǒnggwon ui minjok ron?" ["What is the Meaning of Nationalistic Democracy by the Park Administration?"] *Sasangge Monthly*, XI, no. 12 (December 1963), 78–86. See also Kim sǒn-shik,

The nationalist movement carried with it a challenge to the older generation. The student revolution indicted the entire generation as responsible for the rise of Rhee and the failure to improve the lot of the people. Students even demanded the right to take part in national policy-making. The military revolution actually dislodged the older generation from the power structure and replaced it with a younger breed, calling attention to this "change of generations." The blacklisting of over 5,000 politicians and the ousting of 40 generals "to make room for deserving junior officers" symbolized the impatience for change among the young military leaders, as well as their antipathy toward the old functionaries.[51] The emphasis on youth rather than rank or age symbolized the spirit of both the student and the military revolutions.

Student violence was the appropriate response to the resistance to change of the Rhee regime, given the fact that all avenues to reform were blocked. The military revolution, too, showed a violent reaction to a regime totally incapable of solving social and economic problems. The difference lies in the nature of the regime under attack.

These two revolutions, taken together, seems to fit the pattern of the classical revolutionary cycle—the decline of autocratic despotism, the rise of the moderates, and the emergence of extremists in the wake of the moderates' failure.[52] Hence, the logical inquiry to be made in the succeeding chapters is whether the military rule in Korea simply represents Thermidor reaction in the historic cycle or a new and distinct political phenomenon as it claims the role of innovator.

"Minjok chui wa minju chui" ["Nationalistic Democracy and Democracy"], *Sasangge Monthly*, XIII, no. 11 (November 1963), 50–56. See also Park Chung-hee, *Our Nation's Path: Ideology of Social Reconstruction*, pp. 216–47.

51. *Hanguk Ilbo*, June 4, 1961, p. 1.

52. According to Crane Brinton, the old autocratic system is first replaced by moderates who in turn are supplanted by extremists. For a comparative and analytical study of the Cromwellian, French, American, and Soviet Revolutions, see Crane Brinton, *Anatomy of Revolution* (New York: W. W. Norton, 1938).

Chapter *VI*

CONSOLIDATION OF POWER

The military overthrow of the constitutionally elected government, no matter how justifiable it might have been in terms of inefficacy of the civilian leadership and nobility of the military's intentions, clearly constituted a violaton of legitimacy. Hence it aroused in the Korean intellectual community a general sense of negativism and skepticism. It met with hostility from those who were loyal to the old regime and from those who faced the prospect of more loss than gain from the new order. There was also an inevitable postrevolutionary trauma, stemming from the threat from other aspiring military officers and from the internal power struggle.

To surmount negativism, skepticism, antipathy, and postrevolutionary uncertainty, the military junta immediately undertook several actions: the restoration of stability, the institution of needed reforms, a massive internal and external propaganda campaign, and the creation of an anti-coup mechanism, the Central Intelligence Agency.

The Supreme Council for National Reconstruction (SCNR) and the Beginning of Reform

On May 19, three days after the coup and only one day after the formal assumption of power, the military leadership launched a more constructive approach by changing the name of the junta government to the auspicious title of the Supreme Council for National Reconstruction (SCNR). On the following day, May 20, the thirty-two men of SCNR began to function as the supreme governmental policy-making and policy-executive body. On May 21, the military officers were reassigned as cabinet ministers.[1] The following oath was re-pledged by the military officers who undertook ministerial and administrative tasks:

I do solemnly pledge to the people that I will concentrate my efforts upon strengthening national power for the unification of the nation, developing the national economy, preserving national independence and freedom, strengthening the ties with the U.N. and friendly countries, and overcoming the national crisis through the strengthening of power and effectiveness to combat communism and complete the elimination of corruption and social evils, acting in the basis of the patriotic spirit of the *glorious* armed force.[2]

Such affirmation of high ideals was a deliberate design to win public confidence, but the appointment of Lt. General Kim Hong-il, a 62-year-old retired Army officer, to the post of Foreign Minister and as an SCNR advisor was an earnest act to

1. For a background study of the new cabinet ministers, see *Hanguk Ilbo*, May 20, 1961, p. 1.

2. *New York Times*, May 21, 1961, p. 1, col. 4. This pledge is almost identical to the one which the Turkish junta used on June 24, 1960, at the occasion of the formal assumption of power. The Turkish oath went as follows: "I pledge myself to the service of the Turkish nation, without expecting any reward, and without any other motivations than the principles of morality, justice, law, human rights, and the dictates of my own conscience. I will work for nothing other than the welfare of the nation and for its sovereignty. I will not depart from the goal of rooting the Republic in the new Constitution, and transferring power to the new Parliament. To this I pledge my honor and all that is sacred." Quoted from Walter F. Weiker, *The Turkish Revolution, 1960–1961: Aspects of Military Politics* (Washington, D.C.: The Brookings Institution, 1963), p. 116.

establish stability. General Kim, who had been a Maj. General of the regular Chinese Army, the President of the Military Academy, the South Korean ambassador to Formosa, and a member of the Upper House of the Second Republic, was a senior professional soldier who commanded immense respect from both military officers and civilians.[3] This appointment greatly lessened the initial skepticism which the populace felt toward the military. The retention of the Chiefs of Staff of all the service branches, the retention of the Chairman of the Joint Chiefs of Staff, and the inclusion of all the highest-ranking officers in SCNR had an important stabilizing effect upon national life at the onset of military rule.[4]

On June 6, 1961, the SCNR promulgated the Law Regarding Extraordinary Measures for National Reconstruction. This edict was designed, first, to put the stamp of legality on the coup, and, second, to assume officially all the governing power of the country.[5] It was a document of 24 articles and of fewer than 3,000 words, investing the SCNR with virtually all power—legislative, executive, and a part of the judicial—that had been in the hands of the previous government. (The entire text of this emergency act is found in Appendix 1.)

Article 1, seeking to justify the existence of the military government, stated that "the Supreme Council for National Reconstruction shall be established as the extraordinary measures intended for the reconstruction of the Republic of Korea as a genuine democratic republic by safeguarding the Republic of

3. For more information on Kim Hong-il, see Japan Foreign Ministry, *Kendai chosen zinmei ziten* [*Biographical Dictionary of Modern Koreans*] (Tokyo: Sekai Janarusha, 1962), p. 96.

4. Lt. General Kim Chong-o, Chairman of the Joint Chiefs of Staff; Lt. Gen. Yi Sŏng-ho, Navy Chief of Staff; Lt. Gen. Kim Shin, Air Force Chief of Staff; Lt. Gen. Kim Sŏng-ŭn, Marine Corps Commandant. These gentlemen were the appointees of the Chang government. Lt. Gen. Chang Do-young, Chairman of the SCNR, retained his position as Army Chief of Staff. For documentation of the Orders and Decrees by the SCNR, see *Records of the Korean Military Revolution*, II, 3–19.

5. For the entire context of this law in English, see The Secretariat, Supreme Council for National Reconstruction, *Military Revolution in Korea*, pp. 149–56. For an analysis and interpretation of the law, see Han T'ae-yŏn, *Kukka chaegŏn pisang choch'ipŏb* [*The Law Regarding Extraordinary Measures for National Reconstruction*] (Seoul: Pŏbmun sa, 1961).

Korea against communist aggression and by overcoming the national crisis which resulted from corruption, injustice, and poverty."[6] Article 2 designated the junta as "the supreme governing organ of the Republic of Korea, pending the establishment of a government following the composition of the National Assembly by means of a general election to be held after the completion of the tasks of the military revolution of May 16."[7] Article 9 gave the SCNR all legislative powers which the now-dissolved National Assembly had exercised, as well as the power to determine the national budget.[8]

Also invested in the SCNR were extensive appointive and dismissal powers of key government officials—for example, chiefs of staff, ambassadors, provincial governors, mayors of medium-size cities, justices, and prosecutors.[9] As an explicit warning to those who might engage in antirevolutionary conduct, Article 22 said that "the SCNR may enact special laws in order to punish those who, prior to or after the May 16 Military Revolution, have perpetrated any anti-state or anti-national acts, or counter-revolutionary activities."[10]

The original Constitution was *not* formally suspended; but, Article 24, the last of the SCNR articles, stated: "The provision of the Constitution which may conflict with the Law Regarding Extraordinary Measures for National Reconstruction shall be governed by this Law."[11] Commenting on the sweeping power which the SCNR gave itself, the *New York Times* reported: "The junta assumed all dictatorial powers that not even Rhee had enjoyed."[12]

Once all the government positions were filled, a series of reforms were undertaken by the SCNR in order to win confidence and elicit support from the populace. The first spectacular action was the announcement of the arrest of 4,200 hoodlums and thousands of beggars who were plaguing the urban cen-

6. *Military Revolution in Korea*, p. 149.
7. Ibid.
8. Ibid., p. 151.
9. Ibid., p. 152.
10. Ibid., p. 155.
11. Ibid.
12. *New York Times*, June 7, 1961, p. 1, col. 7.

ters.[13] An even more spectacular action was the parading of the hoodlums in the streets of Seoul on May 24, 1961. They were later turned over to the Public Works Office for "useful contributions" to the state.

Besides such conspicuous and relatively simple "street cleaning," a series of decrees was issued by the Martial Law Command to show its determination for puritanism and austerity.[14] The rationing of rice at restaurants was introduced (Decree No. 3, May 20); a stiffer screening of movies not in harmony with the spirit of revolution was to be enforced (Decree No. 5, May 21); and severe punishment for illegal disposition of military material was to be imposed (Decree No. 6, May 28).[15]

As part of the display of reforming zeal, smugglers, black-marketeers, and usurers came under attack.[16] For smugglers and black-marketeers, the Articles merely required strict enforcement of existing laws, but for usurers, a new law was required, and on May 25 a special decree (SCNR Decree No. 12) was announced. It invalidated the rights of certain creditors in cases where the interest rule was more than 20 percent per annum (the usual rate of private loans between individuals in Korea was from 60 to 80 percent per annum).[17] Of particular significance was that these provisions were to be applied to farmers and fishermen only; commercial, industrial, or other types of loans more urban in occurrence, were not covered. If properly reported, debts incurred by the agricultural and fishing industries might be assumed by the government. That the revolution had been led by officers from rural backgrounds, particularly Park Chung-hee, is well-documented by this prejudicial decree.

13. *Hanguk Ilbo*, May 22, 1961, p. 1. Also announced on the same day was the arrest of over 2,000 communist agents and suspects.

14. The Martial Law Command should be differentiated from the SCNR. The Command was the instrument of control of the SCNR.

15. *Records of the Korean Military Revolution*, II, 46–47.

16. For the arrest records of profiteers and others guilty of business misdemeanors, see Republic of Korea, Office of Public Information, *Uri chŏngbu neun muŏtsŭl ŏttŏkke haewatneun'ga* [*How and What Our Government Accomplished*] (Seoul: Office of Public Information, 1964), p. 132.

17. *Hanguk Ilbo*, May 25 and 26, 1961, p. 1.

Calling for a responsible press, the new regime initiated a policy designed to streamline and control the mass media. Articles 1 and 2 of Decree 11 enjoined press and communication media from operation if they did not possess their own printing facilities or transmitting and receiving equipment.[18] As a result, 1,230 out of the total of 1,573 press and news services were closed down, leaving only 343 which had been in existence prior to April 19, 1960.[19]

Before long, the most reluctant elements in civilian society began to endorse the military government.[20] Apparently they relished the restoration of order and the successful beginning of reform; in any case, they considered the military revolution an accomplished fact. On May 28, less than two weeks after the takeover, the most conservative and outspoken critic of the military junta, *Dong-A Ilbo*, a Seoul daily newspaper with the largest circulation in the nation (over 300,000), came out in support of the military revolution. The editorial on this occasion cautioned:

> . . . It is our conclusion that due to the overinsistence upon democratic legalism prior to May 16, Korea was in danger of a communist success.
>
> The May 16 Military Revolution was undertaken because the situation was critical. It was the last hope for the establishment of liberal democracy in Korea. Henceforth, this military revolution must succeed.
>
> . . . We the citizens must be aware of the great historic meaning and mission of the May 16 Military Revolution and must recognize that the success of the revolution is the only remaining opportunity for the construction of a democratic nation.[21]

Sasangge Monthly, the most influential and prestigious social science journal, carried only a qualified endorsement of the

18. *Hanguk Ilbo*, June 24, 1961. The entire Decree 11 is found there.
19. For a further breakdown on the kinds of news and press services, see Office of Public Information, *Chŏngbu chungyo Sich'aek mit ŏpjŏk* [*Government's Major Policies and Accomplishments*] (Seoul: Republic of Korea, 1961), pp. 40–41. This measure was adopted not to stifle freedom of the press, but to promote the integrity of the press by wiping out spurious presses that sprang up during the Second Republic.
20. See editorial in *Hanguk Ilbo*, May 21, 1961.
21. *Dong-A Ilbo*, May 28, 1961, p. 1.

military government in its June editorial. The journal complimented the military government for its success in "making the citizens respect law, reinvigorating the sagging morale, banishing the hoodlums, punishing the illegal fortune makers, and relieving the debt-ridden farmers and fishermen from privation. . . ." It acknowledged, however, that several problems still existed because of "the inherent difficulty of concurrently executing political, social, and moral reform in an environment so inimical due to hundreds of years of interwoven social evils, mephitic habits, and primitive poverty. . . ." The journal then appealed to the military government, asking that it "resolve all the tasks with precise scientific planning and unfailing resolution. . . ." It then asked the citizens not to follow blindly but "to render self-assured and intelligent support" to the military's nation-rebuilding effort.[22]

In this first stage of the revolution, the junta government asserted its anticommunism, denounced the past regimes, emphasized restoration of law and order, and granted relief to the poor. Next it began to search for an ideological position which would provide long-term justification for its power and facilitate the launching of stage two.

The second stage of the revolution is divided into two phases: first, the military performs the role of the doctor, curing old ills; second, the military acts as the nation's tutor, preparing it for the democratic system. Park Chung-hee used the doctor-patient analogy in commenting on the meaning of the revolution: "The Military Revolution is not the destruction of democracy in Korea. Rather it is a way for saving it; it is a *surgical operation* intended to excise a malignant social, political, and economic tumor. The revolution was staged with the compassion of a benevolent surgeon who sometimes must cause pain in order to preserve life and restore health."[23]

22. "Minjujui wa kunsa hyŏngmyŏng" ["Democracy and the Military Revolution"], *Sasangge Monthly*, IX, no. 6 (June 1961), 4.

23. Park Chung-hee, *Our Nation's Path: Ideology of Social Reconstruction* (Seoul: Dong-A Publishing House, 1962), pp. 197–98. It must be noted that the military junta borrowed extensively from the Egyptian military's revolutionary experience. The statement by Park Chung-hee is almost an exact replica of Nasser's 1954 summary of his entire revolution-

The junta government repeatedly claimed that the revolution was only a temporary suspension of democratic process, not of democratic characteristics. Once the sources of ill were removed and the patient saved, the doctor would change its mission to one of a tutor. As Park wrote, "The aim of our revolution was . . . to lay a solid foundation for rebuilding true democracy" and "to strengthen the autonomous ability of the people." This he proposed to accomplish by implanting and developing among the general public what Park described as "democratic factors."[24] Implicit in these arguments is that democracy is possible first, when the leadership prepares the public for it and, second, when the leadership is given a mandate or has assumed power necessary for such a mission.

This antidemocratic method of democratizing the nation was aptly labeled "Administrative Democracy," and Park proceeded with his task by employing "administrative means" and abandoning "political means."[25] Under such an avowed intention of tutorial rule, the military appointed itself the promoter of democracy, the educator of the public, the foremost exponent of patriotism, and the champion of economic planning. For the first efforts and for the purpose of gaining the confidence of the masses, the junta government inaugurated a massive education or, more accurately, propaganda campaign; later, the first major economic planning was launched with added urgency.

---

ary philosophy: "We are like a father who gives his son medicine, however painful it is to him, for he knows that he saves the life of his child." Gamal Abdel Nasser, in a speech on July 22, 1954, commemorating the second anniversary of Egypt's revolution; quoted from Keith Wheelock, *Nasser's New Egypt* (New York: Frederick A. Praeger, 1960), p. 38.

24. Park Chung-hee, *Our Nation's Path*, p. 208.

25. Ibid., p. 198. This philosophy of "Administrative Democracy" is borrowed from Sukarno's "Guided Democracy," which Sukarno defined as follows: "Yes, indeed, without concealing anything we have made a complete divorce from Western democracy, which is free-right liberalism, but on the other hand since ancient times, we have flatly rejected dictatorship. Guided Democracy is the democracy of the family system without the anarchy of liberalism, without the autocracy of a dictatorship." For more information on Sukarno, see "The Rediscovery of Our Revolution: Political Manifesto," *Political Manifesto Republic of Indonesia of 17th August, 1959* (Department of Information, Republic of Indonesia, n.p., n.d.), p. 62.

Education and Political Propaganda and Development of Anticommunism

With the first issue of the *New Nation Weekly* on August 7, 1961, a massive array of educational and propagandistic materials began to inundate both urban and rural areas. Fifteen million copies of the *New Nation Weekly*—containing various pieces of information on agriculture, current events, and the weekly accomplishments of the junta government—were distributed in the first two years at nominal cost. In addition, millions of copies of national mottoes, anticommunist and antiforeign slogans, pamphlets containing Park Chung-hee's speeches, and listings of government accomplishments were distributed free of charge.[26] Loudspeakers and radio transmitters were also widely employed. In the first two years, the junta government distributed over 20,000 transistor radios and over 1,000 loudspeakers. Eleven new transmitting stations were constructed, and a tremendous increase in the number of government broadcasts followed.[27] Furthermore, from May 16, 1961, to September 30, 1962, 237 films were made and shown to culturally deprived rural audiences free of charge.[28]

The deluge of occasionally educational but mainly propagandistic materials was accompanied by similar efforts directed toward a foreign audience. *Korean Report*, a monthly government publication, was put out in English, French, Spanish, German, and Japanese and was freely distributed to government and educational institutions in the major countries. In addition, thousands of special books and booklets—such as *Korea Moves Ahead, Military Revolution in Korea, The Revolution in Korea, News from Korea, Korea at a Glance,* and *Facts about Korea*—were freely circulated upon request.[29] At the present time, it is known that the Korean government

26. *Records of the Korean Military Revolution*, I, 1739–42.
27. Republic of Korea, *Administrative White Paper* (Seoul: Kwangmyŏng Printing Co., 1962), pp. 400–412.
28. *Records of the Korean Military Revolution*, I, 1742.
29. This information was furnished by the Korean Information Service in Washington, D.C.

spends more money for its "information service" in Washington than any other country except the U.S.S.R.[30]

This intensified propaganda campaign produced two major achievements: publicity for the new military leadership and its activities, and the development of a political consciousness and a sense of popular appreciation of the new government. These propaganda efforts, backed up with relief for the poor and distribution of fertilizer to farmers, apparently made a decisive impact on the rural voters, at least as reflected in their voting on the referendum of the new constitution in December 1962 and on the presidential election in October of the following year.[31]

Creation of the Korean Central Intelligence Agency and Its Activities

A clique that has seized power must guard itself against those who might seek to emulate its successful actions. Therefore, to avoid the fate of the regime that it had deposed, the junta constructed an elaborate and effective security apparatus.

The Central Intelligence Agency was created on June 19, 1961 (Decree No. 619, 1961), and was placed directly under the SCNR. Article 1 defined the functions of this organization as follows: "The Central Intelligence Agency was created directly under the Supreme Council of National Reconstruction in order to supervise and coordinate both international and domestic intelligence activities and criminal investigation by all government intelligence agencies, including that of the military."[32] In other words, the new body was to become the highest and most powerful intelligence and investigatory agency.

The first man appointed to organize the CIA was Kim Jong-pil, who held no position in either the SCNR or the cabinet.

30. The writer was informed of this fact by Mr. Kim Po-sŏng, former Director of the Korean Information Service in Washington, D.C.

31. *Records of the Korean Military Revolution, II,* 550. See also C. I. Eugene Kim, "Significance of the 1963 Korean Election," *Asian Survey,* XVII, no. 1 (March 1964), 765–73.

32. *Hanguk Ilbo,* June 21, 1961, p. 2. For the various activities and arrest records, see *Records of the Korean Military Revolution,* I, 1743–46. For the entire text of Decree No. 619, see Ibid., II, 610.

Kim, utilizing the existing Army Counter Intelligence Corps, built a 3,000-man elite corps to handle all intelligence and investigation work. The first task undertaken by the CIA was a loyalty check which involved the screening of all major political figures and high-ranking government employees. The CIA later announced that it had screened and checked over 41,000 persons, of whom 1,863 were found guilty of some culpable actions or past misdeeds.[33] This clearly served as a serious warning to potential plotters against the revolution.

The CIA, with its unlimited power, emerged as the group to be feared most during the postrevolutionary period. Under the shrewd and capable direction of Kim Jong-pil, the CIA became the eyes and ears of Park Chung-hee, effectively eliminating antirevolutionary elements both within and without the SCNR. From June 1961 to May 1963, thirteen antirevolutionary or counterrevolutionary cases were discovered. Two particular antirevolutionary incidents deserve elbaoration since they shed light on the internal power struggle.

Lt. General Chang Do-young and Major Gen. Kim Dong-ha

On July 4, only six weeks after the coup, Lt. General Chang Do-young relinquished his two remaining positions, that of Chairman of the SCNR and that of cabinet chief. General Chang's dual resignation was announced by him in the following manner:

> From the start of the May Revolution, I felt that my ability and experience was insufficient for me to assume heavy responsibilities as the top man of the revolutionary government. But I assumed the duties temporarily until the proper man could be selected for the sake of the maintenance of order in the nation's emergency.
>
> Now that the foundation of the revolutionary government is established, more positive goals of the revolution should be achieved. For the implementation of the goals, I feel inadequate and I recognize a strong need for a more active and capable person who commands the confidence and respect of the populace. Hence, I am resigning from my position today.[34]

33. Ibid., I, 1746.
34. *Hanguk Ilbo*, July 4, 1961, p. 1. See also *New York Times*, July 4, 1961, p. 1, col. 5.

Resigning with him were three other members of the SCNR who were considered to be his closest associates. Appointed to replace him as the head of cabinet was Song Yo-ch'an, a retired Lieutenant General, who has been in Washington since his resignation from the Army in June 1960.[35] Park Chung-hee, who has long been known as the key figure of the coup, assumed the chairmanship of the SCNR.

At the outset the resignation of Chang and his immediate colleagues seemed to be only the end of the first phase of the revolutionary cycle—the elimination of the frontal figures. Chang was a draftee to the revolution, not an original instigator, as has been noted earlier. The ousting of such a man as Chang, who had his own methods of subterfuge and power politics, was not without repercussions. To forestall the escalation of an internal power struggle, a full-scale purge was initiated.

On July 9 the Deputy Chief of the CIA, Lt. Col. Sŏk Chŏng-sŏn, announced that "the CIA has discovered a plot to assassinate the central figures of the revolution by antirevolutionary forces led by Lt. General Chang Do-young and 45 others."[36] Lt. Col. Sŏk also stated that all 45 officers had been arrested for "their willful forging of factionalism, plotting against the central forces of the revolution, and attempting to eliminate Maj. General Park Chung-hee by assassination."[37] Among these alleged plotters were three members of the SCNR, all of whom had resigned five days earlier with Chang. They were Col. Park Ch'i-ok, the Commander of the paratroop unit, who had furnished 1,000 men at the time of the coup; Maj. General Song Ch'ang-ho, Chairman of the Education and Social Affairs Committee in the SCNR; and Col. Moon Chae-jun, the Chief of the Army Military Police.

On the same day, in a separate announcement, the SCNR gave a detailed account of the attempted counter-coup, and charged Chang with personal ambition for greater power. The

35. Song Yo-ch'an was the former Martial Law Commander during the last days of the Rhee regime and subsequently resigned from the Army; he was sent into exile and went to the U.S.

36. *Hanguk Ilbo*, July 9, 1961, p. 1.

37. Ibid.

logic of events and the information given to the author by many former high-ranking officers of the ROK army strongly substantiate the charge made by the SCNR against the Chang faction. In fact, Chang had been unhappy and uneasy with the promulgation of the "Extraordinary Law" on June 6, which held that the Chairman of the SCNR could not be Army Chief of Staff at the same time.[38] Also on July 9, Chang grudgingly relinquished three of his five positions—those of Army Chief of Staff, Martial Commander, and Defense Minister. He retained only two posts—Chairman of the SCNR and head of the cabinet.[39] Seeing his power directly threatened, he began to consolidate his position by removing both the Park supporters and the Northeastern elements, the latter constituting an overwhelming majority in the SCNR.

Chang began to build his own factional strength with the support of both the Northwestern and Christian leaders. According to the SCNR announcement, Chang sought to install Dr. Paik Nak-jun (George Paik) as the head of the cabinet.[40] Dr. Paik, former president of the Yŏn-sei University in Seoul as well as former president of the House of Councillors (the Upper House under the Second Republic), was a well-known Christian figure of Northwestern origin. Sensitive to Chang's manipulations, the SCNR charged him with the sinister scheme of reviving factionalism in order to overthrow the central and original elements of the revolution.[41] General Chang was sentenced to death by a military court, but he and his underlings were later released by special amnesty and were sent to the U.S., the favorite exile ground for unfortunate Korean politicians and generals.

The SCNR made similar charges of personal ambition and

38. *Records of the Korean Military Revolution*, II, 605. See also Han T'ae-yŏn, *Kukka chaegŏn pisang choch-pŏb*[*The Law Regarding Extraordinary Measures for National Reconstruction*] (Seoul: Pŏbmun sa, 1961), pp. 78–80.

39. *Hanguk Ilbo*, June 6, 1961, p. 1.

40. Ibid., July 9, 1961, p. 1. For more biographical information on Dr. Paik, see *Biographical Dictionary of Modern Koreans*, p. 214.

41. *Hanguk Ilbo*, July 9, 1961, p. 1.

factionalism against the two other former members. Col. Moon Chae-jun, the Commander of the Army Military Police as well as a member of the SCNR, had joined the plot from personal resentment of the CIA, which had become the overlord of the Military Police Command. Col. Park Ch'i-ok, the Commander of the paratroop unit which had made such an important contribution to the coup, had been dissatisfied because he was not appointed to head the newly created Capital Defense Command. Park was a Northwestern-oriented officer.[42]

After the elimination of Chang and his associates, another internal power struggle began to loom, this time between Kim Jong-pil and Kim Dong-ha, the two most important and powerful men next to Park Chung-hee himself. The main source of irritation was the CIA and Kim Jong-pil's power in that organization. Kim Jong-pil, enjoying the complete confidence of Park, exercised intelligence and police power with impunity. The senior members in the SCNR resented Kim and felt threatened by the CIA. Kim was not a member of SCNR and, therefore, was not subjected to its scrutiny.

The long-brewing power conflict between Kim Jong-pil and his key opponent, Marine Major General Kim Dong-ha, came to a head in mid-January 1963 over the organizational structure of a new political party being developed by Kim Jong-pil and his CIA. The Marine General charged that the party, later named Democratic Republican Party, was organized as Kim Jong-pil's personal machine for the promised election in the fall. More fundamentally, Kim Dong-ha opposed the idea creating a political party to perpetuate the military rule.

Kim Jong-pil's CIA in the meantime had resorted to highly irregular methods for raising necessary election funds. They were (1) the importation of 1,642 duty-free automobiles from Japan and their sale at more than double the original price;[43] (2) the importation of 880 duty-free pinball machines; (3) the construction of the Walker Hill Hotel complex at a cost much

42. For a detailed study of the Chang Do-yong case, see *A Complete Study of the May 16 Military Revolution*, pp. 404–12.
43. Normal rate of duty for automobiles is 110 percent.

higher than normally would have been required; and (4) the issuance and irregular manipulation of stocks and bonds. These cases were later to be known as the "Four Major Cases of Grave Suspicion."[44]

Using these highly irregular acts by the CIA as the basis for the case, Maj. General Kim Dong-ha formulated a plan to dislodge Kim Jong-pil entirely from the power structure. The intention was to force Kim Jong-pil's temporary exile and a transfer of power to a civilian body in accordance with the revolutionary pledge.[45] For this purpose, Kim Dong-ha sought support from Lt. General Park Im-hang, Commander of the First Field Army of ROKA, a long-time friend who shared the Northeastern and Manchurian background.[46] Before its maturity, however, the well-intentioned coup was thwarted by the CIA, and Kim Dong-ha and Park Im-hang were both court-martialed in April. Their opposition to the CIA and to Kim Jong-pil had not been totally in vain, for Kim Jong-pil resigned from the chairmanship of the party immediately after the dispute and on February 25, 1963, left on an eight-month foreign junket.

The elimination of Kim Dong-ha and the exile of Kim Jong-pil marked the completion of the internal power struggle. Park Chung-hee remained alone on the pinnacle of power. Also completed was the turnover of the membership of the SCNR. By February 1963, only six of the original thirty-two remained; the rest either had been imprisoned or sent into exile. The number of members in the SCNR was reduced to twenty-two by July 1963, making it more manageable.

By this time, CIA activities guaranteed the elimination of the so-called antirevolutionary elements both within and without the junta government. CIA efficiency meant certain failure to any counter-coup; it was the prime reason for the continuation of the military in power. Kim Jong-pil's personal character and his high-handedness as the director of the CIA became a major

44. For a detailed study of this case, see *Hanguk Ilbo*, September 25, 1963, p. 2.
45. *A Complete Study of the May 16 Military Revolution*, pp. 473–84.
46. Ibid.

political issue in the fall election of 1963. Park's junta government was bitterly criticized for what the opposition called "politics by Intelligence" and "politics by Investigation."[47]

Hanguk Ilbo cautiously endorsed the CIA: ". . . The CIA was of necessity created during the postrevolutionary period, first, to coordinate and centrally direct all the activities of intelligence and investigation and, second, to gather policy data necessary for national policy making." The paper, however, proposed the following in regard to the Intelligence Agency. ". . . Upon the termination of the military rule, intelligence, investigative and other related governmental functions must not, in any condition, reside outside or above the three branches of the governmental or beyond political scrutiny." It went on to warn its readers about the ever-present possibility of another revolution: ". . . It must be remembered soberly that the violation of fundamental rights by those who should have defended them results in the desertion of them by the people and would lead to a recurrence of violent reaction like the one manifested in the April 19 Student Revolution. . . ."[48]

The net effect of the CIA activities with regard to the intrarevolutionary power struggle was the almost total elimination of officers with North Korean backgrounds. First, Chang Do-young and his cohorts were eliminated; next, Kim Dong-ha and Park Im-hang, the two most powerful Northeastern elements, were purged. All seven Lt. Generals ousted after the coup were officers of North Korean birth. One major observation that can be made from the CIA activities is that the elimination of both Kim Dong-ha and Park Im-hang virtually terminated the long honeymoon between Park and the Northeastern elements which had been so decisively important in staging the coup and in ousting the Northwestern elements afterward.

No one was greatly surprised when the cabinet of the Third Republic was announced in December 1963: no *Northwestern* men, civilian or military, were appointed; and only one *Northeastern* man, Chung Il-gwon—who is credited with saving the

47. *Hanguk Ilbo*, October 12, 1963, p. 1.
48. Ibid., October 12, 1963, p. 2.

career of Park Chung-hee in 1948—was given a post.[49] Seven of the twenty cabinet posts went to men from the Southeastern Kyŏng-sang Province. Indeed, a new power structure emerged on a geographical line with the help of the CIA.

The First Five-Year Economic Plan

In order to make a full assessment of the military in politics, mention must be made of the epoch-making First Five-year Economic Development Program inaugurated by the junta.[50] On January 13, 1962, the SCNR made public the entire program, including projected goals, of the First Five-Year Plan. The plan was the culmination of six months of arduous preparation by the Economic Planning Council, which had come into being on July 22, 1961.[51]

Under the rather auspicious name of "guided capitalistic system," defined by the SCNR as "economic policies based upon the principle of free enterprise, respecting the freedom and originality of private citizens," the policies provided that the Government either directly participate in or indirectly use inducement policies in key sectors and other major fields; that is, the government began to undertake a massive economic development by the infusion of capital and by the institution of government controls over the economy.[52] The plan called for a $2,500,000,000 investment from domestic, foreign, public, and private money sources. It was designed to increase the gross national product by 40.7 percent during the five years of the plan

49. For the roster and biographical records of the new cabinet members, see *Hanguk Ilbo*, December 18, 1963, p. 1.

50. The Three-Year Economic Development Plan and the Five-year Economic Development Plan were drafted under the Rhee and Chang regimes respectively, but neither of them was implemented, partly because of lack of vigor and partly because of the change in political power.

51. For the structure and functions of the Economic Planning Council, see *Hanguk Ilbo*, July 22, 1961, p. 1.

52. Republic of Korea, Office of Public Information, *Korea Moves Ahead* (Seoul: Office of Public Information, 1962), p. 66. For a further study, see "Long-term Economic Development," *Korea Journal*, II, no. 10 (October 1962), 5–19. and Lee Joe-won, "Perspective for Economic Development and Planning in South Korea," in Andrew C. Nam, ed., *Studies in the Developmental Aspects of Korea* (Kalamazoo, Mich.: Western Michigan University, 1969), pp. 30–56.

and to achieve an annual average growth rate of 7.1 percent. For this rather ambitious project, the government was to assume 53 percent of the industrial investments.[53]

The plan concentrated on the following points:

1. Establishment of energy supply sources—electric power and coal.

2. Elevation of income by means of increasing the agricultural products and correcting the structural imbalance of the national economy.

3. Expansion of key industries and the formation of indirect social capital.

4. Utilization of idle industrial facilities, especially an increase in the employment, preservation, and development of national land.

5. Improvement of the balance of international payments, primarily by increasing exports.[54]

The plan placed supreme emphasis on heavy industry and agriculture to the almost total neglect of consumer products and social welfare. The program of national economy was strongly influenced by the mercantilistic philosophy, an old doctrine which holds that the creation of an export surplus is the prime means for increasing national economic wealth. The industrialization program in such a context was geared to industrial self-sufficiency, thereby reducing foreign imports to a minimum. The plan encouraged exports by granting generous export subsidies.[55]

Such an economic program was not to be undertaken through nationalization of industries and farm collectivization, but through the creation of public corporations to handle the government-sponsored industries. Government protests to the contrary, the program was clearly socialistic in terms of establishing and operating basic industrial plants. The SCNR ve-

53. Republic of Korea, Economic Planning Board, *Summary of the First Five-Year Economic Plan, 1962–66* (Seoul: Economic Planning Board, 1962), p. 31. See also C. Wolf, Jr., "Economic Planning in Korea," *Asian Studies*, II (December 1962), 22–28.

54. *Korea Moves Ahead*, p. 66.

55. For a critical analysis of the plan, see Ch'oi Ho-chin, "Major Problems Involved in the Program," *Korean Affairs*, I, no. 1 (March/April 1962), 1–6.

hemently eschewed the word "socialism," and used a new euphemism, "guided capitalistic system." The passionate abnegation of socialism and the formal adherence to capitalism testify to the paradoxical nature of the military revolution, which had overthrown the democratically elected government in the name of democracy. Nevertheless, the transparent attempt to uphold the capitalistic system in theory—in the face of contrary practice—seemed to have been politically motivated by the desire to retain the aura of anticommunism in whose name the revolution was perpetrated.

In carrying out the plan, the junta government relied heavily upon civilian economists who had been educated in the U.S. in recent years. The first chairman of the Economic Planning Council, Kim Yu-t'aek, was also Vice-Chairman of the Cabinet and was the first civilian to regain a cabinet post under the junta government.[56]

What was especially remarkable about the plan was the progress it achieved despite the political uncertainty throughout all of 1962. In the first two years of military rule, 1961–1963, exports more than doubled from $40,878,000 to $85,300,000; coal output increased from 5,884,000 tons in 1961 to 8,858,090 tons in 1963; and cement production expanded to 778,898 tons in 1963 from 522,832 tons in 1961.[57] These are some of the indisputable accomplishments of the Five-year Economic Development Plan. As early as the summer of 1962, W. W. Rostow, commenting on Korea's economic future, stated that "South Korea is going to pick up and go."[58]

Economists and social scientists talk of the inevitable sacrifice which economic planning entails, and they often predict that the future of a given government in underdeveloped countries depends on how well the government satisfies the insatiable appetite of the impatient masses. Such an observation has

---

56. The first chairman of the Economic Planning Council, Mr. Kim Yu-t'aek, was the former president of the Bank of Korea.

57. *Economic Statistics Yearbook, 1964* (Seoul: Bank of Korea, 1964).

58. W. W. Rostow, former M.I.T. economics professor and Special Assistant to presidents John F. Kennedy and Lyndon B. Johnson, was interviewed by *U.S. News and World Report* for the May 7, 1962, issue. See Vol. LII, p. 67.

undeniable validity, but governments have fallen more often because of their inability or unwillingness to undertake effective development programs than because of public demands for consumer benefits. The civilian government in Korea had fallen, at least in part, because it failed to undertake a program of serious economic development. The military could not be charged with a similar error. Instead, it laid an economic foundation for national progress as well as for its own ultimate security.

Of considerable importance is the apparent absence of force and coercion in the implementation of the program. Judging from the present perspective, Korea might prove in the near future that economic self-sufficiency can be achieved without resorting to painful methods of total collectivism and forced savings, provided that guidance and aid from friendly advanced nations continue and that proper and determined leadership is present. If the Korean model of a "guided capitalistic system," to use their phrase, bears economic fruit, it could serve as the noncoercive alternative to the communist approach.

In the final analysis, during the most critical period of the first eighteen months following the coup, the junta successfully negotiated the uncharted and often precarious roads. The country once again regained its equilibrium and began to envision stability and growth under a new order. But for its price, the nation had to live with the revived authoritarian and administrative rule so long ingrained in Korean body politics.

TABLE 9. *Percent of Party Votes in the 1963 Korean Presidential Election by Special Cities and Provinces*

		Percent of Total Valid Votes		Percent of Total Voting	Total Registered Voters
	Park	Yun	Others		
Special Cities				%	
Seoul	30.2%	65.1%	4.7%	(77.5)	1,676,262
Pusan	48.2	47.5	4.3	(80.1)	665,545
Provinces					
Kyonggi	33.1	56.9	10.0	(85.9)	1,492,207
Kwangwon	39.6	49.1	11.3	(88.8)	938,143
Ch'ungch'ong (north)	39.8	48.9	11.3	(86.9)	.. 657,380
Ch'ungch'ong (south)	40.8	49.4	9.8	(87.1)	1,278,294
Cholla (north)	49.4	41.5	9.1	(86.1)	1,076,248
Cholla (south)	57.4	35.9	6.7	(75.5)	1,687,302
Kyongsang (north)	55.7	36.1	8.2	(85.8)	1,940,975
Kyongsang (south)	61.7	29.9	8.4	(86.9)	1,427,810
Cheju	69.9	22.3	7.8	(88.6)	144,849
Total	46.7	45.1	9.2	(85.0)	12,985,015

SOURCE: Compiled from the figures given by the Central Election Management Committee on October 17, 1963. Reprinted with permission from C. I. Eugene Kim, "Significance of the 1963 Korean Election," *Asian Survey*, IV, no. 3 (March 1964), 771.

NOTE: Invalidated votes are included in total voting percentage figures.

TABLE 10. *Percent of Major Party Votes in the Assembly Elections of Special Cities and Provinces, 1963*

Special Cities	Number of Seats	Democratic-Republican Party %	Minjung Party %	Democratic Party %
Seoul	(14)	21.9(2)	28.3(7)	22.7(4)
Pusan	(7)	36.5(6)	28.2(1)	18.4(−)
Provinces				
Kyonggi	(13)	26.6(7)	21.4(5)	15.9(1)
Kwangwon	(9)	30.7(7)	13.0(−)	17.3(1)
Ch'ungch'ong (North)	(8)	30.4(6)	19.2(1)	8.1(−)
Ch'ungch'ong (South)	(13)	31.9(8)	21.8(3)	9.9(−)
Cholla (North)	(11)	32.0(7)	21.2(4)	14.2(−)
Cholla (South)	(19)	31.1(12)	18.7(3)	8.5(1)
Kyongsang (North)	(20)	38.2(19)	13.8(1)	8.9(−)
Kyongsang (South)	(15)	40.0(13)	16.0(1)	13.3(1)
Cheu	(2)	40.3(2)	2.9(−)	9.3(−)
Total	(131)	32.4(88)	19.3(22)	13.1(8)
Number of Contested Districts	(131)	131	128	120
Districts Won	(131)	88	22	8
Proportional Representation	(44)	22	14	5
Total Seats	(175)	110	41	13

Table 10 continued on next page

TABLE 10. *(cont.)*

Special Cities	Liberal Democratic Party %	Party of the People %	Percent Voting %	Total Registered Voters
Seoul	8.1(1)	8.4(−)	57.5	1,772,518
Pusan	2.4(−)	4.7(−)	67.8	685,676
Provinces				
Kyonggi	4.6(−)	10.3(−)	68.2	1,428,181
Kwangwon	6.9(1)	12.6(−)	75.3	823,551
Ch'ungch'ong (North)	10.9(1)	9.7(−)	78.1	693,909
Ch'ungch'ong (South)	5.8(−)	10.6(2)	75.1	1,303,355
Cholla (North)	8.3(−)	5.3(−)	72.8	1,143,748
Cholla (South)	13.6(3)	7.6(−)	72.1	1,794,274
Kyongsang (North)	7.7(−)	10.4(−)	75.4	2,031,691
Kyongsang (South)	5.0(−)	5.9(−)	80.1	1,490,310
Cheju	9.9(−)	4.8(−)	81.4	151,680
Total	7.6(5)	8.6(2)	71.9	13,318,893
Number of Contested Districts	111	109		
Districts Won	6	2		
Proportional Representation	3	0		
Total Seats	9	2		

SOURCE: Computed on the basis of the figures given in the *Hanguk Ilbo*, November 29, 1963, adjusted to the later corrections. The figures for total registered voters are taken from the *Dong-a-Ilbo*, November 8, 1963. Reprinted with permission from C. I. Eugene Kim, "Significance of the 1963 Korean Election," *Asian Survey*, IV, no. 3 (March 1964), 772–73.

NOTE: Numbers in the parentheses under the party columns are the number of seats won. Percent voting includes the votes received by seven minor parties and the invalid votes.

Chapter VII

CHANGE OF MANTLES

The Transfer of Government

At 12:00 noon, August 12, 1961, Park Chung-hee, the Chairman of the SCNR, announced that the military would relinquish power to the civilian government in May 1963, following a referendum on a new constitution in March of the same year. This public pledge of a specific date for the transfer of power considerably relieved the tension and uneasiness among the intellectuals and the American authorities. After reluctantly subscribing to the pledge, *Hanguk Ilbo* in an editorial gently adjured the military: ". . . In the accomplishment of the revolutionary goal, the military must more widely employ civilian talent and must learn to respect civilians."[1]

Heartened by the August 12 pledge of relinquishment, and aware that nothing could be gained by a negative attitude toward the firmly entrenched Park regime, the U.S. gradually became reconciled to the existence of the junta. The acceptance became official in September when President Kennedy invited

1. *Hanguk Ilbo*, August 13, 1961, p. 1.

General Park to pay a visit to Washington.[2] On November 14, 1961, following talks between President Kennedy and Chairman Park a joint communiqué was issued reaffirming mutual friendship and the determination to serve the cause of freedom and democracy. Aside from these perfunctory statements of friendship, the communiqué contained an unusual pledge from Chairman Park to restore civilian rule within two years. The communiqué stated: "The Chairman reiterated the solemn pledge of the revolutionary government to return the government to civilian control in the summer of 1963, as he declared in the statement made on August 12, 1961."[3] This personal assurance to President Kennedy was to have major political significance in the spring of 1963, when the military sought to repudiate its pledge and to prolong its rule for four more years.

The political crisis of March and April 1963 requires close study, for it marked a turning point in the intramilitary power struggle and in the future of civilian rule. However, several important events preceding the political crisis in the spring of 1963 must be reviewed before the crisis itself can be discussed.

In preparation for the promised general election, the junta drafted a new Constitution with sweeping changes in governmental structure and eligibility for political candidacy. A national referendum on the Constitution was held on December 17, 1962. The new Constitution, emphasizing the supreme importance of a strong President, changed the once-powerful legislative branch into a feeble unicameral body. The President would be elected by direct popular vote, not by the legislature as in the previous Constitution; the President would appoint the Premier and cabinet members without legislative consent; the President would also enjoy the power to ratify treaties, initiate legislation, dispatch and receive diplomatic envoys, exercise supreme command of the Armed Forces, order emergency financial and economic dispositions, issue ordinances, and pro-

2. Council on Foreign Relations, *The United States in World Affairs, 1961* (New York: Harper & Row, 1962), pp. 231–33.
3. Council on Foreign Relations, *Documents on American Foreign Relations, 1961* (New York: Harper & Row, 1962), p. 333.

claim martial law.[4] Also included in the Constitution for the first time was the provision enjoining independent politicians from running for public office and requiring every candidate for the National Assembly to obtain a party nomination (Article 38, par. 3). This provision was designed, of course, to insure a strong party government which would eliminate uncommitted and often unpredictable elements in the National Assembly.

These basic changes evoked outraged protests from civilian politicians and intellectuals. Both groups viewed them as the first step toward an autocratic government which would have the support of the one strong party with government backing.

A law professor from Korea University perceptively summed up the gist of the controversy on the new Constitution:

In view of the fact that the Korean constitution subscribes to the principle of the separation of powers, the constitution must contain more meaningful checks and balances. . . .

. . . There is an inherent danger in the present Constitution that presidential power could easily be expanded and be abused. The purpose of constitutional government is to limit those who exercise political power, thereby safeguarding the rights and freedom of the individual citizens.

. . . Viewed from such a fundamental standpoint, the new Constitution must contain more specific balances and checks upon the executives.[5]

Opposing this view was Rupert Emerson, Professor of Political Science at Harvard University and the key advisor in drafting the new Constitution. Emerson considered a strong presidency as the only alternative to political instability in Korea, which has not yet been fully disciplined in the rigors of a parliamentary system. To reiterate, the new Constitution can

4. Articles 48, 64, 71, 72, 73, and 74. For the entire text and an interpretation of the new Constitution, see The Council of the Constitutional Amendment, *Hŏnpŏb kaehŏnan haesŏl* [*An Exposition of the Constitutional Amendment*] (Seoul: Republic of Korea, 1962). See also "New Basic Law Builds Foundation for Stable Strong Third Republic," *Korean Report*, II, no. 9 (November/December 1962), 4–8.

5. Han Dong-sŏb, "Saehŏnpŏbŭl pip'anhanda" ["A Critique of the New Constitution"], *Sasangge Monthly*, X, no. 12 (December 1962), 56–58.

be regarded as a resurgence of the administrative tradition which has deep roots in the Korean past.[6]

The national referendum gave surprising results: 8,339,333 out of 10,585,998, or 78.8 percent, voted in favor of the new Constitution. Even the city of Seoul, the citadel of political cynicism and opposition to military rule, voted for the Constitution by an overwhelming vote of 779,468 yeas and 239,933 nays, or 74.6 percent.[7] The outcome of the national referendum was taken as the "vote of confidence" for the 19-month-old military rule. On the following day, General Park issued a statement in which he thanked the people for their approval of the new Constitution:

With the overwhelming popular support displayed in the national referendum, the revolutionary government is now even more encouraged and determined to carry out the revolutionary tasks of the nation, rebuilding democracy on the soil of Korea.

As witnessed by the nation, the voting was carried out in an atmosphere of freedom and fairness unprecedented in the political history of Korea. The referendum has established a new milestone in the nation's tradition of democracy.[8]

Civilian politicians cautioned the military not to be misled by the outcome of the referendum, for it could very well be interpreted as a manifestation of the people's desire to have a civilian government at the earliest possible moment.[9]

On December 26, 1962, the new Constitution was formally promulgated; three important laws pertaining to the forthcoming election immediately followed.[10] In the months of Jan-

6. For more information on the historical import of this third Constitution, see C. I. Eugene Kim, "South Korean Constitutional Development: the Meaning of the Third Constitution," *Papers of the Michigan Academy of Science, Arts and Letters*, XLIX (1964), 301–12.

7. "Nation's First Referendum Approves New Constitution," *Korean Report*, II, no. 9 (November/December 1962), 3.

8. Ibid.

9. Hong Soon-il, "On Current Political Phenomena," *Korean Affairs*, II, no. 1 (1963), 98.

10. Early in January 1963, the SCNR announced the Election Law and Law Governing Political Parties. These enactments introduced a new proportional representation system, imposed various requirements for party formation, and placed restrictions on party finances, membership, and activities. Also the number of election districts were reduced from the

uary and February, the ban of political activities was partially lifted and a number of civilian politicians were freed from the restrictions on their political activities under the Political Activities Purification Act, a law adopted by the SCNR in 1961. With seeming prospects of a general election in the fall, various political parties began to make their presence known. But in spite of the exigency of forming a united front by the civilian leaders, they failed to pull their strength together in order to form a single political party or an alliance of all the opposition political parties.

In the meantime, the junta's party—Democratic Republican Party—was rapidly being whipped into shape under the skillful direction of Kim Jong-pil and his CIA staff. To capitalize on the disunity among the civilian forces, the SCNR announced its decision on an early election and the DRP hurriedly nominated General Park as its presidential candidate. These two acts marked the beginning of the forthcoming political crisis. Civilian leaders were enraged as they viewed these moves as a transparent scheme to deny them necessary time to get organized for an effective election campaign, and as a blatant reneging of Park's earlier promise not to seek the presidency. At this juncture, to compound the situation, a serious policy difference within the SCNR surfaced over the vital issue of junta's role during the future election. General Song Yo-ch'an, who served as Head of Government, and Marine General Kim Dong-ha, chairman of the Standing Committee on Economic and Financial Affairs of the SCNR, in a separate move, came out opposing the perpetuation of the military's rule by seeking electoral positions.[11]

Confronted with stiff resistance from all directions, Chairman Park relented. On February 23, he promised to give up his nomination and to postpone the election. Four days later Park reiterated the SCNR's decision to observe its original pledges and simultaneously sought reciprocity from the civilian leaders with the following promises:

---

previous 233 to 131 by enlarging the election districts—a move designed to achieve gerrymandering against the civilian candidates.

11. *Hanguk Ilbo,* January 20–30, 1963.

1. To maintain political neutrality of the armed forces and uphold the pledge of support to the new civilian government;
2. To retain by the new civilian government the spirit of the April 19 and May 16 revolutions;
3. To permit military officers to run for government, remain in office or return to military duties, according to individual choice;
4. To prevent reprisals after the transfer of government and recognize the legitimacy of the May 16 Revolution;
5. To guarantee the status of those employed by the revolutionary government after the revolution;
6. To give preferential employment to capable reserve soldiers;
7. To stop all political disputes and initiate new policies for national reconstruction;
8. To maintain the integrity and dignity of the new Constitution;
9. To cooperate in the settlement of ROK-Japanese normalization negotiations on a supra-partisan basis.[12]

Relishing these meek statements by Park, the civilian politicans plunged into a wild and undisciplined electioneering. New parties formed. New factions emerged from the existing parties. Criticism toward the junta became more vocal. Political uncertainty once again loomed large. Compounding the situation further was the appearance of the armed troops for political action. On March 5, scores of soldiers, presumably at the instigation of the junior officers, staged a demonstration in front of the SCNR, calling for an extension of military rule. They also threatened to take up arms "if the government were turned over to corrupt politicians."[13]

Amid the highly perplexing and tense situation, Park began to develop a second thought about the military's planned retirement. On March 7, in a speech at the headquarters of the First Field Army in the city of Wonju, he hinted that he might not relinquish power to the civilian leaders if they would precipitate another political crisis.[14] During this uncertain period, the incipient division between the young Colonels (Kil Chae-ho, Oh Ch'i-sŏng, Kim Hyŏng-wook) and the senior members of the SCNR (Park Im-hang, Kim Chong-o, Yi Chu-il and Kim

12. *Hanguk Ilbo*, February 27 and 28, 1963.
13. *Dong-A Ilbo*, March 15 and 16, 1963.
14. *Korea Annual*, 1964, pp. 139–45.

Dong-ha) became more pronounced. The junior members, citing the deteriorating political scene as well as questioning the desirability of restoring civilian rule, pressured the chief of the junta into reconsidering his plans. On March 16, Park Chung-hee apparently in the interest of maintaining the harmony within the SCNR and possibly to avoid bloodshed, reversed his pledges by announcing that he needed more time "to guarantee the birth of a sound civilian government" and "to complete the revolutionary tasks." Thus canceling the forthcoming general election, he proposed that there be a referendum "to let the people decide on the continuation or the termination of junta rule."[15] This reversal of the policies of the SCNR touched off what is known as "the spring crisis of 1963."

Massive protests from domestic sources were evident. Huh Chung, the elder statesman who did such a splendid job during the interim government immediately after the fall of Rhee, responded by saying, "The prolongation of the military is a major tragedy for the Korean people." Yun Po-sǒn, the President of the Second Republic who stayed on until March 1962, said that "Park had burned the democracy which had just begun budding." Shin Sang-ch'o, a leading intellectual and a practicing politician who had supported the military earlier, said, "The philosophy of the perpetuation of the military has stemmed from the policy of the 'military first'; it is unthinkable to have another special class in a country striving for popular sovereignty."[16]

A series of demonstrations by politicians and students also expressed considerable reservation with Park's decision, but the most formidable pressure came from the United States, to whom Park had unequivocally pledged that he would turn over power to the civilian government in the spring of 1963. On March 25 the State Department issued a carefully worded statement:

The military junta's effort to continue military rule for four more years has created a difficult situation in Korea. We believe that prolongation of military rule could constitute a threat to stable and ef-

15. Shin Sang-ch'o, "Minjujui ui chungdaneǔn ǒpda" ["Democracy Cannot Be Interrupted"], *Sasangge Monthly*, XI, no. 3 (March 1963), 111.
16. Ibid., pp. 112–13.

fective government, and we understand that this whole matter is being reexamined by the Korean Government.

We hope the junta and the major political groups in Korea can work out together a procedure for a transition to civil government that will be acceptable to the nation as a whole.[17]

On March 22, at a press conference responding to questions on the Korean situation, President Kennedy gave a noncommittal answer: "We are anxious for stability in the area."[18] It was later reported, however, that President Kennedy sent a stern message to General Park urging him not to renege on the earlier pledge.[19]

Reviewing the political and intramilitary crisis, A. M. Rosenthal, the *New York Times* correspondent, observed: "Park and others are under counter-pressure from several groups of angry young officers who are insisting on continuous military rule. These officers are bitter about U.S. 'interference' and say they are in a mood to go it alone."[20] A *New York Times* editorial also assessed the difficult situation in which Park had placed himself: "On one side General Park is under heavy pressure from army subordinates to perpetuate the present military regime. On the other side he faces mounting agitation from civilian politicians and sections of the public for the restoration of civilian rule."[21] "General Park," the editorial advised, "would do well to revert to his earlier plan for an elected government. The weaknesses that have been developing in his regime suggest that an increasing division and even civil strife would be in prospect if it continues indefinitely in power."[22]

With the possible threat that the "armed forces tigers" might get out of control, General Park faced a situation which could

17. Council for Foreign Relations, *Document on American Foreign Relations, 1963* (New York: Harper, 1964), p. 312. See also Lincoln White, "Korea," *Department of State Bulletin,* XLVIII (1963), 573.

18. On April 2, the White House announced only that it had given the junta what is described as a friendly warning against the perpetuation of unconstitutional government. See the *New York Times,* April 3, 1963, p. 1, col. 6. This information also came from a personal interview with several Korean correspondents in Washington during the summer of 1964.

19. *New York Times,* March 22, 1963, p. 1, col. 7.

20. Ibid., March 27, 1963, p. 1, col. 4.

21. Ibid., March 22, 1963, p. 8, col. 1.

22. Ibid.

have developed into control of the SCNR by its radical junior members. There is no public record concerning the debates of the SCNR during this crucial moment. Park, however, cautiously announced on April 6 that the intended referendum on the proposal to extend military rule be put off to the end of September 1963 and that the junta permit immediate resumption of political activities by civilian opposition groups. On July 8 Chairman Park pledged again to transfer the government within a year. The crisis gradually subsided, but not without leaving casualties: Kim Dong-ha and several other senior officers were totally eliminated as political powers and were later incarcerated.

From this crisis, several observations can be made. First, the moderate voice that supported the restoration of civilian rule succumbed to the strong desire of the younger officers of the junta. The gustation of power and privilege and the fear of reappraisal could have very well motivated the junior officers to repudiate the earlier pledges but what seemed to have led them to choose a more hazardous course was their basic objection to the reestablishment of a dysfunctional political system that South Korea had known under the civilian leadership during the Rhee and Chang periods. Thus implicit in this observation was the repudiation of the kind of democracy that was practiced earlier and simultaneous adherence to a more functional administrative rule. Second, General Park once again proved himself to be the stabilizing force even though he rode through the stormy crisis in a haphazard fashion. He clearly demonstrated his ability in dealing with extreme demands from within and without the junta, and successfully prevented the disintegration of the junta and the further polarization in civilian-military relations. As a result, he emerged as the undisputed leader as well as a more mature and skillful politician.

Once the storm was past, political activities resumed. On May 27 Park Chung-hee was unanimously nominated as the presidential candidate of the Democratic Republican Party, and he immediately launched his campaign. It was announced that Park would retain his post as Chairman of the SCNR and as Acting President even if he retired from active duty, "to avoid creating a political vacuum preceding the scheduled elections."[23]

On August 30, in an impressive military ceremony, General Park ended his 17-year-old tumultuous military career in order to prepare for the forthcoming presidential election slated for October 15. He made some profoundly revealing statements. Talking of his personal background and of the unfinished revolutionary tasks, he said:

> I was born, like many of you, in a poor farming family. Ever since I became a soldier, I have worn the uniform as a military servant of the people and have never thought my life or body to be my own. I sought to perform my duty as a soldier and to seek the truth of life in the military service. Today, however, not having fully achieved the revolutionary objectives as soldier, I must become a civilian in order to further the ideals of the revolution.
>
> . . . The May Revolution was not a simple change of political system; not the reorganization of the external order, nor the emergence of a new class. The ultimate objective of our revolution is to eliminate the unfortunate legacies from our ancestors of mutual hatred and factionalism, waste, confusion, indolence, and dishonesty and to put an end to this contaminated national history, in order to construct the independent, prosperous Fatherland of tomorrow.
>
> . . . A pan-national revolution must be developed leading to our goal of political and economic independence. The revolutionary goals are prosperity and democratic republicanism.
>
> . . . I . . . will end this message of retirement with the hope that never again will any soldier be forced along such an unfortunate pathway as the one I have trod.[24]

Park's formal retirement from the military on August 30 set the tempo of the election campaign at full speed. The removal of the names of all but a few of the politicians from the blacklist already had started the rush of serious electioneering. In opposition to Park's Democratic Republican Party, six civilian parties emerged. Only the Civil Rule Party under the leadership of Yun Po-sŏn, President of the Second Republic, offered major opposition. Both Huh Chung, the leader of the People's Party,

23. "Chairman Unanimously Nominated Presidential Candidate: Gen. Park Expresses Willingness to Run on the DRP Ticket," *Korean Report*, III, no. 4 (June 1963), 3.

24. Supreme Council for National Reconstruction, *General Park Chunghee: His Address at the Ceremony of Retirement* (Seoul: Office of Public Information, 1963).

and Song Yo-ch'an, the presidential nominee of the Liberal Democratic Party, withdrew from the presidential race.[25] Following a bitter and intensive two-month campaign,[26] the elections were held on October 15 in an atmosphere later described by a U.N. observer as "the most honest and peaceful election in fifteen years of Korean history."[27]

The election outcome was almost a photofinish: Park defeated Yun by a vote margin of 181,126 out of a total vote cast of over 11 million.[28] As expected, Park lost heavily in the urban areas but gained heavily in the rural areas, particularly in the Southeastern Kyŏngsang Province. One significant point is that Park did not receive a majority vote, but only 46.7 percent of the total votes cast; thus Park could have been defeated had the civilian opposition been united.[29] Another noteworthy point is that Park failed to receive substantial support from the so-called military areas along the Demilitarized Zone. These are the areas where the bulk of the 600,000-man ROK Army is stationed. In Ch'ŏlwon, Hwach'ŏn, Ch'unch'ŏn, and Wonju in the Kwangwon Province—cities which serve as the unit headquarters of several Army Corps and the First Field Army—Park won only 33 to 42 percent of the vote.[30]

Seriously concerned about the close election outcome, Professor Rupert Emerson later sent a personal letter to the *New*

25. For a summation on all seven presidential candidates, their platforms, and mottoes see *Hanguk Ilbo*, September 5, 1963, p. 4.

26. Mr. Yun Po-sŏn and his campaign manager committed a blunder by hinting that Park had been a Communist with the remark, "There are too many Communists among those who are born in the Southeastern Kyŏngsang Province." This ungentlemanly accusation, according to many observers, cost Yun the election. Note and compare the election returns by provinces in table 9, p. 122.

27. *New York Times*, October 19, 1963, p. 24, col. 1.

28. For the detailed election outcome, see table 9, p. 122.

29. For a detailed analysis of the presidential elections on October 15 and the National Assembly election on November 26, see C. I. Eugene Kim, "Significance of the 1963 Korea Elections," *Asian Survey*, IV, no. 3 (March 1964), 765–73. See also Ch'oi Sŏk-ch'e, "Daet'ongyŏng sŏngojonui punsŏk" ["An Analysis of the Presidential Elections"], *Sasangge Monthly*, XI, no. 11 (November 1963), 35–45.

30. Kim, "Significance of the 1963 Korea Election," p. 770. See also Kim Myŏng-whoi, "The Presidential Election in Korea, 1963," *Korean Affairs*, II, nos. 3–4 (1963), 375.

York Times, in which he suggested that the close election "should serve as a warning to General Park and his associates that military rule is eyed with suspicion and hostility by large numbers of Koreans." "Civil liberties," he continued, "must be scrupulously safeguarded if the popular will is to make itself effective and if the people are to be given a sense of participation in their government."[31]

Park's victory was in fact a blessing for the future of democracy in Korea. Had the military lost, it can be safely assumed that the military would have ignored the electoral outcome and continued its rule even though such rule would have meant a total destruction of constitutionalism. Undoubtedly this action would have irrevocably impeded any future attempt to establish a democracy. The narrow victory had a stultifying effect upon the ego of the military leadership which had been overconfident as a result of the success on the national referendum the year before.

Alarmed by the narrow base of the popular mandate, Park's Democratic Republican Party waged an even more vigorous election campaign for the election of the National Assemblymen. On November 26 Park's party won an overwhelming majority: 110 seats out of a total of 175, while the four minor opposition parties took the remaining 65 seats. The recurring phenomenon of civilian disunity was again the principal reason for the civilians' failure to capture at least workable minority strength.[32] Once again, the defeat of civilian opposition was a political blessing, for had Park's party lost, it could have ignored the defeat. The consequence of such action needs no elaboration.

On December 17 at an austere ceremony, Park Chung-hee took the oath of office as the third President since South Korea's independence in 1948. At the inauguration, appealing for popular support, he stated: "The new government will establish a strong economic and social foundation, consolidate the united

31. *New York Times*, October 27, 1963, p. 8, col. 5.
32. For a breakdown of the seats among the different parties, see table 10, pp. 123–24.

strength of the nation, and strengthen our ties with the U.S. and all freedom-loving peoples of the world."[33] Thus came to an end the military regime which had ruled the country by fiat for two years, seven months, and a day. Korea began its third attempt in fifteen years at nation-building. This time, however, the effort would be made under a strong presidential system, thus formally adhering again to the administrative tradition that long undergirds the Korean body politic.

The Third Republic and International Relations, 1963–1969

The Park administration has greatly improved the national image both within and without. Internationally, Korea has emerged as an active member of the world community, improving the quantity and quality of its diplomatic relations. The number of countries maintaining diplomatic relations with Korea has jumped to 87, up from 25 in 1961, and resident embassies have increased to 25, up from 13 in 1961. In addition, South Korea participates in 18 specialized agencies in the U.N. and 220 other international organizations. This active international involvement reflects the Park regime's successful drive to open diplomatic channels with nonaligned nations—a flexibility that was unthinkable during the Rhee period.

In 1966 Korea hosted the first major Conference of Asian nations. From June 14 to June 16, the Ministerial Meeting for Asian and Pacific Cooperation (ASPAC) was held in Seoul, attended by ten foreign ministers from Japan, Thailand, Australia, the Philippines, Nationalist China, South Vietnam, Malaysia, New Zealand, and Laos. This meeting, convened to serve as the basis for future regional cooperation for economic development and stability, bore fruit in the same year with the establishment of the Asian Development Bank under the leadership of Japan. Another major achievement was the normalization of diplomatic relations with Japan, a thorny issue that was finally settled in 1965. On March 9 of the following year, Kimura Chisoshichi, the first Japanese ambassador to Korea since 1909, assumed his

33. *Korea Times*, December 18, 1963, p. 1.

diplomatic duties in Seoul, and Korea sent Kim Dong-cho to Tokyo as its ambassador to Japan.

The Park administration, determined to implement the economic development program, risked its own continuance in power by pushing through this restoration of diplomatic relations. It demonstrated its willingness and ability to undertake an action—rapprochement with Japan—which would undoubtedly rekindle the old and virulent anti-Japanese feeling. Negotiations were resolutely executed in spite of student demonstrations and determined obstructions by the political opposition. The outcome of the Normalization Treaty, in which Japan promised Korea $800,000,000 in loans and grants, will not be determined for some time. Park had realistically placed a high priority on the country's need for Japanese economic assistance and technological guidance. Clearly the future of Asia is to be greatly influenced by the new era of cooperation of these two nations.

The most ambitious international engagement of Korea today is the military commitment to South Vietnam.[34] With 45,000 combat troops in Vietnam—because of strong pressure from the United States—the Park administration further solidified the Korean-American alliance. Of no small importance is the distinguished combat records of the Korean units serving in Vietnam, which has won international acclaim for Korea.

The Park government was also successful in negotiating several important economic concessions from the U.S. The U.S. agreed (1) to purchase from Korea a large quantity of war materials used in Vietnam by both U.S. and South Vietnamese troops; (2) to pay Korean troops in U.S. dollars at a rate of about one-fourth that of their American counterparts; and (3) to employ a large number of Korean civilian technicians for the reconstruction program in South Vietnam. (There are more than 20 thousand Korean civilians employed in Vietnam.) Also, during the summer of 1966, the United States finally agreed to

34. See the author's article, "Korea's Involvement in Vietnam and Its Political and Economic Impact," *Asian Survey*, X, no. 6 (June 1970), 519–32.

sign the long-desired Status of Forces Agreement between the two nations. This gives considerable jurisdiction to Korean civil authorities and enables Korean civil courts to try U.S. troops who commit crimes outside military compounds.

On the most critical matter of international importance— national unification—the Park regime has been very rigid and has continually insisted that present political and economic circumstances render negotiations premature. At the same time, the Park administration has recognized the United Nations as the ultimate arbiter of this vexing question. South Korea clearly is reluctant to chance the possible political and economic disruption which might occur in the event of a sudden merger with North Korea.

Economy: Achievements and Problems

The Park regime's policy of "economy first" has resulted in a spectacular industrial growth since 1961 and particularly since 1966, when the Second Five-Year Plan was inaugurated on the strength of the highly successful First Five-Year Plan. The nation's gross national product—the most accurate indicator of economic health—jumped from an average rate of about 8 percent during the period 1962–1965 to a phenomenal 13.4 percent in 1966 and 8.9 percent in 1967 in spite of a 6 percent decline in agricultural output due to a severe drought and a subsequent flood.[35] According to the latest report, the GNP (after the price adjustment) leaped to 18 percent in 1969.[36]

The most dynamic sector in the nation's economy has been manufacturing, the mainstay of South Korea's industrial strength. The annual growth of manufacturing accelerated

35. *United Nations Economic Survey of Asia and the Far East*, 1964, 1965, 1966, 1967, Vols. XV, XVI, XVII, XVIII.

36. "Recent Development of the Korean Economy, "*Korean Report*, IX, no. 3 (July–September 1969), 10–11. See also "Korean Economy Continues to Meet Ambitious Growth Goals, "*International Commerce*, LXXVI (October 1968), 24–26. *Monthly Review* (Seoul: Korean Exchange Bank), has current and useful information on various economic activities of Korea. See also U.S. Department of State, Agency for International Development, *U.S. Foreign Aid in East Asia: Proposed Fiscal Year 1970 Program* (Washington, D.C., 1969), pp. 10–14.

from 12 percent increase per annum during 1962–1964 to 18 percent per annum during 1965–1966, and in the first half of 1968 industrial output grew in excess of 25 percent over the corresponding half of 1967.[37] Now manufacturing accounts for almost one-third of the entire GNP, up from 21 percent in 1967 and 14 percent in 1968. By the end of 1969 it was anticipated that manufacturing would surpass agriculture as the largest contributor to the total GNP. This marks a striking departure from what was traditionally a low-yielding agrarian economy to a high-yielding industrial economy. From all indications—savings, capital formation, and exportation—the present trend of industrial expansion is expected to continue for some time to come.

Closely related to economic growth is the volume of foreign trade. Both exports and imports have risen almost exponentially during the past several years. Earnings from exports have more than quadrupled since 1962, surpassing $250 million in 1966, $360 million in 1967, and $500 million in 1968. The ambitious target for 1969, $700 million, was also reached.[38] The significance of this rapid increase in export earning was that four-fifths of it came from manufactured products. This figure is quite a contrast to the exports of the 1950s, when two-thirds of the sales abroad, amounting to a mere $30 million a year, consisted of agricultural and mineral raw materials. Such a rapid economic gain naturally spurred the rise of per capita income, which rose from $120 in 1963 to $205 in 1969; simultaneously, unemployment dropped from 8.1 percent to 4.7 percent during the corresponding period.[39]

What has made South Korea a "capitalist showcase" is the direction, guidance, and massive assistance rendered by the government to stimulate private incentive and establish firm industrial policies. To promote the export industries, for in-

---

37. Bank of Korea Report appeared in *Dong-A Ilbo*, September 24, 1968.

38. "Korea's Export Trade in 1968 Envisions a Further 40% Growth," *Korean Report*, VIII, no. 2 (April–June 1968), 12–13. *Monthly Review* (Seoul: Korean Exchange Bank) contains monthly reports on import and export records.

39. *Dong-A Ilbo*, February 11, 1970.

stance, the government introduced a series of promotional measures that included export subsidies, liberal credits, and tax incentive; it also initiated a licensing system that favors firms with good export records. Also, in order to activate idle capital, government-supported banks raised interest rates on time-deposit savings to 25.2 percent per annum (at one point to 30 percent per annum). In addition, foreign investment regula-

TABLE 11.   *Several Key Economic Indicators for South Korea*

Years	1958	1963	1964	1965	1966	1967	1968	1969
Industrial Production[a]	57	100	108	127	155	194	258	305[b]
Mining	36	100	110	114	126	130	113	
Manufacturing	62	100	107	126	156	200	275	
Electricity	68	100	122	147	176	223	273	
Foreign Trade[c]								
Exports		16	87	119	175	250	320	455
Imports		378	560	404	463	716	996	1,468
Balance		−362	−473	−285	−288	−466	−676	−1,013
Gross National Product		3,211	3,476	3,734	4,234	4,612	4,612	
Per Capita Income[d]		120	126	132	146	155	171	205

Source: Data mainly from *U.N. Statistical Yearbook* and *Monthly Review* (Foreign Exchange Bank, Seoul).
[a]1963=100. [b]As of September 1969. [c]Million Dollars. [d]Dollars.

tions have been greatly liberalized, and a realistic and floating exchange system was introduced in 1964 as a capital inducement measure. Indeed, foreign capital inflow has become an important source of capital formation in the last several years. In contrast to a meager $48 million in 1965, the inflow in 1966 jumped to $250 million and in 1968 it surpassed $350 million.[40] As a result, domestic deposits have been increasing at a rate of 30 to 35 percent during the past several years.[41]

40. "Korean Economy Continues to Meet Ambitious Growth: U.S. Share of Commercial Imports up Strongly," *International Commerce*, LXXIV, no. 42 (October 14, 1968), 24–26. See also Yim Young-il, "Foreign Influence on the Economic Change in Korea," *Journal of Asian Studies*, XXVIII, no. 1 (November 1968), 77–100. *Korean Week*, III, no. 4 (February 28, 1970), 2.
41. *Monthly Review*, III, no. 6 (June 1969), 3.

To assure a sustained growth, the government improved the transportation and communication systems, both of which are owned or financed by the government. The railroads were modernized; harbor facilities were expanded; and the highway system was vastly improved.[42] A four-lane expressway, now complete, linking Seoul and Pusan will have a far-reaching economic impact as well as military implications.

Another noteworthy development closely related to economic growth is the slowing down of population growth as a result of an extensive birth control program. A population expansion rate of 3.0 percent during 1955–1965 has been brought down to 2.4 percent in 1969.[43] A further reduction to 2 percent is planned by the terminal year of the Second Five-Year Plan. The visible result of planned parenthood is shown by the fact that, relative to the entire population, the number of those four years old and under declined from 18.2 to 15.7 percent in the period 1960–1966.[44]

In spite of these notable gains, there are many economic problems that are left unsolved. One that still looms large in South Korea is its repayment obligations.[45] With more than two and a half billion dollars of outstanding foreign debts, plus an additional foreign loan of a half-billion dollars earmarked for 1970–71, there is serious concern that South Korea is overloading its repayment capability. In 1970, repayment on principle and interest will reach $171.91 million, and it will top $235 million in 1972.[46] These figures represent roughly 14 to 20 percent of Korea's projected annual earnings, surpassing the 9 percent repayment and foreign-earnings ratio which the present government has pledged to maintain.[47] Also, considering the

42. U.S. Department of State, *U. S. Foreign Aid in East Asia: Proposed Fiscal Year 1970 Program,* 9–14.
43. This information was provided during an interview with a public health official from the Korean Population Control Center, Seoul, Korea, in March 1970.
44. *Dongwha Annual, 1968,* p. 424.
45. *Dong-A Ilbo,* January 20, 1970.
46. *Korean Week,* III, no. 2 (January 30, 1970), 2.
47. Derek Davis, "Seoul Searching," *Far Eastern Economic Review,* XLIII, no. 2 (January 9, 1969), 53–54.

continuing decline in United States aid and the anticipated reduction of Korea's earnings from Vietnam, which together represent about 20 percent of the total sources of foreign income, Korea's ability to meet foreign obligations may be seriously questioned.[48] Of course, the two major suppliers of capital—the United States and Japan—might agree to a request to defer repayment. Such a request, however, would surely compromise Korea's political and economic integrity. Widespread concern about a Japanese economic invasion already exists for more than 10,000 Japanese businessmen have penetrated into virtually all sectors of the Korean economy.

Another problem that chronically plagues the Korean economy is the trade deficit. After considerable progress toward narrowing the gap during the period 1963–1966, the imbalance began to rise sharply. In the following three years the deficit rose to a high in 1969 of nearly one billion dollars. The rising demand for more sophisticated machinery as the economy becomes more complex and the increasing demand for luxury goods as income rises will make the trade imbalance even harder to redress in the future. What disturbs this writer is that the Park government has not adopted any measures to alter the trend. On the contrary, in February 1970 the government lifted so-called "prior permit" restrictions on imports of all Japanese goods.[49] This is surely a step in the wrong direction, given the fact that Japan already enjoys a 10 to 1 advantage in trade with Korea. Incidentally, since diplomatic normalization South Korea has emerged as the second-largest buyer of Japanese merchandise, surpassed only by the U.S. Correction of the trade deficit is a matter of economic and political exigency if South Korea is to sustain an orderly growth without jeopardizing economic solvency or political integrity.

An equally serious problem lies in the agricultural sector. Unfavorable weather conditions from 1966 to 1968, combined

48. See the author's article, "Korea's involvement in Vietnam and Its Political and Economic Impact," *Asian Survey*, X, no. 6, (June 1970), pp. 519–32.

49. *Korean Week*, III, no. 3 (February 14, 1970), 1.

with the assignment of top priority to the requirements of industry and export, resulted in farm production increases at an annual rate of 5 percent as contrasted with 25 percent in the industrial sector.[50] Given a population growth rate of 2.4 percent and a rising demand for high-calorie intake in recent years, the country must rely upon a massive import of foreign grain. In fact, according to a recent announcement by the Ministry of Agriculture, domestic grain production will provide only 83 percent of the nation's needs in 1970, thus requiring importation of 1,880,000 tons of various foodstuffs from abroad. Such importation will cost $250 million which, incidentally, represents one-fourth of the entire projected earnings from exports in 1970.[51] One ironical footnote to this need to import grain is that a half-million tons of rice will be bought from Japan, the country which used to be the principal consumer of Korean rice. Even in 1969 Japan had already furnished Korea with 300,000 tons of rice.[52] The original goal of achieving self-sufficiency in the food supply by the terminal year of the Second Five-Year Plan, 1971, appears remote indeed.

Another serious outcome of assigning priority status to heavy industry and the export trade was the rise of many opulent entrepreneurs, whose conspicuous consumption has emphasized the inequitable distribution of wealth. Thus far, very little has been done to mitigate this growing imbalance, even though it threatens the orderly growth of the nation's economy and the social stability of the country.

In spite of these significant shortcomings, the future of Korea's economic health is optimistic. Recent loans from the World Bank and the continuing inflow of foreign capital seem to support this observation. Thus, barring a worldwide depression or the resumption of war between the divided halves, South Korea may be able to achieve its goal of economic self-reliance in the mid-1970s.

50. U.S. Department of State, *U.S. Foreign Aid in East Asia: Proposed Fiscal Year 1970 Program*, p. 13.
51. This announcement by the Ministry of Agriculture appeared in *Korean Week*, III, no. 2 (January 30, 1970), 2.
52. *Dong-A Ilbo*, December 4, 1969.

Civil Liberties

Under the Park government, as expected, the least advancement has been in the area of civil liberties. In terms of the procedural aspect of law enforcement, very little or nothing has been done. In fact, all the ignominious traditional methods of executing the law, including the "third degree," still prevail. The relationship between public servants, particularly the police, and individual civilians has altered little. The former still act with arbitrary arrogance; the latter respond with fear but not respect. The rise of the CIA with practically unlimited power to investigate and to detain any person accused of aiding the enemy has severely restricted the right to dissent and to criticize the regime in power.

The concept of due process as the backbone of law enforcement has not yet been embraced by the present government. In fact, the present regime has taken a somewhat regressive position in this regard. Not only has it strengthened the draconian National Security Act of 1960, but it has also added an even more prohibitive Anti-Communist Act. Under these two sweeping pieces of legislation, any kind of antigovernment activity, including critical speeches and writings, may be designated as "sympathizing with communism or communists" or "aiding antigovernment organizations," thus constituting a criminal act. A brief look at several controversial cases will shed some light on the problems of safeguarding basic civil liberties.

The first case involves the opposition legislative candidate Kim Chae-hwan and the New Democratic Party to which Kim belonged and by which he was named to the tenth position on the proportional representation ticket. Kim was arrested on June 1, 1967, just eight days before the voting, for allegedly receiving political funds from a communist-front organization in Japan and for paying an enormous sum (more than $100,000) to the New Democratic Party as the price for his nomination as a party candidate. In spite of Kim's public renunciation of his candidacy before the election and of conflicting and dubious evidence presented by the prosecution, the CIA and the police used this case as a pretext for the search and seizure of the account books from the headquarters of the opposition party. The sacking of the office of the principal opposition party on the eve of the national election was an entirely unwarranted action regardless of Kim's background. And this unfortunate incident was interpreted by many administration-supported candidates as a direct involvement of the government on their behalf. As a result, the overzealous DRP candidates employed highly irregular campaign tactics, seriously marring the voting process on June 8.[53]

The second case deals with the well-publicized episode of a spy ring based in East Berlin. A total of 34 Korean professors and students largely from Western Europe were brought back and charged with espionage activities for North Korea. The trial was conducted in an atmosphere of sobriety and propriety, and the subsequent appeals were handled with due process. The significance of this case does not lie in the proceedings of the trial, but in the aftermath of the court action. In the summer of 1968, some time after the announced sentences of the defendants—which were not as severe as anticipated in view of the gravity of the offense—mysterious incidents began to occur. First, anonymous threatening letters were sent to the judges who handled the case and to the opposition New Democratic Party members, as well as to key figures in the press corps covering the case. The letters gave explicit warning not to interfere with anticommunist activities. Later, wall posters containing similar threats appeared in the center of the capital city. National Assembly requests that those responsible be unmasked and identified have met with only half-hearted government efforts in this direction. The content of the warnings and the lukewarm attitude of the government led to the belief that the whole event was a scheming concoction by one of the government agencies which enjoys maximum legal immunity.

The timing of this entire episode was regrettable. The Park regime needed to shore up public confidence following the dis-

53. The aftermath of the election crisis is discussed in a later section. See pp. 150–52.

orderly election and the subsequent political crisis of the preceding year. Instead, it seemed to either condone highly unsavory political tactics or to be helpless to control high-powered government agencies. If the present regime is to command a continuing mandate from the increasingly sophisticated citizenry, it must make clear that this kind of incident will not recur, and that if it should, the government would assume full responsibility.

In the fall of 1968 another distressing case came to public attention. Several key members of the Dong-yang News Agency, one of the oldest and most prestigious press services in Korea, were prosecuted and many other newsmen "screened" on the charge of divulging military secrets regarding the defense deployment of South Korean troops. As a result of this case, the CIA was given complete freedom to determine the sensitivity of military information in the future. Such power could easily lead to a censorship of the press, or at best might subject the press corps to the whims of the government.

In the winter of 1968 a similar incident occurred. Several members of the opposition paper, *Dong-A Ilbo*, were summoned and interrogated by the CIA for an article exposing financial misdealings involving the acquisition of government permission to secure foreign loans. Some of the leading figures of the Park regime were connected with the irregularities. The frequent subjection of reporters to "screening," interrogation, or even prosecution by the police and the CIA seriously jeopardized the basic freedom of the press. Such actions create an atmosphere of political repression.

Granted, a country like Korea, beleaguered by threats from the belligerent communist North and laboring under urgent and massive domestic developmental programs, needs stringent law enforcement; but undue obsession with communist witchhunting and suppression of normal political action must be avoided if the present regime is to win public confidence. Especially because of its reform nature, the Park regime must exercise a policy of prudence and tolerance rather than a policy of prohibition or intimidation.

The Politics of the 1967 General Elections

The Presidential Election of May 3 / The outcome of the May presidential election was more or less a foregone conclusion. Considering the unprecedented record of economic progress, the political stability achieved during the preceding years, the chronic disunity of the civilian opposition, and the formidable, well-financed, and well-managed party apparatus of the incumbent candidate, the reelection of Park Chung-hee was hardly in doubt. Moreover, the reluctance and apathy shown by such civilian political luminaries as Park Soon-ch'ŏn, Paik Nak-jun (George Paik), and Yi Pŏm-sŏk to endorse Yun Po-sŏn, the principal opposition candidate, virtually precluded Yun from serious contention. Park's landslide victory was therefore not a surprise. The only surprise was the margin of victory was not greater than 1,160,000 votes. Park received 5,688,000 against Yun's 4,526,000 out of a total of slightly less than 11 million votes cast. The remaining one million votes were shared by the five other minor candidates.[54]

Several brief observations can be made regarding the outcome of this election. *First,* this was, without doubt, a free and honest election devoid of discernible foul play, particularly by the party in power. Confident of overwhelming victory, the Park government strictly maintained political neutrality. Even the perennial opposition paper, *Dong-A Ilbo,* praised the orderly manner in which the election was conducted. *Second,* the relatively narrow margin of victory by Park represented a growing political maturity among the Korean public. Unlike Egypt and Pakistan, where the quasi-military regimes of similar nature claimed more than 80 to 90 percent of votes during their postrevolutionary periods, the Korean voters—in spite of Park's impressive economic accomplishments—seemed to be still hesitant to support the regime which has an unconstitutional history.

Just after the presidential election, a Korean visitor to the

54. C. I. Eugene Kim, "Patterns in the 1967 Korean Election," *Pacific Affairs,* XLI, no. 1 (Spring 1968), 60–70.

United States remarked that most intellectuals and urban voters had voted for Yun, the opposition candidate, not because he was a more attractive and able alternative, but because voting for him would reduce the margin of victory for Park, whose reelection in their view was a certainty. Such a move was a deliberate act to caution the ruling regime against being overconfident.

The rise of political sophistication was further demonstrated by the shift of the voting pattern. In spite of numerous negative votes by the intellectuals, Park came out much stronger in the urban areas, where he had made the poorest showing in 1963. On the other hand, Park lost heavily in the rural regions of the Southwest, where he had been in considerable favor before. The support he received in the urban centers seems to have resulted from the profitable impact of the intensive economic development programs; the rural Southwestern provinces, however, were registering their displeasure at receiving such low priority. Only in the rural Southeastern Kyŏngsang Province did Park score a particular success; there he amassed an even greater majority in 1967. The explanation for this is simple: in locating the bulk of new industrial plants in this region, Park was showing his partiality to his home province.

A clear correlation exists between benefits incurred and regional reaction to the regime in power. This supports the contention that Koreans had made great strides toward political maturity.

Third, there was a marked reversal in voting returns in the so-called "military regions" along the Demilitarized Zone. Un-

TABLE 12. *Comparison of the Urban and Rural Vote (by Thousands)*

		Park	Yun	Others
1967	Rural	3,870 (52.2%)	3,150 (42.4%)	440 (5.4%)
	Urban	1,790 (50.4%)	1,340 (37.7%)	420 (12%)
1963	Rural	3,488 (50.8%)	2,713 (39.5%)	163 (5.1%)
	Urban	1,214 (57.8%)	1,833 (57.1%)	669 (9.7%)

SOURCE: *Dong-A Ilbo,* May 5, 1967.

like 1963, when Park lost heavily in these regions, in 1967 he received substantial support from the military personnel in the frontier towns of Ch'ulwon, Whach'un, Ch'unch'ŏn, and Kangnung. As a whole, his votes in 1967 exceeded 60–65 percent compared to 32–40 percent on the previous occasion.[55]

The increasing acceptance of the former military general by those in active service is highly significant. It indicates military endorsement of the originally controversial policy whereby South Korea has committed 45,000 combat troops to Vietnam. Furthermore, sympathetic identification with the quasi-military regime by the majority of the soldiers creates an atmosphere in which antigovernment conspiracy would be extremely hazardous. Intramilitary stability and a healthy relationship between the military and the present government might lead Park's government to relax its control over the military, a step which would have important political implications.

In summary, the return of Park was, indeed, a political blessing. Without his victory serious political and military disruption might have taken place, interrupting the present development program. All in all, Park's reelection can be taken "as an augury of continuing political stability. . . and economic progress."[56]

The Parliamentary Election of June 8, 1967 and Its Aftermath / The presidential election in May was a bitter lesson to the disunited civilian opposition. In order to allay the crushing defeat, the major antiadministration party, the New Democratic Party, under the new and able leadership of Dr. Yu Chin-o, mounted a vigorous and determined campaign as soon as it could gather its strength. However, the odds against the opposition party winning a majority in the National Assembly were almost insurmountable. The four other splinter parties refused to form a united front against the ruling Democratic Republican Party (DRP), once again sapping the potency of the civilian counterforce. As a three-year-old minority party, the New Democratic Party's campaign was seriously

---

55. C. I. Eugene Kim, "Patterns in the 1967 Korean Election," *Pacific Affairs*, XLI, no. 1 (Spring 1968), 60–70.
56. *New York Times*, May 5, 1967, p. 14.

marred by inadequate financial resources, poor management, and inefficient coordination of partisan activities. The individual party endorsees were forced to wage isolated contests largely on their own.

Lined up against this opposition was the well-oiled party machinery supported by almost unlimited funds and the power of the government. Also, to insure a comfortable majority in the legislature, the DRP deployed its 1,500,000 members in every electoral district and gave them specific missions. In addition, the case of Kim Chae-hwan[57] and the overeagerness on the part of the Park government to recapture control of the Assembly created such a frenzy that the individual party nominees felt free to employ a variety of highly irregular tactics.[58] In view of such organization, the outcome of the June election was hardly in doubt. What was surprising was the unexpectedly large margin of defeat suffered by the New Democratic Party. The President's party carried all but 27 of 131 electoral districts, and claimed 130 of the 175 seats in the National Assembly, 13 seats more than the two-thirds majority required to amend the Constitution.[59]

The election returns touched off two major crises—one political, the other constitutional. In condemnation of the widespread election irregularities and in response to the virtual domination of the National Assembly by the administration's party, the legislative boycott was staged by minority assemblymen. With only 44 seats in the 175 member National Assembly —one seat taken by a splinter Masses Party—the opposition force resorted to tactics of deliberate obscurantism. As a result, the legislative branch came to a complete stand-still. Also there was a recurrence of a familiar phenomenon, street demonstrations against the election outcome. This post-election crisis in 1967 was more than a political crisis. It represented a constitutional

57. See p. 145.
58. After the election, no less than 3,800 cases of voting violations were reported, and many of them led to criminal prosecution and the disqualification of several of the newly elected candidates.
59. According to the proportional representation system, the DRP was given an additional 27 out of 44 P.R. seats, with the remaining 17 seats going to the New Democratic Party.

crisis. The control of two-thirds of the legislature by the President's party was tantamount to the birth of a legal leviathan with constitution-making power. The government now had the power to *initiate* constitutional amendment, an ominous possibility since no administration-sponsored constitutional changes ever failed to be ratified in a national referendum.

In the face of such crucial political and constitutional questions, the opposition party, with support from students and intellectuals, staged a determined battle to secure some kind of balance in the legislature by forcing the DRP to admit its misdeeds and to expel those clearly guilty of election fraud. In order to placate the aroused public and to assuage the boycotting minority assemblymen, the DRP finally yielded with a series of concessions. The Park government admitted irregularities during the election and promised to take necessary legal action against those who were responsible. The majority DRP agreed to form a thirteen-member parliamentary committee to probe the voting disturbances. The most important concession was that the ruling party reduced the margin of majority to a level below the critical two-thirds by expelling and easing out sixteen DRP members accused of the most serious violations.

It is significant that a determined and vociferous minority party with strong support from a concerned public was able to exert enough pressure to obtain desired results from the dominant party. The Park regime exhibited considerable political finesse in choosing to conciliate the opposition rather than suppress or intimidate it. This parliamentary democracy was a real departure from the policies of the First Republic.

Many basic qualities which make the legislative chamber a great hall of debate and deliberation are still lacking, however. The majority party too frequently acts with impatience, impulsiveness, and even arbitrariness, while the frustrated minority party too often resorts to political obscurantism and personal defamation. It is still possible for immature acts to take place. For example, when the budget bill was being considered in December 1967, only three minutes of debate were devoted to it, and on another occasion an opposition lawmaker threw human waste at cabinet members. The need for improvement in political discipline and for tolerance and respect for the opposition is unmistakable.

Perhaps the most important after effect of the June election was the brief rise of Dr. Yu Chin-o as a civilian political leader. Dr. Yu, the architect of the first Constitution of the republic in 1948, is a long-time educator, president of the prestigious Korea University (the seedbed of Korean nationalism), and an unadulterated political purist without prior partisan involvement. He is a unique political figure who could command unqualified respect and deference from friends and foes alike. In him the opponents of the present regime could have found a new leader, but his retirement from political life in 1969 and the rise of Yu Chin-san in early 1970 as the spokesman of the opposition considerably weakened any chance for unseating the incumbent in the 1971 general elections.

Chapter *VIII*

THE PRESENT
IN PERSPECTIVE

An old Korean aphorism claims that "even rivers and mountains alter in ten years." After being in power more than ten years since the fateful day in May 1961, the Park regime too has undergone inevitable changes simultaneously altering the overall scenery of the republic. Previously dominant civilian politicians have been gradually pushed aside by ex-soldiers and former military officers have formed a new Gibraltar of power in the political arena. Within the military structure a new locus of power, initially considered as transitory, seems to have been established firmly enough to exude a distinct aura of permanence. Under this new and powerful leadership reinforced by the executive-dominant administrative system, the nation has enjoyed stability and order in the political field and a considerable prosperity in the economic sector. But the economic affluence and political stability, in the absence of a long-term ideology, are intensifying moral laxity in both public and private sectors, thus nullifying the revolutionary spirits and commitment of the present regime. In order to bring this discussion up to date, brief assessment of the whole gamut of the recent military political phenomena follows.

The Military and Its Relationship with the Present Regime

All three service branches, particularly the predominant Army, have undergone a major shift in the locus of real power. The ranking generals in the Army and Navy, all of them products of the Military English School, have either retired from active service or have been removed from the mainstream of power in the military. The mantle of leadership and control over the hierarchy within the Army has been assumed by the members of the second and the eighth classes of the Officers Candidate School, the mainstay of the military coup of 1961.[1] This power turnover, as expected, has had some of the most far-reaching ramifications to date with regard to intramilitary and civil-military relations.[2]

The major significance of this new power alignment is the fusion of civil and military authority in the hands of those who were either actively involved in or closely associated with the coup; the "civilianized" government of Park Chung-hee is largely dominated by former comrades-in-arms. This concentration of power, plus the estrangement of many leading civilians from active politics, has introduced a unique kinship between the Chief Executive and the military. This is now being maintained by continuous reliance upon a number of informal factors.

In the first place, there is the unwritten but rigid *seniority system*, determined by duration of service or dog-tag numbers, which carries over from the military into the government. With all the ranking generals out of the running, President Park derives his seniority from his position vis-à-vis the active military officers. A second source of his "kinship relations" with the military comes from "class loyalty," a shared fraternity of mili-

1. Kang I-sŏp, "Yuksa p'alkisaeng" ["The 8th Class of the Military Academy"], *Shindong-A* (September 1964), pp. 170–98.
2. All but one member of the first class of the OCS left active service, Sŏh Chong-ch'ŏl, Commander of the 1st Field Army in charge of frontier defense. His presence in the service was regarded as more political window dressing within the military structure.

tary comrades of the same vintage. By positioning classmates in all the strategic spots, President Park maintains strict control over the Army. As of late 1969 all five corps commanders—the position between the division and the Field Army commanders—are members of the second class of OCS, and many division commanders and staff officers of corps are members of the eighth class.

A third source of subordinates for President Park are those from a common geographical background. Geographical section, marked by linguistic dialect and peculiarities of loyal customs, traditionally has encouraged group loyalty and factional rivalry. President Park utilizes this to his own advantage: he summons and enjoys the almost complete support and allegiance of officers of Southeastern origin. In return, he gives them particularly favorable assignments.

Should these more or less informal measures fail to guarantee Park's position vis-à-vis the armed services, he has a final persuader: the Army Counter-Intelligence Corps (CIC), not to be confused with the CIA, which is technically a civilian agency founded by Kim Jong-pil. A purely military agency, the CIC is under Park's direct control and maintains a strict surveillance over all high-ranking officers and their relationships to each other. Hence this body acts as a deterrent to would-be revolutionaries and also guards against the rise of disruptive factionalism within the military. This powerful security organ, until 1969 led by several different members of the eighth class of the OCS, now is commanded by General Kim Chae-kyu, a member of the second class to which Park belongs.[3]

Of special importance is the fact that the military has been pacified by a series of positive actions. The most significant accomplishment has been the successful wooing of former generals to the government. Paik Sŏn-yŏp, the former head of the Northwestern faction within the military, joined the Park gov-

3. On October 20, 1969, the government announced the creation of a new super Army Security Command and the appointment of Maj. General Kim Chae-kyu as its first commander. Although information regarding the functions of this body is not yet clear, they are believed to be of a more political nature, since it is to be located under the President.

ernment as Minister of Transportation in 1969, and Yi Han-rim, the Commander of the First Field Army at the time of the coup and the key member of the Northeastern group, was appointed Minister of Construction in the same year. Of course, Premier Chung Il-gwon, the durable former leader of the Northeastern faction, still retains his position. Also, many other officers who initially opposed the coup d'état have since been serving in the government.[4] This highly convivial state of affairs seems to be a result of two principal factors: President Park's earnest desire to create an atmosphere of consensus within the military and the willingness of the former rivals to bury their hatchets and join the mainstream of political power. Whatever is the governing reason for this harmony, President Park deserves a high mark for his statesmanship.

The second measure introduced was the equalization of the salary scale between the military and civil servants. Formerly, military personnel received only token payment, owing to the predominant philosophy that military service is more a civic responsibility than a professional career. As a result, a private first class previously received monthly pay of less than one dollar; a second lieutenant earned about ten dollars. A series of preferential salary increments removed the civil-military income disparity so that a military career became more reasonable in terms of livelihood. Now a second lieutenant earns $50 per month and a general's salary ranges from $200 to $300.

A third step was to free the military from the pressure of providing political funds to the party in power. As discussed earlier, the major portion of financial contributions to the regime had been extracted from the military. Of course, money was raised by either disposing of war materials or by diverting the funds allocated for the sustenance of troops. On the strength of the rising economy the Park government now relies on the civilian sector for needed political funds. Indeed, restoring the financial integrity of the military removed a major source of the

4. General Ch'oi Kyŏng-rok is now ambassador to Mexico and General Kang Moon-bong is representing Korea in Sweden. General Kang Young-hoon, once imprisoned for his alleged counterrevolutionary activities, will soon head a government-subsidized research institute in Washington, D.C.

civil-military dysfunction and improved the morale of soldiers.

Park's decision to send combat troops to South Vietnam—under strong pressure from the United States—also produced several desirable aftereffects on the Korean Army.[5] Aside from gaining actual combat experience, which the troops badly need in view of increasing belligerence from the communist North, they are receiving a tangible monetary reward. Operating as a part of the Allied Forces, Korean personnel are paid in American dollars—about one-fourth of the U.S. counterpart—and are given access to the American post exchanges. The average savings of frugal officers is said to be three to four thousand dollars from one tour of duty. Now that more than half the entire officer corps and practically every graduate of the regular four-year Military Academy completes at least one tour of duty, this unfortunate conflict in Southeast Asia has considerably improved the economic status of the Korean Army.[6] Another major byproduct of the military involvement in Vietnam is an opportunity to tighten the chain of command all the way from the Commander-in-Chief down to the smallest fighting units, making any kind of disruptive action within the military highly unlikely. Park's pro-military outlook thus began to engender a favorable attitude among the troops, a trend demonstrated by the outcome of the 1967 presidential elections. In the so-called "military regions" along the Demilitarized Zone, the percentage vote for President Park soared from 32–40 in 1963 to 60–65 in 1967.[7]

With skillful employment of carrot and stick, the Park regime has maintained intramilitary stability as well as firm control over the military. Any kind of disruptive movement within the military seems to be unlikely in the foreseeable future. The questions remaining to be answered are those which require long-term consideration. How will the internal power makeup

5. See the author's article, "South Korea's Involvement in Vietnam and Its Economic and Political Impact," *Asian Survey*, X, no. 6 (June 1970), 319–33.
6. More than a quarter of a million South Korean troops have served in combat duty in Vietnam during the past five years.
7. See p. 150.

of the military and the quasi-civilian dominance over the military be affected by the gradual receding of the graduates of the old Officers Candidate School? How will the rapidly emerging graduates of the regular four-year military academies react to the present power configuration as they become the key staff and line officers? The last question requires especially serious consideration, because the members of the first class of the Military Academy, graduated in 1955, already have been promoted to Lieutenant Colonel, and many of them now occupy some of the key positions in Army Headquarters or in combat units.

What must be emphasized here is the tight esprit de corps among classmates and fellow alumni of the Academy. Class loyalty, which has been mentioned as a major source of cliquishness, prevails even more strongly among these young officers. The former cadets, unlike their predecessors with the OCS background, have undergone a much longer period of communal activities, most of which required individual sacrifice for the welfare of the class as a whole. Another source of class solidarity is professional elitism, which these officers share as the recipients of superior and rigorous education and training in an environment almost identical to that of West Point or Annapolis. Also to be noted is the highly selective recruitment process to which these career officers have been subjected before their admission to the Academy. Indeed, there is a marked difference in terms of quality and professional commitment between the Academy graduates and the OCS products. (The latter were required to have a marginal middle school education and received only three or six months of training before being commissioned as Second Lieutenants.)

On the strength of group loyalty, class cohesion, and the professional elitism which the Academy graduates share, they could be organized quite easily into a highly motivated, disciplined force if the present quasi-military government or any future civilian regime should fail to deliver what the military considers to be crucial to the nation's welfare. It must also be remembered that a majority of these former cadets come from rather indigent economic backgrounds and that a susceptibility to revolutionary activity is high among them (one need only recall the experience of the Japanese in the 1930s).

Fully aware of the potential threat posed by this professional officer corps, the astute Park regime has been making a serious effort to deemphasize the differentiation between the Academy, OCS, and ROTC products. In addition, a policy of "divide and rule" has been applied to neutralize Academy-trained officers from any kind of group activities. The especially bright ones have been absorbed into the system, and various schemes to keep these officers under control have thus far been effective.

What is now needed is the replacement of short-term tactics with a long-term design to restore the concept of civil supremacy and to sustain intramilitary stability. The first step to be taken should be a gradual and deliberate relaxing of centralized control over the military in order to facilitate the transition of the civil-military relationship from a *personal, informal,* and *factional* one to an *impersonal, formal,* and *constitutional* one. A serious effort should be made to prevent a recurrence of the extra-legal alliance between the two by rooting out the tendency of senior officers to build personal empires. In short, the Park regime must move away from a cliquish power structure and must simultaneously undertake development of a truly legal basis of authority.

The Park regime must also cease to exhort the revolutionary behavior of 1961, lest it be emulated by other self-righteous officers. At the same time, intensive indoctrination and inculcation of the concept of military subordinance to civilian authority should be conducted in order to draw a firm line of demarcation between military professionalism and civilian politics. Without the restoration of the legal pre-eminence of civilian authority, the second stage of modernization, political development, would be tantamount to building a house on sand.

Clear criteria for military assignment and promotion must also be instituted to attack a major source of discontent. Likewise, there should be a continuous and realistic adjustment of the military pay scale, not only to maintain the present standard of living, but also to upgrade living conditions. There is no better morale booster than a salary increment, which would greatly improve the image of civilian government at the same time. Without these preparatory measures, any alteration in the power balance maintained by the quasi-military government could produce problems of formidable magnitude. The Park regime still faces the monumental task of creating lasting and stable civil-military relations based on constitutionalism.

The New Politics in the "Civilian" Sector

The elections of 1963 and 1967 basically altered the political substructure as well as the superstructure of South Korea. The seemingly transient military intrusion into civilian politics has become what appears to be a permanent political phenomenon. An almost new political order has emerged, for most of the old guard who had dominated politics and business during the Rhee and Chang periods have departed from the scene. Some died from old age and others from illness caused by personal despair after being swept away from the mainstream of politics.[8] Many others simply retired or faded away into obscurity during the period of political inactivity imposed upon them by the Park regime.[9] Only a few joined the dominant force.[10]

Something about the new political order can be learned from studying the extent to which professional soldiers have permeated the present civilian power structure. With regard to active participation in the government 40 out of 95 holders of cabinet posts have had professional military backgrounds since the civilianization of the regime in December 9, 1963. Ten out of 11 directorships of independent regulatory commissions and 32 of 59 ambassadorial posts have been held by inactive military officers (as of 1968). In the National Assembly, 36 out of 174 seats in the Sixth Assembly (1963–1967) and 37 out of 175

8. Notably, Syngman Rhee died in 1965 while he was in exile in Hawaii, and John M. Chang succumbed to a liver infection in 1966.

9. Song In-sang, Han Hee-sŏk, Yun Po-sŏn, to name a few, have retired from active politics. The blacklisting of former politicians was officially lifted on August 3, 1968, after seven years.

10. Among those well-known political figures now adapted to the ruling party are Paik Du-jin, former Premier under Rhee; Yun Ch'i-young, former Home Minister and key member of Rhee's regime and party; and Ch'oi Hee-song, a prominent North Korean refugee.

seats in the Seventh Assembly (1967) have been held by retired military figures. Also, in the administrative departments 14 percent of high-ranking civil servants and political appointees have had military backgrounds to varying degrees.[11]

A similar trend is apparent in the economic sphere. Since the coup in 1961, retired ranking generals have freely moved into top-level positions in the multimillion dollar government corporations, many of which have been created subsequent to the military takeover. As of early 1969, 33 of 42 major publicly-financed industrial establishments have been, or still are, headed by former military officers. Industrial positions, like some of the overseas ambassadorial assignments, have been given away as if they were retirement presents.[12] In addition to those who have made successful conversions to governmental or political life, there are more than 2,000 former officers with the rank of Major or above now engaged in some form of civilian activity. In many cases, these men hold positions of great influence because of their knowledge of and contact with the dominant power structure.

Aside from such quantitative advancement to positions of influence, there is a qualitative influx of former generals and colonels into key governmental offices—from the head of state down to the bureau chiefs in the more sensitive positions. The following list of key officials and their former military ranks shows the extent of military entrenchment in the governmental process as of the winter of 1969:

1. The President of the Republic (Head of State)
   Park Chung-hee, General, Army*
   Presidential Secretariat Senior Secretaries
   Political Affairs: Kim Sang-bok, Lt. General, Army
   Civil Affairs: Yu Sŏng-won, Brig. General, Army
   Public Information: Kang Sang-uk, Brig. General, Army

11. Yo Hoon, "Social Background of Higher Civil Servants in Korea," *Koreana Quarterly*, IX, no. 1 (Spring 1968), 51–52.

12. Park Jin-sŏk, Yi Sŏng-ho, Kim Il-hwan, Yun T'ai-il, Park T'ae-jun, Ahn Ki-sŏng, Kim Yong-bae, and Song Yo-ch'an are a few of those heading industrial corporations owned and operated by the government.

* All ranks are those held at the time of retirement from active duty.

Protocol: Cho Sang-ho, Colonel, Army
General Affairs: Kim Won-hui, Brig. General, Army

2. Central Intelligence Agency
   Director, Kim Kye-won, Lt. General, Army

3. The Prime Minister (Head of Government)
   Chung Il-gwon, General, Army

4. The Minister of Defense
   Chung Nae-hyŏk, Lt. General, Army

5. The Minister of Home Affairs (National Police and Internal
   Security)
   Park Kyŏng-won, Lt. General, Army

6. The Minister of Construction
   Yi Han-rim, Lt. General, Army

7. The Minister of Transportation
   Paik Sŏn-yŏp, General, Army

8. The Minister of Agriculture and Forestry
   Cho Si-hyŏng, Maj. General, Army

9. The Chairman, Committee of Agriculture and Forestry,
   the National Assembly
   Yi Chong-gun, Brig. General, Army

10. The Chairman, Committee on Commerce and Industry, the
    National Assembly
    Kil Chong-sik, Colonel, Army (former CIA officer)

11. The Chairman, Committee of Foreign Affairs, the National
    Assembly
    Ch'a Chi-ch'ŏl, Colonel, Army

12. The Chairman, Committee on Home Affairs, the National
    Assembly
    Yi Sang-mu, Colonel, Army

13. The Chairman, Judiciary Committee, the National Assembly
    No Chee-p'il, Brig. General, Army

14. The Chairman, Committee on National Defense, the National
    Assembly
    Min Pyŏng-gwon, Lt. General, Army

15. The Chairman, Committee on Steering and Planning, the
    National Assembly
    Yi Pyŏng-whi, Colonel, Army

Not only do ex-officers dominate the government superstructure, but they also control the Democratic Republican Party, the political arm of the Park regime with a massive membership of 1,500,000 and almost unlimited financial resources. Until last year the Chairman of the party was Kim Jong-pil. Although he is now outside the party, his personal influence over partisan matters has not abated much. The Secretary-General of the party, the overseer of administrative activities, is Kil Chae-ho, Park's fellow revolutionary from the outset of the coup. Park Chung-hee is the head of the party as the President of the DRP.

Clearly, the Park regime is quasi-military, the free elections of 1967 notwithstanding. Confronted now with stepped-up guerrilla activities from the communist North, the regime might undergo another period of consolidation along military lines. Ex-officers are so deeply entrenched in, and so well adapted to, the mainstream of political and economic life that they will remain as a nucleus of political strength and will influence Korean politics for many years to come. Thus in terms of *realpolitik* any attempt to dislodge the former military officers from the power center might have far-reaching consequences since it would have a disruptive effect upon the entire power structure and the administrative process of recent origin.

The means by which the Park government formulates and implements national policies is largely governed by the military approach to the adaptation and execution of goals. National policies are drawn up and carried out like a war plan. After a careful calculation of all the measurable variables in terms of a specific objective, all the available means and resources are applied to achieve the desired end. Discarded during such a process are administrative trivialities and the concern for material and human costs. A good example of the military way of executing a task is the urban renewal projects now being undertaken in Seoul under the personal direction of Mayor Kim Hyŏn-ok, a former Army officer and a close confidant of President Park. Since becoming mayor, Kim has pushed through numerous and expensive road expansion and slum clearance programs in spite of the outcry against his high-handed tactics from the press and the opposition side in the legislative chamber. Even the thirty-year-old city planning scheme originally drafted by the Japanese was finally implemented at the expense of thousands of residents of the affected areas. The normalization of diplomatic relations with Japan despite widespread opposition, the successful conclusion of the First Five-Year Plan, and the introduction of long overdue educational reform at the middle school level are positive examples of the success of a military-type determination.

The Park regime's highly centralized decision-making system reflects the military staff system. At the apex of the present hierarchy there is what is known as a "mini-cabinet" comprised of the presidential secretaries who hold cabinet status.[13] Functioning as the eyes, ears, and sometimes even as the conscience of the President, they exert enormous influence upon the adoption of executive policies. They also form a buffer between the President and the many civilian-oriented cabinet ministers in the State Council and the heads of the local governmental units. The significance of this staff system is the dominant presence of the former military officers. As has been noted earlier, five of seven key secretaries are former Army officers. Only those involved with economic matters and the press do not have military backgrounds.

Park delegates to his cabinet ministers and to other key officials a clear-cut authority and expects them to exercise it fully. As long as they remain loyal to Park and devoted to their assignments, they are consistently backed. This contributes to relatively low cabinet turnover and to a governmental stability unknown during the Chang and Rhee periods.

Of greater importance than the procedural character of governance are the priorities of the present regime. Rather than tackling the philosophic aspect of political modernization, the Park government has opted for the more immediate and concrete task of economic development as the first order of business. Under the "economy first" policy the entire nation's energy and resources have been concentrated on the increase of gross national product and the expansion of exportation. Today the new slogan, "Production, Exportation, Anticommunism," not

13. Paik Sang-ki, "A Study of Decision-making Process in the Chung-Wa-Dae," *Koreana Quarterly*, II, no. 2 (Summer 1969), 38–50. See also *Dong-A Ilbo*, March 23, 1968.

only inspires national policy but also commands popular attention on the walls of sprawling buildings in the cities.

The "economy first" policy carries with it a high propensity to put the first priority on those industries that are closely associated with military capabilities: cement, petroleum, railroads, and fertilizer. The cement industry, which multiplied itself each year during the last seven years, now produces more than 5,000,000 tons, a tenfold increase since the coup. Of course, cement is a key item, and its uses range from the construction of reenforced bunkers at the front to the super-highway in the rear. The burgeoning of the oil and chemical industries also has a clear military implication: gaining "logistical independence" from the United States, upon whom the Republic of Korea Army has been totally dependent for petroleum and munition supplies.

The Park Regime at the Crossroads

Institutionalization of political innovations occurred during the present leadership's first years in office. Inertia gave way to a "puritanic" zeal for social and economic reform. The lethargic public was rejuvenated by a new emphasis on hard work and personal morality, which resulted in the successful completion of administrative programs. In the past several years, however, a serious reversal in this process has occurred. As the ex-officers have grown accustomed to their seemingly permanent positions of power, their reform zeal has waned. The revolutionary leadership, never having had an ideology, lacks a long-term political program. A product of modern scientific pragmatism, it has no *Weltanschauung* and/or high moral goal. In the midst of economic progress and apparent political stability, a clear, moral direction does not exist. Indeed, during the past several years, the present regime has proved either incapable or unwilling to stamp out recurring public corruption and graft.[14]

14. According to an official government report, cases involving financial irregularities among public officials have been increasing by 30 to 40 percent a year. In the first half of 1969 alone, more than 4,000 public officials have been reprimanded for a variety of misdemeanors and felonious conduct. See *Dong-A Ilbo*, December 5, 6, and 7, 1969.

There is also a dangerous tendency to associate the country's destiny with the permanence of the ruling body, for last year a constitutional amendment removed the third-term limitation from the office of President. Recurring corruption, the regime's unwillingness to relinquish power, and increasing public apathy project another ominous sign. For the future of the Third Republic and for the sake of the present leadership, this study concludes with a caveat.

The Park regime in Korea must be reminded that the process of nation-building does not end with economic expansion and swift processing of a developmental plan. Indeed, these represent only the beginning of multifaceted and multilinear development. Now that the country is nearing national economic self-sufficiency and, at the same time, has achieved some degree of institutionalization, the three following measures must be taken if the country is to make continued forward progress toward the ultimate goal of modernization: the creation of a moral society with material abundance.

First, in order to increase political output it is imperative to decentralize the system by granting added autonomy to the lower levels. Given the chance for specialization and adaptation of institutions to occur, the political system will be strengthened and stabilized.

Second, the present Park regime must undertake an immediate and agonizing self-appraisal if it is not to forfeit what President Park himself called "the historic mission of performing a surgical operation to eliminate corruption and to eradicate other social evils and to inculcate a free and wholesome moral and mental attitude among the people." After nine years, recurring dysfunction portends future difficulty. The once-vigorous reform spirit which earned the Park regime public support at the outset seems to be dissipating, and creeping complacency and lethargy seem to supplant the earlier revolutionary zeal. If the regime is not to be a victim of its own successes, reaffirmation of revolutionary pledges is urgently needed.[15]

15. See the author's article, "Moral Imperative in Political Development: A Caveat to the Park Regime in Korea," *Asian Forum*, I, no. 3 (October 1969), 43–45.

Finally, if the Park regime is indeed an innovating and modernizing regime, it must assume the role of political reformer. Crystallization of a new ideology is a matter of utmost exigency; economic expansion cannot indefinitely be regarded as a surrogate to political ideology. A new purposeful ideology, based upon a higher moral value, is needed if the leadership is to stir or capture the imagination and creativity of its people. Indeed, the present regime is at the crossroads. It might degenerate, following the long historical line of administrative tyranny, or it might usher in a new era of innovative governance based on liberal democracy.

Chapter *IX*

A COMPARATIVE VIEW

There are two major schools of thought on the potential of the military as a modernizing force in developing nations: one holds that the military can perform such a function, and the other seriously questions it.[1] From this debate a number of observations regarding the general pattern of the military revolution and its nation-building role have emerged. In this study of comparative politics it seems fitting to conclude this work by treating Korea's military experience during the past nine years in the perspective of these two opposing schools.

Edward Shils, one of the most learned and elder scholars in the field of comparative politics, makes a strong case against military intrusion into civil politics. In discussing various detrimental qualities of the military as an innovating force, he emphasizes that the military is not a complete regime given its

1. The leading skeptics of the military's ability to undertake an effective and lasting developmental change are Edward Shils, S. E. Finer, and Eduardo Santos, while Lucian Pye and Samuel Huntington comprise the sympathetic school. Of course, there are many others who have dealt with a particular military revolution in an area or in a nation. Consult Robert E. Ward on Japan, John J. Johnson on Latin America, and Sydney Fisher on the Middle East.

limited educational preparation and practical experience. As an incomplete regime, he argues, the military places more stress on order and clean-up than on progress, and when it has a program for progress, its ideas are rather scant and unimaginative even where well-intentioned. Also like all non-hereditary oligarchies, Shils continues, the military has no provision for succession and like other totalitarian hierarchies, it allows no place for opposition.[2]

S. E. Finer, an articulate voice on civil-military relations, almost totally dismisses any possible constructive role by the military in the political area by stressing the general pattern of the military's "degeneration into absolutism."[3] He also argues that temporary gains in terms of restoring order and stability are far outweighed by the losses resulting from military rule. Eduardo Santos, a leading student of Latin American military situations, bases his objection to military rule on the military's lack of "humanism": "Accustomed to the blind obedience of their inferiors, the dry voices of command, and the narrow horizon of their profession, the military leadership lack the courage to rectify mistakes, to ask for and listen to advice, to have patience, to realize that one owes one's power to the will of the people."[4] In a similar vein, Manfred Halpern and Morris Janowitz, in their attempts to conceptualize the military phenomenon in developing nations, points out that the military approach to problem-solving is detrimental to the political process. Janowitz argues that military leaders are conditioned to regard any problem as amenable to direct and simple scientific action, that they shun and are repulsed by "indirect solution and the willingness of political leaders to temporize as a way of solving problems."[5] Halpern registers his reservations

2. Edward Shils, "Political Development of the New States," in John J. Johnson, ed., *The Role of the Military in Underdeveloped Countries* (Princeton: Princeton University Press, 1962), pp. 52–67.

3. S. E. Finer, *Man on Horseback: The Role of the Military in Politics* (New York: Frederick A. Praeger, 1962).

4. Eduardo Santos, "Latin American Realities," *Foreign Affairs*, XXXIV, no. 4 (June 19, 1956), p. 256.

5. Morris Janowitz, *The Military in the Political Development of New Nations: An Essay in Comparative Analysis* (Chicago: University of Chicago Press, 1964), pp. 89–92.

by emphasizing the military's obsession with discipline, hierarchy, obedience, and rigidity.[6]

These concerns and fears expressed by interested scholars seem to have only limited relevance to the Korean case. The military did not place its supreme effort on order, but on progress and organization-building except during the initial stage of the revolution. Developmental progress was not just "scant and unimaginative" but precise and well-conceived, as records of the economic growth indicate. The military oligarchy did not degenerate into absolutism nor permanently silence the opposition. Rather, it demonstrated an uncanny ability to absorb the former political opponents and counter-revolutionaries into the power structure. Indeed, the Park regime exhibited a greater degree of "humanism" and leniency in dealing with political enemies than did the civilian leadership under Rhee. President Park gained a popular mandate through an effective political organization and through an undeniable, concrete record of economic achievement, not through the imposition of massive terror or extensive employment of fraudulence or deception. It was flexible, not rigid, in its diplomatic relations, even with countries having diplomatic ties with North Korea. It was also pragmatic and nondoctrinaire in regard to economic development and was willing to modify its programs whenever the situation warranted. In comparison with Rhee, Park was quite moderate and restrained in exercising his authority.

These scholars tend to treat the rise of the military as equivalent to the total retreat of the civilian elite. Certainly this was not the case in Korea. What the military leadership *did not do* was replace civilian administrative personnel nor alter the existing public and private institutions. Not only were the capable people retained in spite of their earlier political involvement as the appointees of previous regimes, but also many well-known and idle civilian talents were mobilized for economic planning and governmental efficiency. At the same time, the leading financiers and industrialists were left alone, after initial inconvenience, to operate their enterprises despite their

6. Manfred Halpern, *The Politics of Social Change in the Middle East and North Africa* (Princeton: Princeton University Press, 1963), p. 258.

financial irregularities in the past. The result of this policy has been continuity and stability in the administrative and economic sectors.

These comments, however, should not be construed as implying that the present quasi-military leadership has been entirely pure and problem-free. Quite the contrary is true, given the problem of succession as demonstrated by the 1969 constitutional amendment to remove the third-term limitation and given a myriad of other unsolved economic and social problems. Nevertheless, it seems fair to say that performance under the present regime has been relatively better than that of the previous civilian leadership, but it still falls far short of what it should be as an innovating force.

With an opposite viewpoint on military potential as a modernizing force are two important scholars, Samuel Huntington and Lucian Pye.[7] Huntington, viewing the reform coup as a genuine alternative in nations without a constitutional tradition of peaceful change, stated: "The alternative to social revolution appears to be a progression of reform coups. Reform coups are the products of the drives for westernization and modernization. Frequent coups are signs of change and progress. Not all coups, to be sure, produce reforms, but virtually all reforms are produced by coups. . . ."[8]

Supporting Huntington's thesis on the potential role of the military, the MIT group under the leadership of Lucian Pye reported: "The military—the one traditional social order likely to survive the process of social change—may be able to play

7. Lucian W. Pye, "The Armies in the Process of Political Modernization," in John J. Johnson, ed., *The Role of the Military in Underdeveloped Countries*, pp. 86–87. Also consult the special study done on this topic by The MIT group in 1960: MIT, The Center of International Studies, *United States Foreign Policy: Social and Political Change in the Underdeveloped Countries and Its Implication for United States Policy*, Study No. 10 (Washington, D.C.: Government Printing Office, 1960). For more sympathetic studies on individual nations, see Guy J. Pauker, "Southeast Asia as a Problem Area in the Next Decade," *World Politics*, II, no. 3 (July 1959). 325–45; see also K. J. Newman, "Pakistan's Preventive Autocracy and Its Cause," *Pacific Affairs*, XXXII (March 1959), 18–33.

8. Samuel P. Huntington, *Changing Pattern of Military Politics* (Glencoe, Ill.: The Free Press of Glencoe, 1962), pp. 39–40.

a role in promoting mobility while maintaining stability, in facilitating change while preventing chaos. Upon the efficiency with which the military sector can be made to perform this role may hinge the successful outcome to the transition in many societies."[9] In his companion studies on the military in developing nations, Pye alluded throughout to the military as the last remaining cohesive and disciplined unit with modern orientation; hence it is destined to assume the role of modernization. He even admonished those who hold a negative outlook toward the military: "In seeking a realistic estimate of the potential role of the military in the political development of particular countries it is necessary to avoid being excessively influenced by ideological considerations which may be relevant only in advanced societies. We have in mind, particularly, the western stereotype of the military as a foe of liberal values. . . . And we must expect many paradoxes."[10]

Somewhat at variance with the foregoing observations by those who have a more positive outlook on military potential, the Korean military revolution was not envisioned and undertaken by officers who articulated or subscribed to a reform philosophy. The original instigators of the coup were almost reactionary revolutionaries who unequivocally eschewed both communism and socialism and, at the same time, held a serious reservation about the suitability of western democracy in a developing nation such as Korea.[11] For this reason, the military's rise in Korea did not touch off a social revolution which uproots and alters the basic socioeconomic structure. Rather, it was a

9. MIT, *United States Foreign Policy: Social and Political Change in the Underdeveloped Countries and Its Implication for United States Policy,* in Roy C. Macridis and Bernard E. Brown, *Comparative Politics: Notes and Readings* (Homewood, Ill.: Dorsey Press, 1961), p. 529.

10. Lucian W. Pye, "The Armies in the Process of Political Modernization," in John J. Johnson, ed., *The Role of the Military in Underdeveloped Countries*, pp. 86–87.

11. Those generals known for their progressive and liberal attitudes and for their clean records adamantly opposed the coup. They include Lt. General Kang Young-hoon, Lt. General Ch'oi Kyŏng-rok, Maj. General Kim Ŭng-soo, and Lt. General Kim Hyŏng-il. The last officer still opposes the Park regime, while the former generals made peace with the present regime.

simple change of leadership, euphemistically called "the ex-change of generations," at the expense of the civilian politicians.

Second, the civilian leadership in Korea was not supplanted by the military because the latter was the only remaining co-hesive force capable of undertaking modernization, but largely because there was intramilitary dysfunction and civilian tam-pering with the military. The failure of the civilian leadership as a modernizing force only provided the military with a justifi-cation for the former's overthrow; it was not the immediate cause of the revolutionary undertaking. In this respect, the Korean coup cannot be treated as mere "reactive militarism" against the civilian regime, as Professor Janowitz has labeled it.[12] Indeed, unlike similar upheavals in Pakistan, Burma, and Turkey—where the military coup was the work of the top mili-tary hierarchy—the Korean coup was undertaken by second and third echelon officers in the military.

Third, the initial success of the military as an innovating force was not so much a result of training and modern technical know-how as it was the urgency of success that the situation required. As a revolutionary enterprise which overthrew a constitutionally elected government, not some hereditary mon-arch or despotic usurper of power, the military coup had to demonstrate a sincere and honest nation-building spirit by ini-tiating developmental programs if it was to justify its extra-constitutional action. Particularly the questionable personal history of its revolutionary leader, Park Chung-hee, compelled the regime to undertake and succeed in its innovating task if it was to convince the public and the military establishment of its authenticity as a bona fide reform government. Indeed, it was almost in haphazard fashion that the Park regime plunged into the task of modernization. The military's honest and frantic effort to forge ahead at the initial period generated enough momentum to carry the regime through a successful conversion of the junta government to a civilianized regime. Once the

---

12. Janowitz, *The Military in the Political Development of New Na-tions*, pp. 89–92. Janowitz seems to include the Korean coup in the cate-gory of "reactive militarism" as a reactive against the corrupt civilian regime.

wheels began to roll, desperation developed into genuine commitment. Of course, scientific orientation toward problem-solving, organizational theory for efficiency and stability, and youthful enthusiasm and impatience with inertia all greatly facilitated the developmental programs that the Park administration conceived.

Another major factor for which the Park regime owes its success is found in Kim Jong-pil, the mastermind of the revolution. Without his ability as an organizational genius, the CIA and the Democratic Republican Party could not have developed into such functional institutions, so vital to the military leadership during the uncertain postrevolutionary period and so useful later in assisting the nonviolent transition to a "civilian" regime. The successful implementation of the entire developmental program could not have been achieved without the stability assured by these political organizations. What can be concluded from this almost fortuitous success of the present leadership is that modernization is not really as complex and difficult as has been supposed. It can occur if there is a determined leadership with organizational skill, whether it be civilian or military, committed to such a goal. In Korea, a few hundred military officers threw themselves into the task of developmental change and quickly learned at first hand the arts of innovative changes—at least in such functional areas as the economy and public administration.

Another significant development is that former military officers have in the last ten years become managerial experts in both private and public sectors. Korea, which did not possess a large number of civilian experts and managers (particularly in the economic sector), was in great need of managerial expertise in the wake of the economic upsurge of recent years. It was natural that the ex-officers with newly acquired know-how fill the vacuum, not by wholly replacing their civilian counterparts but by complementing them. Continuous civilianization, plus increasing interaction among the civilian and military elites, considerably obscured the civil-military duality of the first years of the military revolution.

There are also other factors and developments which make

the Korean military experience different from others. No other developing nation since World War II has been under such close American scrutiny and support. The United States built the Korean Army from a nonentity to a vast modern army of 600,000, and it still exercises operational control over the Korean forces and provides them with basic logistical support. It is also the American aid in materials and planning that served as the basis for economic recovery, and it is American-inspired anticommunism that underlies Korean political ideology. In view of the close ties between the two countries, the American role in the various stages of the emergence of the military, whether openly demonstrated or not, cannot be overlooked.

Also, in contrast to other nascent nations under similar direct or indirect military rule, political ecology is quite different in Korea. Political consciousness and the literacy rate are both high.[13] Indeed, in the non-Western world, Korea ranks second only to Japan in education and voting participation. What should thus be recognized is that Korea was a relatively fertile ground for modernization prior to the inauguration of the developmental design of the present leadership. What Korea needed was a proper direction from political leadership.

Against this background, it is difficult to identify the Korean military coup with one particular pattern or with a universal hypothesis. In different countries, diverse sociopolitical and military factors govern the political actions of both civilians and the military. For this reason it is advisable to treat each nation's experience in its particular context rather than in a broad, more general framework—a point which Professor J. C. Hurewitz eloquently argues in his recent study on the Middle Eastern military in politics.[14] It is hoped, in conclusion, that the study of the Korean military experience contributes to the important question of the military in politics today.

13. Publication and consumption of newspapers and other library materials in Korea far exceed that from all the Arab world.

14. J. C. Hurewitz, *Middle East Politics: The Military Dimension* (New York: Frederick A. Praeger, 1969).

APPENDIXES,
BIBLIOGRAPHY,
AND INDEX

The Law Regarding Extraordinary Measures
for National Reconstruction

Promulgated on June 6, 1961

Chapter I. General Provisions

Article 1: Establishment of the Supreme Council for National Reconstruction.

The Supreme Council for National Reconstruction shall be established as the extraordinary measures intended for the reconstruction of the Republic of Korea as a genuine democratic republic by safeguarding the Republic of Korea against Communist aggression and by overcoming the national crisis which resulted from corruption, injustice and poverty.

Article 2: Status of the Supreme Council for National Reconstruction.

The Supreme Council for National Reconstruction shall have the status of the supreme governing organ of the Republic of Korea, pending the establishment of a government following the composition of the National Assembly by means of a general election to be held after the completion of the tasks of the May 16 Military Revolution.

Article 3: Basic Rights of the Citizen.

The basic rights of the citizens provided for in the Constitution shall be guaranteed to such extent as is not inconsistent with the fulfillment of the tasks of the Revolution.

Chapter II. Composition of the Supreme Council for National Reconstruction

Article 4: Supreme Councilors.

(1) The Supreme Council for National Reconstruction shall be composed of the Supreme Councilors elected from among the officers on active duty of the National Armed Forces who are deeply imbued with the cause of the May 16 Military Revolution.

(2) The number of the Supreme Councilors shall be neither more than thirty-two (32) nor less than twenty (20).

(3) The Supreme Councilors shall be elected by a majority vote of the Supreme Councilors duly seated upon the recommendation of not less than five (5) Supreme Councilors.

(4) The Supreme Councilors shall be precluded from holding additional offices except the Head of Cabinet and military posts; and the Chairman of the Supreme Council for National Reconstruction shall be precluded from holding any other offices except the Head of Cabinet.

Article 5: Election of the Chairman and the Vice-Chairman.

The Supreme Council for National Reconstruction shall elect one Chairman and one Vice-Chairman from among the Supreme Councilors by a majority vote of the Supreme Councilors duly seated.

Article 6: Duties of the Chairman.

(1) The Chairman of the Supreme Council for National Reconstruction shall maintain order in the Supreme Council for National Reconstruction, regulate its proceedings, supervise performance of its duties, and represent the Supreme Council for National Reconstruction.

(2) When the Chairman is unable to perform his duties for any reason, the Vice-Chairman shall act in his stead.

(3) When both the Chairman and the Vice-Chairman are unable to perform their duties for any reason, the youngest Supreme Councilor shall act in their stead.

Article 7: Voting.

Unless otherwise provided for in this Law, the Constitution, or the Law of the Supreme Council for National Reconstruction, the attendance of a majority of the Supreme Councilors duly seated and votes of a majority of Supreme Councilors present shall be necessary for decisions of the Supreme Council for National Reconstruction.

Article 8: Standing Committee.

(1) There shall be established the Standing Committee of the Supreme Council for National Reconstruction, in order to deal with matters delegated thereto, to a prescribed extent, by the Supreme Council for National Reconstruction.

(2) Necessary matters relating to the Standing Committee mentioned in the preceding paragraph shall be stipulated by the Law of the Supreme Council for National Reconstruction.

Chapter III. Powers of the Supreme Council for National Reconstruction

Article 9: Exercise of the Powers of the National Assembly.

The Powers of the National Assembly provided for in the Constitution shall be exercised by the Supreme Council for National Reconstruction.

Article 10: Decision on Budget Bill.

The attendance of not less than two thirds of the Supreme Council duly seated and votes of a majority of the Supreme Councilors present shall be necesary for the adoption of the Budget Bill.

Article 11: Exercise of the Powers of the President by Proxy.

When the President is in default or unable to perform his duties for any reason, his powers shall successively be exercised by the Chairman of the Supreme Council for National Reconstruction, the Vice-Chairman thereof and the Head of Cabinet.

Article 12: Powers of the Supreme Council in regard to the Executive Matters.

The following matters shall require decision by the Supreme Council for National Reconstruction:

1. Proclamation and termination of Martial Law;

2. Appointments and removal of the Chairman of the Joint Chiefs of Staff, the Chief of Staff of each Armed Force, and the Commandant of the Marine Corps, and other important military affairs;

3. Awarding of honors and granting of amnesty, commutation and rehabilitation;

4. Approval for the appointment of the Prosecutor General and the Chief Prosecutors, the Chairman of the Board of Audit, the Chairman of the Inspection Commission, the Presidents of National Universities, Ambassadors, and Ministers, and other public officials designated by Law, and managers of important Government-operated enterprises.

Article 13: Control over the Cabinet.

(1) The powers of the State Council, as provided for in paragraph (1), (2), and (12), Article 72 of the Constitution and elsewhere therein, shall be exercised by the Cabinet under the direction and control of the Supreme Council for National Reconstruction.

(2) The Cabinet shall assume collective responsibility to the Supreme Council for National Reconstruction.

Article 14: Composition of the Cabinet.

(1) The Cabinet shall be composed of the Head of Cabinet and other Cabinet Members.

(2) The Head of Cabinet shall be appointed by the Supreme Council for National Reconstruction.

(3) The appointment mentioned in the preceding paragraph shall be made by a majority vote of the Supreme Councilors duly seated.

(4) The Cabinet Members shall be appointed by the Head of Cabinet with the approval of the Supreme Council for National Reconstruction.

(5) The number of the Cabinet Members shall be neither more than fifteen (15) nor less than ten (10).

Article 15: Resignation en bloc of the Cabinet and removal of Cabinet Members.

(1) The Supreme Council for National Reconstruction may resolve resignation en bloc of the Cabinet by the concurring votes of not less than two-thirds of the Supreme Councilors duly seated.

(2) The Supreme Council for National Reconstruction may resolve a removal of a Cabinet Member by a majority vote of the Supreme Councilors duly seated.

Article 16: Explanation of Cabinet Members.

The Head of Cabinet and other Cabinet Members may attend the meetings of the Supreme Council for National Reconstruction and present their opinions.

Article 17: Control over the Executive Powers pertaining to the administration of Justice.

The major programs of the Executive Powers pertaining to the Administration of Justice shall be directed and controlled by the Supreme Council for National Reconstruction.

Article 18: Composition of the Supreme Court and Appointment of the Chief Justice and the Justices of the Supreme Court.

(1) The Supreme Court shall be composed of the Chief Justice and Justices.

(2) The Chief Justice and Justices shall be appointed by the

President upon the recommendation of the Supreme Council for National Reconstruction.

(3) The recommendation mentioned in the preceding paragraph shall be made by a majority vote of the Supreme Councilors duly seated.

Article 19: Appointment of Judges.

(1) Judges, other than those mentioned in the preceding Article, and the Director of the Office of Court Administration shall be appointed by the Chief Justice with the approval of the Supreme Council for National Reconstruction.

(2) The assignment of the judges including and higher than the Chiefs of District Courts shall be made by the Chief Justice with the approval of the Supreme Council for National Reconstruction.

Article 20: Appointment of Heads of Local Autonomous Bodies.

(1) The provincial governors, the Mayor of Seoul Special City, the mayor of a city with a population of not less than 150,000 inhabitants shall be appointed by the Cabinet with the approval of the Supreme Council for National Reconstruction.

(2) Heads of the local autonomous bodies, other than those mentioned in the preceding paragraph, shall be appointed by the provincial governors.

Chapter IV.   Miscellaneous Provisions

Article 21: Amendment of the Law regarding Extraordinary Measures for National Reconstruction.

The provisions of the Law may be amended with the motion by not less than ten (10) Supreme Councilors and by concurring votes of not less than two thirds of the Supreme Councilors duly seated.

Article 22: Special Law, Revolutionary Court and Revolutionary Prosecution Division.

(1) The Supreme Council for National Reconstruction may enact special laws in order to punish those who, prior to or after the May 16 Military Revolution, have perpetrated any anti-state or anti-national unjust acts, or counter-revolutionary activities.

(2) There may be established the Revolutionary Court and the Revolutionary Prosecution Division in order to dispose of the criminal cases prescribed in the preceding paragraph.

Article 23: Application Mutatis Mutandis.

(1) The Constitutional provisions on the National Assembly and the State Council shall apply mutatis mutandis of the Supreme Council for National Reconstruction and Cabinet respectively.

(2) The Ordinance of the State Council provided for in the Constitution shall be issued at the Ordinance of the Cabinet.

Article 24: Relationship with the Constitution.

The provisions of the Constitution which may conflict with the Law regarding Extraordinary Measures for National Reconstruction shall be governed by this Law.

Supplementary Provisions

1. This Law shall be in effect on and after the date of its promulgation.

2. The Supreme Council for National Reconstruction and the Cabinet in existence at the time of enforcement of this Law shall be regarded as having been constituted in accordance with this Law; and the Chairman and the Vice-Chairman of the Supreme Council for National Reconstruction, and the public officials and the managers of the Government-operated enterprises appointed by the Supreme Council for National Reconstruction or the Cabinet, shall be regarded as having been elected or appointed in accordance with this Law. Provided, however, that the concurrently assigned post in contravention of the provisions in the provision of paragraph 4, Article 4 of this Law, shall be relinquished within five days from the date of promulgation of this Law.

3. The decrees and proclamations of the Military Revolutionary Committee and of the Supreme Council for National Reconstruction at the time of enforcement of this Law shall have the same effect as this Law or the laws enacted pursuant thereto.

4. The judges and the Director of the Office of Court Administration at the time of enforcement of this Law shall continue in office until such time as their successors shall be appointed in accordance with the provisions of Article 18 or Article 19 of this Law.

5. All provisions concerning the Constitutional Court shall be suspended.

The Supreme Council
for National Reconstruction Law

Promulgated on June 10, 1961
Amended on July 3, and August 22, 1961
Law No. 618

Chapter I. Assembly and Organs

Article 1: Convocation.
A plenary meeting of the Supreme Council for National Reconstruction shall be convened whenever deemed necessary by the Chairman, or whenever requested by the Standing Committee or by eight or more Supreme Councilors.

Article 2: Sort of Committees.
The Supreme Council for National Reconstruction shall have a Standing Committee, Sub Committees and a Planning Committee, and may establish a Special Committee, if necessary.

Article 3: Standing Committee.
(1) The Standing Committee shall act for the Supreme Council for National Reconstruction in matters delegated by the Supreme Council.
(2) The Standing Committee shall be composed of the Chairman,

the Vice-Chairman of the Supreme Council and the chairman of the sub-committees.

Article 4: Standing Committee Chairman.

(1) The Chairman of the Supreme Council shall be the Standing Committee Chairman.

(2) In case of the absence of the Chairman, the Vice-Chairman shall act in his stead.

(3) In case of the absence of both the Chairman and Vice-Chairman, the oldest of the committee members shall act in their stead.

Article 5: Sub-Committees.

(1) The sub-committees and their jurisdiction shall be as follows:

1. Sub-Committee on Legislation and Justice:

(a) Matters pertaining to the jurisdiction of the Ministry of Justice and the Revolutionary Prosecution Division.

(b) Matters pertaining to the jurisdiction of the Secretariat of the State Council.

(c) Matters pertaining to the jurisdiction of the Inspection Commission.

(d) Matters pertaining to the judicial administration of the courts, court martial and Revolutionary Court.

(e) Matters pertaining to the review of the system, form, and wordings of law bills.

(f) Matters pertaining to the general administrative management.

(g) Matters pertaining to the jurisdiction of the Board of Audit.

(h) Matters not specifically pertaining to the jurisdiction of other sub-committees.

2. Sub-Committee on Home Affairs:

(a) Matters pertaining to the jurisdiction of the Ministry of Home Affairs.

(b) Matters pertaining to the jurisdiction of the Central Intelligence Agency.

(c) Matters pertaining to the jurisdiction of the Central Election Committee.

3. Sub-Committee on Foreign Affairs and National Defense:

(a) Matters pertaining to the jurisdiction of the Ministry of Foreign Affairs.

(b) Matters pertaining to the jurisdiction of the Ministry of National Defense.

(c) Matters pertaining to the jurisdiction of the Headquarters of the Joint Chiefs of Staff; Army, Navy, and Air Force Headquarters; and Marine Corps Command.

4. Sub-Committee on Finance and Economy:
   (a) Matters pertaining to the jurisdiction of the Ministry of Finance.
   (b) Matters pertaining to the jurisdiction of the Office of Monopoly.
   (c) Matters pertaining to the jurisdiction of the Office of Ex-Royal Property Custody.
   (d) Budget and Audit.
   (e) Matters related to the approval of reserve fund disbursement.
   (f) Matters pertaining to the jurisdiction of the Economic Planning Board.
   (g) Matters pertaining to the jurisdiction of the Office of Supply.
   (h) Matters pertaining to the jurisdiction of the Ministry of Agriculture and Forestry.
   (i) Matters pertaining to the jurisdiction of the Agricultural Research Institute.
   (j) Matters pertaining to the jurisdiction of the Ministry of Commerce and Industry.
   (k) Matters pertaining to the jurisdiction of the Office of Marine Affairs.
5. Sub-Committee on Transportation and Communications:
   (a) Matters pertaining to the jurisdiction of the Ministry of Transportation.
   (b) Matters pertaining to the jurisdiction of the Ministry of Communications.
6. Sub-Committee on Education and Social Welfare:
   (a) Matters pertaining to the jurisdiction of the Ministry-of-Education.
   (b) Matters pertaining to the jurisdiction of the Atomic Energy Institute.
   (c) Matters pertaining to the jurisdiction of the Academy of Science and the Academy of Arts.
   (d) Matters pertaining to the jurisdiction of the National Reconstruction Movement Headquarters.
   (e) Matters pertaining to the jurisdiction of the Ministry of Health and Social Welfare.
   (f) Matters pertaining to the jurisdiction of the Ministry of Public Information.
7. Sub-Committee on House Steering and Planning:
   (a) Matters related to the steering of the Supreme Council for National Reconstruction.
   (b) Matters related to the Supreme Council for National Re-

construction Law and the Supreme Council for National Reconstruction Regulations.

(c) Matters pertaining to the jurisdiction of the Secretariat of the Supreme Council for National Reconstruction.

(d) Matters pertaining to the jurisdiction of office of public information of the Supreme Council for National Reconstruction.

(e) Matters related to the Library of the Supreme Council for National Reconstruction.

(f) Matters pertaining to the jurisdiction of the Capital Defense Command.

(g) Matters pertaining to the jurisdiction of the Planning Committee of the Supreme Council for National Reconstruction.

(2) When the Executive branches have been newly established, abolished, or merged, or when otherwise deemed necessary, the Supreme Council may by virtue of its decision newly establish, abolish or merge its sub-committees and modify their respective jurisdiction.

Article 6: Functions of Sub-Committees.

(1) A sub-committee shall, in accordance with the provisions of the preceding Article, formulate basic policies of the State and examine measures and petitions, with regard to matters within the jurisdiction thereof.

(2) The Sub-Committee on Finance and Economy shall not increase the sum of the budget which has been decided by each sub-committee.

(3) A sub-committee may, with the approval of the Chairman of Supreme Council or the Chairman of Standing Committee, inspect the national administration within the jurisdiction thereof.

Article 7: Fixed Number of the Members of the Sub-Committee.

The fixed number of the members of the sub-committee shall be less than seven:

Provided that the fixed number of the members may be increased or decreased by the decision of the Supreme Council for National Reconstruction.

Article 8: Chairman of Sub-Committee.

Chairman of the sub-committee shall be appointed by the Chairman of the Supreme Council from among the Supreme Councilors with the approval of the Supreme Council upon the recommendation of the Chairman of Standing Committee.

Article 9: Advisory Members in the Sub-Committee.

(1) A sub-committee may have advisory members.

(2) Advisory members shall be commissioned by the Chairman

of Supreme Council upon the recommendation of the chairman of each sub-committee.

(3) Advisory members shall give advice upon the request by the Sub-Committee concerned.

(4) Advisory members may express views on the plenary meeting of the Supreme Council or Standing Committee by the decision of the Council or the Committee.

Article 10: Professional Staff Members, Etc.

(1) The sub-committee may have professional staff members and administrative personnel.

(2) Professional staff members shall be appointed by the Chairman of the Supreme Council upon the recommendation of the chairman of each sub-committee concerned.

(3) Professional staff members may express views at the plenary meeting of the sub-committee concerned.

Article 11: Planning Committee.

The Planning Committee shall conduct researches and studies relating to State Policies, and shall provide advice and suggestions to the Supreme Council under the control of the Standing Committee, sub-committees or special committees.

Article 12: Composition of Planning Committee.

The composition of the Planning Committee and other necessary matters thereof shall be made in accordance with the Regulation of the Supreme Council for National Reconstruction.

Article 13: Appointment of Planning Committee Chairman.

The Chairman of the Planning Committee shall be appointed by the Chairman of the Supreme Council from among the officers on active duty of the National Armed Forces with the approval of the Supreme Council for National Reconstruction.

Article 14: Planning Committee Members.

(1) Members of the Planning Committee shall be appointed or commissioned by the Chairman of the Supreme Council upon the recommendation of the Chairman of Planning Committee.

(2) Planning committee members may express views at the plenary meeting of the Supreme Council or other committee by its decision.

Article 15: Chairman of Special Committee.

The chairman of special committee shall be appointed by the Chairman of the Supreme Council from among the Supreme Councilors with the approval of the Supreme Council.

Article 16: Headquarters of National Reconstruction Movement.

(1) The Headquarters of National Reconstruction Movement

shall be established under the Supreme Council for the purpose of enhancing national movement for national reconstruction.

(2) The Headquarters of National Reconstruction Movement shall have one Director and other necessary staff personnel.

(3) Necessary matters pertaining to the provisions of the preceding two paragraphs shall be provided for otherwise by law.

Article 17: Appointment of Director, National Reconstruction Movement Headquarters.

The Director of the National Reconstruction Movement Headquarters shall be appointed by the Chairman of the Supreme Council with the approval of the Supreme Council for National Reconstruction.

Article 18: Central Intelligence Agency.

(1) A Central Intelligence Agency shall be established under the Supreme Council for the purpose of countering indirect aggression of the Communist forces and to remove obstacles to the execution of the revolutionary tasks.

(2) The Central Intelligence Agency shall have one Director and other necessary staff personnel.

(3) Necessary matters pertaining to the provisions of the preceding two paragraphs shall be provided for otherwise by law.

Article 18–II: Inspection Commission.

(1) An Inspection Commission shall be established under the Supreme Council for the purpose of inspecting illegality of public officials in carrying out their duty and administrative affairs.

(2) Necessary matters pertaining to the organization and functions of the Inspection Commission shall be provided for otherwise by law.

Article 19: Secretariat of the Supreme Council.

(1) A Secretariat of the Supreme Council shall be established to conduct the official business of the Supreme Council.

(2) A Secretariat of the Supreme Council shall have a Secretary-General and other necessary staff personnel.

(3) Necessary matters pertaining to the provisions of the preceding two paragraphs shall be provided for by the Regulation of the Supreme Council for National Reconstruction.

Article 20: Appointment of Secretary-General.

The Secretary-General of the Supreme Council shall be appointed by the Chairman of the Supreme Council with the approval of the Supreme Council for National Reconstruction.

Article 21: Duties of the Secretary-General.

The Secretary-General shall under the direction and supervision of the Chairman of the Supreme Council, conduct the official business of the Supreme Council, direct and supervise the officials under his jurisdiction.

Article 22: Office of Public Information.
(1) An Office of Public Information shall be established to administer the public information affairs of the Supreme Council for National Reconstruction.

(2) The Office of Public Information shall have one Director and other necessary staff personnel.

(3) Necessary matters pertaining to the provisions of the preceding two paragraphs shall be provided for by the Regulation of the Supreme Council for National Reconstruction.

Article 23: Capital Defense Command.
(1) The Supreme Council for National Reconstruction may set up a Capital Defense Command.

(2) Necessary matters pertaining to the provision of the preceding paragraph shall be provided for otherwise by law.

Article 24: Advisors.
The Chairman and the Vice-Chairman of the Supreme Council may have less than ten advisors as advisory organs respectively.

Chapter II. Meetings

Article 25: Quorum.
The Supreme Council for National Reconstruction shall sit with the attendance of majority of the Supreme Councilors duly seated.

Article 26: Proposal of Measure.
With support of not less than three Supreme Councilors, a Supreme Councilor may propose a measure.

Article 27: Presentation of a Budget Bill.
The Executive shall present a bill of budget stipulated in the Article 91 of the Constitution prior to the first day of November each year.

Article 28: Measure abolished at a Committee.
(1) A measure, upon which a sub-committee or special committee has decided not to report to the plenary meeting of the Supreme Council, shall not be put under discussion of the Supreme Council. Provided, however, that even such a measure should be submitted to the Supreme Council in case five or more Supreme Councilors, within five days after the date of report by the committee, so request.

(2) When there is no request set forth in the provision of the preceding paragraph, the measure shall be abolished.

Article 29: Non-deliberation of the same matters twice.
A rejected matter may not be deliberated again without the consent of ten or more Supreme Councilors.

Article 30: Motion for Revision.
(1) A motion for revision to a measure shall, under the joint signature of three or more Supreme Councilors, be presented in advance to the Chairman of Supreme Council for National Reconstruction. Provided, however, that a motion for revision to a budget bill shall require the support of not less than ten Supreme Councilors.

(2) A revision to a measure reported by a sub-committee after examination shall become a subject for discussion without seconding.

(3) A substitute for a measure shall be presented to the Chairman of the Supreme Council during the examination of an original measure in a sub-committee, and the Chairman shall refer the substitute to the said sub-committee.

Chapter III. Miscellaneous Provisions

Article 31: Formulation of Regulations.
The Supreme Council for National Reconstruction may formulate regulations concerning the internal rules and execution of business of the Supreme Council for National Reconstruction or its subsidiary organs.

Article 32: Assignment of Military Personnel and Other Public Officials.
The Chairman may request the Executive to send necessary military personnel and other public officials.

Article 33: Library of Supreme Council.
The Library provided for under Article 24, National Assembly Law, shall be deemed the Library of the Supreme Council for National Reconstruction.

Article 34: Application Mutatis Mutandis.
The provisions of the existing National Assembly Law. Administration Inspection Law, Law on Testimony and Expert Opinion at National Assembly and Service Regulations of National Assembly Secretariat shall apply mustatis mutandis insofar as they do not conflict with the provisions of this Law. Provided, however, that the number of personnel prescribed under Article 70, 102, (2) and 142 of National Assembly Law shall be three or more, and the number of personnel prescribed under Article 29, 139, 147 and 175 of the said law shall be five or more.

Supplementary Provisions

(1) This law shall be effective on and after the date of its promulgation.

(2) The committee chairman, committee members, advisors and other personnel already appointed for commissioned by the Supreme Council Chairman at the time of the promulgation of this Law shall be deemed to have been appointed or commissioned under this law.

(3) The personnel of the House of Representatives Secretariat and the House of Councilors Secretariat shall be deemed to have been dismissed simultaneously with the enforcement of this Law.

Supplementary Provision (July 3, 1961)

This law shall be effective on and after the date of its promulgation.

Supplementary Provision (August 22, 1961)

This law shall be effective on and after the date of its promulgation.

Appendix *3*

The Constitution of the Republic of Korea

Promulgated on July 17, 1948
Amended on December 26, 1962
Amended on October 21, 1969

Preamble

We, the people of Korea, possessing a glorious tradition and history from time immemorial, imbued with the sublime spirit of independence as manifested in the March 1st Movement in the year of Kimi (A.D. 1919), now being engaged in the establishment of a new democratic Republic on the basis of ideals as manifested in the April 19th Righteous Uprising and the May 16th Revolution, determined:

To consolidate national unity through justice, humanity and fraternity,

To eliminate outmoded social customs of all kinds,

To establish democratic institutions,

To afford equal opportunities to every person,

To provide for the fullest development of the capacity of each individual in all fields of political, social and cultural life,

To help each person discharge his duties and responsibilities,

To promote the welfare of the people at home and to strive to maintain permanent international peace and thereby to ensure the security, liberty and happiness of ourselves and our posterity eternally.

Do hereby amend, through national referendum, the Constitution, ordained and established on the Twelfth Day of July in the year of Nineteen Hundred and Forty Eight A.D., on this Twenty Sixth Day of December in the year of Nineteen Hundred and Sixty Two A.D.

Chapter I. General Provisions

Article 1.
(1) The Republic of Korea shall be a democratic Republic.
(2) The sovereignty of the Republic of Korea shall reside in the people and all state authority shall emanate from the people.

Article 2.
The conditions necessary for being a Korean national shall be determined by law.

Article 3.
The territory of the Republic of Korea shall consist of the Korean Peninsula and its accessory islands.

Article 4.
The Republic of Korea shall endeavor to maintain international peace and renounce all aggressive wars.

Article 5.
(1) Treaties duly ratified and promulgated in accordance with this Constitution and the generally recognized rules of international law shall have the same effect as that of the domestic law of the Republic of Korea.
(2) The status of aliens shall be guaranteed in accordance with international law and treaties.

Article 6.
(1) All public officials shall be servants of the entire people and shall be responsible to the people.
(2) The status and political impartiality of public officials shall be guaranteed in accordance with the provisions of law.

Article 7.
(1) The establishment of political parties shall be free and the plural party system shall be guaranteed.
(2) Organization and activities of a political party shall be democratic and political parties shall have necessary organizational arrangements to enable the people to participate in the formation of political will.
(3) Political parties shall enjoy the protection of the State. However, if the purposes or activities of political party are contrary to the basic democratic order, the Government shall bring action against it in the Supreme Court for its dissolution and the political party shall be dissolved in accordance with the decision of the Supreme Court.

Chapter II. Rights and Duties of the Citizen

Article 8.

All citizens shall have the dignity and value as human beings, and it shall be the duty of the State to guarantee fundamental rights of people to the utmost.

Article 9.

(1) All citizens shall be equal before the law and there shall be no discrimination in political, economic, social, or cultural life on account of sex, religion or social status.

(2) No privileged castes shall be recognized, nor ever be established in any form.

(3) The awarding of decorations or marks of honor in any form shall be effective only for recipients and no privileged status shall be created thereby.

Article 10.

(1) All citizens shall enjoy personal liberty. No person shall be arrested, detained, searched, seized, interrogated or punished except as provided by law, and shall not be subject to involuntary labor except on account of a criminal sentence.

(2) No citizen shall be subject to torture of any kind, nor shall be compelled to testify against himself in criminal cases.

(3) The warrant issued by a judge upon request from a prosecutor must be presented in case of arrest, detention, search or seizure. However, in case the criminal is apprehended *flagrante delicto* or in case where there is danger that a criminal, who committed a crime subject to imprisonment for three years or more in long term, may escape or destroy evidence, the investigating authorities may request an *ex post facto* warrant.

(4) All persons who are arrested or detained shall have the right to prompt assistance of counsel. When criminal defendant is unable to secure the same by his own efforts, the State shall assign a counsel to the use of the defendant as provided by law.

(5) All persons who are arrested or detained shall have the right to request the court for a review of the legality of the arrest or detention. When a person is deprived of personal freedom by other private individual, he shall have the right to request the court for a remedy.

(6) In case the confession of a defendant is considered to have been made against his will by means of torture, act of violence, threat, unduly prolonged arrest, deceit etc., or in case the confession of a defendant is the only evidence against him, such confession shall

not be admitted as evidence for his conviction nor shall he be punished on the basis of such a confession.

Article 11.
(1) No person shall be prosecuted for a criminal offense unless such act constitutes a crime prescribed by law at the time it was committed, nor shall he be placed in double jeopardy.
(2) No restrictions shall be imposed upon the political rights of any citizen nor shall any person be deprived of the property right by means of retroactive legislation.

Article 12.
All citizens shall have freedom of residence and of the change thereof.

Article 13.
All citizens shall have freedom of choice of occupations.

Article 14.
All citizens shall be free from violation of their residence. In case of search or seizure in the residence, the warrant of a judge must be presented.

Article 15.
The privacy of correspondence of all citizens shall be guaranteed.

Article 16.
(1) All citizens shall enjoy freedom of religion.
(2) No State religion shall be recognized, and religion and state shall be separated.

Article 17
All citizens shall enjoy freedom of conscience.

Article 18.
(1) All citizens shall have freedom of speech and press, and freedom of assembly and association.
(2) Licensing or censorship in regard to speech and press or permit of assembly and association shall not be recognized. However, censorship in regard to motion pictures and dramatic plays may be authorized for the maintenance of public morality and social ethics.
(3) The standard for publication installations of a newspaper or press may be prescribed by law.
(4) Regulation of the time and place of outdoor assembly may be determined in accordance with the provisions of law.
(5) The press or publication shall not impugn the personal honor or rights of an individual, nor shall it infringe upon public morality and social ethics.

Article 19.

(1) All citizens shall have freedom of science and arts.

(2) The rights of authors, inventors and artists shall be protected by law.

Article 20.

(1) The right of property of all citizens shall be guaranteed. Its contents and restrictions shall be determined by law.

(2) The exercise of property rights shall conform to public welfare.

(3) In case of expropriation, use or restriction of private property for public purposes, due compensation shall be paid in accordance with the provisions of law.

Article 21.

All citizens who have attained the age of twenty shall have right to elect public officials in accordance with the provisions of law.

Article 22.

All citizens shall have the right to hold public office in accordance with the provisions of law.

Article 23.

All citizens shall have the right to submit written petitions to any State authority in accordance with the provisions of law. The State authority shall be obliged to examine such petitions.

Article 24.

(1) All citizens shall have the right to be tried in conformity with the law by competent judges as qualified by the Constitution and law.

(2) Citizens who are not on active service or employees of the military forces shall not be tried in the court-martial except in case of espionage on military affairs and in case of crimes in regard to sentinel, sentry-posts, provision of harmful food, and prisoners of war as defined by law, and except when they are under an extraordinary state of siege in the territory of the Republic of Korea.

(3) All citizens shall have the right to speedy trial. The criminal defendant shall have the right to a public trial without delay in the absence of justifiable reason.

Article 25.

In case the criminal defendant under detention is found innocent, he shall be entitled to a claim against the State for compensation in accordance with the provisions of law.

Article 26.

In case a person has suffered damages by unlawful acts of public officials done in the exercise of their official duties, he may request for redress from the State or public entity; however, the public officials concerned shall not be exempt from liabilities.

Article 27.

(1) All citizens shall have the right to receive an equal education correspondent to their abilities.

(2) All citizens who have children under their protection shall be responsible for their elementary education.

(3) Such compulsory education shall be free.

(4) Independence and political impartiality of education shall be guaranteed.

(5) Fundamental matter pertaining to the educational system and its operation shall be determined by law.

Article 28.

(1) All citizens shall have the right to work. The State shall endeavor to promote the employment of workers through social and economic means.

(2) All citizens shall have the duty to work. The contents and conditions of the duty to work shall be determined by law in conformity with democratic principles.

(3) Standards of working conditions shall be determined by law.

(4) Special protection shall be accorded to the working women and children.

Article 29.

(1) Workers shall have the right to independent association, collective bargaining and collective action for the purpose of improving their working conditions.

(2) The right to association, collective bargaining, and collective action shall not be accorded to the workers who are public officials except for those authorized by the provisions of law.

Article 30.

(1) All citizens shall be entitled to a decent human life.

(2) The State shall endeavor to promote social security.

(3) Citizens who are incapable of making a living shall be protected by the State in accordance with the provisions of law.

Article 31.

All citizens shall be protected by the State for purity of marriage and health.

Article 32.

(1) Liberties and rights of the citizens shall not be ignored for the reason that they are not enumerated in the Constitution.

(2) All liberties and rights of citizens may be restricted by law

only in cases deemed necessary for the maintenance of order and public welfare. In case of such restriction, the essential substances of liberties and rights shall not be infringed on.

Article 33.
All citizens shall have the duty to pay taxes levied in accordance with the provisions of law.

Article 34.
All citizens shall have the duty to defend the national territory in accordance with the provisions of law.

Chapter III. Organs of Government

SECTION I. THE NATIONAL ASSEMBLY

Article 35.
The legislative power shall be exercised by the National Assembly.

Article 36.
(1) The National Assembly shall be composed of members elected by universal, equal, direct and secret elections of the citizens.

(2) The number of the members of the National Assembly shall be determined by law within the range of no less than one hundred and fifty and no more than two hundred and fifty persons.

(3) Any person desiring to become a candidate for the National Assembly shall be recommended by the political party to which he belongs.

(4) Matters pertaining to the election of the members of the National Assembly shall be determined by law.

Article 37.
The terms of office of the members of the National Assembly shall be four years.

Article 38.
A person shall lose his membership in the National Assembly during his tenure when he leaves or changes his party, or when his party is dissolved. However, the provisions of this article shall not apply in case of changes in party membership caused by amalgamation of parties or in case he has been expelled from his party.

Article 39.
No member of the National Assembly shall concurrently hold other public or private positions as determined by law.

Article 40.
All members of the National Assembly shall be prohibited from seeking, through abuse of their position, any rights or interests in

property or position, or from facilitating the securing of the same in behalf of others, by means of contract with, or disposition of, a State or public agency or any enterprise determined by law.

Article 41.
(1) During the sessions of the National Assembly, no member of the National Assembly shall be arrested or detained without the consent of the National Assembly except in case of *flagrante delicto.*

(2) In case of apprehension and detension of a member prior to the opening of the session, such member shall be released during the session upon the request of the National Assembly except in case of *flagrante delicto.*

Article 42.
Members of the National Assembly shall not he held responsible outside the National Assembly for opinions expressed or votes cast within the Assembly.

Article 43.
(1) A regular session of the National Assembly shall be convened once every year in accordance with the provisions of law.

(2) In case of extraordinary necessity, the Speaker of the National Assembly shall publicly notify the convocation of an extraordinary session of the National Assembly upon the request of the President or one-fourth or more of the members duly elected and seated.

(3) The period of regular session shall not exceed one hundred and twenty days and the extraordinary session thirty days.

Article 44.
The National Assembly shall elect one Speaker and two Vice Speakers.

Article 45.
Unless otherwise provided for in the Constitution or in law, the attendance of more than one half of the members duly elected and seated and concurrence of more than one half of the members present shall be necessary for decisions of the National Assembly. In case of a tie vote, the matter shall be considered to be rejected by the National Assembly.

Article 46.
The session of the National Assembly shall be open to the public. However, it may not be open when so decided upon with the concurrence of more than one half of the members present.

Article 47.
Bills and other subjects submitted to the National Assembly for deliberation shall not be abandoned for the reason that they are not

decided upon during the session. However, it shall be otherwise in case the tenure of the members of the National Assembly has expired.

Article 48.
Bills may be introduced by the members of the National Assembly or by the Executive.

Article 49.
(1) Each bill passed by the National Assembly shall be sent to the Executive and the President shall promulgate it within fifteen days.

(2) In case of objection to the bill, the President may, within the period referred to in the preceding paragraph, return it to the National Assembly with the written explanation of his objection, and may request its reconsideration. The President may do the same during the adjournment of the National Assembly.

(3) The President may not request the National Assembly to reconsider the bill in part or with proposed amendments.

(4) In case there is a request for reconsideration of a bill, the National Assembly shall reconsider it and if the National Assembly repasses the bill in the original form with the attendance of more than one half of the member duly elected and seated, and with concurrence of two-thirds or more of the members present, the bill shall become a law.

(5) If the President does not promulgate the bill or does not request the National Assembly to reconsider it within the period referred to in the first paragraph the bill shall become a law.

(6) The President shall without delay promulgate the law as determined in accordance with the foregoing paragraphs (4) and (5). If the President does not promulgate a law within five days after it has been determined under the foregoing paragraphs, or after it has been returned to the Executive under paragraph (4), the Speaker shall promulgate it.

(7) A law shall become effective twenty days after the date of promulgation unless otherwise stipulated.

Article 50.
(1) The National Assembly shall deliberate and decide upon the national budget.

(2) The Executive shall formulate the budget for each fiscal year and submit it to the National Assembly within one hundred and twenty days before the beginning of a fiscal year. The National Assembly shall decide upon the budget within thirty days before the beginning of the fiscal year.

(3) If the budget is not adopted within the period referred to in the foregoing paragraph, the Executive may, within the limit of revenue and in conformity with the budget for the previous fiscal

year, disburse the following expenditures until the adoption of the budget by the National Assembly:

1. The emoluments of public officials and basic expenditures for the conduct of administration.

2. Maintenance costs for agencies and institutions established by the Constitution or law and the obligatory expenditures provided by law.

3. Expenditures for continuous projects already provided in the budget.

Article 51.

(1) In case it shall be necessary to make continuous disbursements for a period of more than one fiscal year, the Executive shall determine the length of the period for such continuous disbursements. The continuous disbursements shall be approved by the National Assembly.

(2) The establishment of a reserve fund for unforeseen expenditures not provided in the budget or for any disbursement in excess of the budget shall be approved by the National Assembly in advance. The disbursement of the reserve fund shall be approved by the subsequent session of the National Assembly.

Article 52.

When it is necessary to amend the budget because of circumstances arising after the adoption of the budget, the Executive may formulate a supplementary revised budget and submit it to the National Assembly.

Article 53.

The National Assembly shall, without the consent of the Executive, neither increase the sum of any item of expenditure nor create new items of expenditure in the budget submitted by the Executive.

Article 54.

When the Executive plans to issue national bonds or to conclude contracts which may create financial obligation for the State outside the budget, it shall have the prior decision of the National Assembly.

Article 55.

The items and rates of all taxes shall be determined by law.

Article 56.

(1) The National Assembly shall have the right of concurrence to the ratification of treaties pertaining to mutual assistance or mutual security, treaties concerning international organizations, treaties of commerce, fishery, peace, treaties which shall cause a financial obligation for the State or nationals, treaties concerning the status of alien forces in the territory, or treaties related to legislative matters.

(2) The National Assembly shall also have right of concurrence to the declaration of war, to the dispatch of the armed forces to foreign states or to the stationing of alien forces in the territory of the Republic of Korea.

Article 57.

The National Assembly may inspect the administration of the State, demand the production of necessary documents, the appearance of a witness in person, and the furnishing of testimony or opinions. However, the National Assembly shall not interfere with judicial trial, or criminal investigation in process or prosecution.

Article 58.

The Prime Minister, the State Council members and Representatives of the Executive may attend meetings of the National Assembly or its committees to report on the state of administration or to state opinions and answer questions, and upon request from the National Assembly, its committees, or from more than thirty members of the National Assembly, they shall appear in any meeting of the National Assembly and answer questions.

Article 59.

(1) The National Assembly may advise the President the removal of the Prime Minister or any State Council member.

(2) The advice of the preceding paragraph shall have the concurrence of more than one half of the members of the National Assembly duly elected and seated.

(3) When the advice referred to in paragraphs (1) and (2) is submitted, the President shall agree thereto unless there is special reason to be otherwise.

Article 60.

(1) The National Assembly may establish rules concerning its agenda and internal regulations, provided they are not contrary to law.

(2) The National Assembly shall review the qualification of its members and take disciplinary action against its members.

(3) The concurrence of two-thirds or more of the members of the National Assembly duly elected and seated shall be required for the expulsion of any member.

(4) No action shall be brought to court with regard to the disposition under paragraphs (2) and (3).

Article 61.

(1) In case the President, the Prime Minister, Cabinet members, Head of the Executive Ministry, Judges, members of the Central Election Committee, members of the Board of Audit and Inspection and other public officials designated by law have violated this Con-

stitution or other laws in the exercise of their duties, the National Assembly shall have power to pass motions for their impeachment.

(2) The motion for impeachment, pursuant to the preceding paragraph, shall be proposed by thirty members or more of the National Assembly. The vote of more than one half of the members of the National Assembly duly elected and seated shall be necessary to institute impeachment. Provided, that the motion of an impeachment against the President shall be proposed by fifty members or more of the National Assembly, and the concurrence of a two-thirds or more of the members of the National Assembly duly elected and seated shall be required to an impeachment against the President.

(3) Any person against whom impeachment has been instituted shall be suspended from exercising his power until the impeachment has been tried.

Article 62.

(1) An Impeachment Council shall be established to try impeachment.

(2) The Impeachment Council shall be composed of the Chief Justice of the Supreme Court, who shall serve as Chairman, three justices of the Supreme Court, and five members of the National Assembly. However, in case of trial for impeachment of the Chief Justice, the Speaker of the National Assembly shall become the Chairman of the Council.

(3) The concurrence of six or more members of the Impeachment Council shall be required for the decision on impeachment.

(4) The decision on impeachment shall not cause other than dismissal from public position. However, it shall not exempt the impeached person from civil or criminal liability.

(5) Matters pertaining to the impeachment trial shall be determined by law.

SECTION II. THE EXECUTIVE

1. The President

Article 63.

(1) The executive power shall be vested in an Executive Branch headed by a President.

(2) The President shall represent the State vis-a-vis foreign states.

Article 64.

(1) The President shall be elected by a universal, equal, direct and secret ballot of the people. However, in case of vacancy in the office of the President with remaining term of two years or less, the President shall be elected by the National Assembly.

(2) Citizens who are qualified to be elected to the National Assembly and who, on the date of the Presidential election, shall have

resided continuously within the country for five years or more and have attained the age of forty years or more, shall be eligible to be elected to the Presidency. In this case, the period during which a person is dispatched overseas on official duty shall be considered as a period of domestic residence.

(3) Any person desiring to become a Presidential candidate shall be recommended by the political party to which he belongs.

(4) Matters pertaining to the Presidential election shall be determined by law.

Article 65.

(1) When more than one Presidential candidate have received the highest number of votes in the popular Presidential election, they shall be voted by the National Assembly in open session attended by more than one half of the members of the National Assembly duly elected and seated, and the person receiving a plurality shall be elected the President.

(2) When there shall be only one Presidential candidate, he shall not be elected unless he has received a one-third or more votes of total number of electors.

Article 66.

(1) In case of the election of the President by the National Assembly, the person who receives a two-thirds or more votes of the members of the National Assembly attended by two-thirds or more of its members duly elected and seated shall be elected the President.

(2) If no person shall receive the number of votes referred to in the preceding paragraph, a second voting shall be conducted and if no person shall receive the same number of votes referred to in the preceding paragraph, and there was only one person with the highest votes, a final voting shall be conducted between the person with the highest votes and one with next highest votes, or between the persons with the highest votes in case there were more than one person with the highest votes, and the person who shall receive a majority of votes in such election shall be elected the President.

Article 67.

(1) The President shall be elected within seventy to forty days before the term of the incumbent President expires.

(2) In case of vacancy in the office of the President, an election shall be held immediately. The same shall apply in case the President-elect dies, or loses his qualification as President due to decisions of the court or other reasons.

Article 68.

(1) Before the President assumes his office he shall take the following oath: "I do solemnly swear before the people that I shall

observe the Constitution, defend the State, promote freedom and welfare of the people and shall faithfully execute the duties of the office of the President."

(2) The members of the National Assembly and justices of the Supreme Court shall witness the Presidential oath referred to in the preceding paragraph.

Article 69.

(1) The term of the office of the President shall be four years.

(2) In case of vacancy in the office of the President, the successor shall hold office during the remaining term of his predecessor.

(3) No President shall be elected more than three terms consecutively.

Article 70.

In case of vacancy in the Office of the President or of his inability to perform his duties, the Prime Minister and the members of the State Council in consecutive orders as determined by law shall act as the President.

Article 71.

The President shall conclude and ratify treaties, accredit, receive or dispatch diplomatic envoys, declare war and conclude peace.

Article 72.

(1) The President shall exercise supreme command of the National Armed Forces in accordance with the provisions of the Constitution and law.

(2) The organization and formation of the National Armed Forces shall be determined by law.

Article 73.

(1) When in time of civil war, in a dangerous situation arising from foreign relations, in case of natural calamity or on account of a grave economic or financial crisis, it is necessary to take urgent measures for the maintenance of public safety and order, the President shall have power to take minimum necessary financial and economic dispositions and to issue ordinances having the effect of law, provided, however, that the President shall exercise such power only when it is not possible to convene the National Assembly in time.

(2) The President shall have power to issue ordinances having the effect of law only when it is necessary for the national security under the state of armed hostilities, and when it is not possible to convene the National Assembly in time.

(3) The ordinances or dispositions set forth in paragraphs (1) and (2) shall be reported without delay to the National Assembly for approval.

(4) If the approval referred to in the preceding paragraph is not obtained, such ordinances or dispositions shall lose their effect there-

after. However, any law, revised or repealed by such ordinances, shall be duly reinstated from the time they were disapproved by the National Assembly.

(5) The President shall announce to the public without delay the circumstances and reasons in connection with paragraphs (1) and (2).

Article 74.

The President may issue Presidential ordinances concerning matters that are within the scope specifically delegated by law and that are required for the enforcement of law.

Article 75.

(1) The President shall, in time of war, armed conflict, or similar national emergency when there is a military necessity or when it is necessary to maintain the public safety and order by mobilization of the military forces, proclaim a state of siege in accordance with the provisions of law.

(2) The state of siege shall consist of an extraordinary state and a precautionary state.

(3) Under the proclaimed state of siege, special measures may be taken, in accordance with provisions of law, with regard to the warrant system, freedom of speech, press, assembly and association, or with regard to the rights and the powers of the Executive or the Judiciary.

(4) The President shall immediately notify the National Assembly of the proclamation of state of siege.

(5) When the National Assembly so requests, the President shall lift the proclaimed state of siege.

Article 76.

The President shall appoint public officials in accordance with the provisions of the Constitution and law.

Article 77.

(1) The President may grant amnesty, commutation and rehabilitation in accordance with the provisions of law.

(2) In granting general amnesty, the President shall receive the consent of the National Assembly.

(3) Matters pertaining to amnesty, commutation, and rehabilitation shall be determined by law.

Article 78.

The President shall award decorations and other honors in accordance with the provisions of law.

Article 79.

The President may attend and address the National Assembly or express thereto his view by written message.

Article 80.

The acts of the President in accordance with law shall be executed by written document, and all such documents shall be countersigned by the Prime Minister and the members of the State Council concerned. The same shall apply to the military affairs.

Article 81.

The President shall not hold concurrently the offices of the Prime Minister, the State Council, the head of any Executive Ministry, or other official and private positions as determined by law nor engage in private business.

Article 82.

The President shall not be charged with criminal offence during his tenure of office except for insurrection or treason.

2. The State Council

Article 83.

(1) The State Council shall deliberate on important policies that fall within the power of the Executive.

(2) The State Council shall be composed of the President, the Prime Minister, and the members of the State Council whose number shall be no more than twenty and no less than ten.

Article 84.

(1) The Prime Minister shall be appointed by the President, and members of the State Council shall be appointed by the President upon the proposal of the Prime Minister.

(2) No military personnel shall be appointed as the Prime Minister or a member of the State Council unless he has retired from active service.

(3) The Prime Minister may recommend to the President the removal of members of the State Council from office.

Article 85.

(1) The President shall be the Chairman of the State Council.

(2) The Prime Minister shall assist the President and shall be the Vice Chairman of the State Council.

Article 86.

The following matters shall be referred to the State Council for deliberation:

(1) Basic plans on State affairs, and general policies of the Executive;

(2) Declaration of war, conclusion of peace and other important matters pertaining to foreign policy;

(3) Proposed treaties, legislative bills, proposed ordinances of the President;

(4) Proposed budgets, closing accounts, basic plan on disposal of

State properties, conclusion of contract creating financial obligation for the State, and other important financial matters;

(5) Proclamation and termination of a state of siege;

(6) Important military affairs;

(7) Matters pertaining to the request for convening the extraordinary sessions of the National Assembly;

(8) Awarding of honors;

(9) Granting of amnesty, commutation and rehabilitation;

(10) Matters regarding the determination of jurisdiction between Executive Ministries;

(11) Basic plans concerning delegation or allocation of powers within the Executive;

(12) Evaluation and analysis of the administration of the State affairs;

(13) Formulation and coordination of important policies of each Executive Ministry;

(14) An action for the dissolution of a political party;

(15) Examination of petitions pertaining to executive policies submitted or referred to the Executive;

(16) Appointment of the Prosecutor General, the Presidents of the National Universities, Ambassadors, the Chief of Staff of each armed service, Marine Corps Commandant, diplomatic ministers, other public officials designated by law, and the managers of important State-operated enterprises;

(17) Other matters presented by the President, the Prime Minister or a State Council member.

Article 87.

(1) The National Security Council shall be established to advise the President on the formulation of foreign military and domestic policies related to the national security prior to their deliberation by the State Council.

(2) The meeting of the National Security Council shall be presided over by the President.

(3) The organization, the scope of functions, and other matters pertaining to the National Security Council shall be determined by law.

3. The Executive Ministries

Article 88.

Heads of Executive Ministries shall be appointed by the President from among the State Council members upon the proposal of the Prime Minister.

Article 89.

The Prime Minister shall supervise, under orders of the President, the Executive Ministers in their administration.

Article 90.

The Prime Minister or the head of each Executive Ministry may, under the delegation of powers by law or Presidential ordinances, or *ex officio,* issue ordinances of the Prime Minister or the concerning matters that are within their jurisdiction.

Article 91.

The establishment, organization, and the scope of functions of each Ministry shall be determined by law.

4. The Board of Inspection

Article 92.

The Board of Inspection shall be established under the President to inspect the closing accounts of revenues and expenditures, the account of the State and other organizations as determined by law, and to inspect the administrative functions of the executive agencies and public officials.

Article 93.

(1) The Board shall be composed of no less than five and no more than eleven members including its Chairman.

(2) The Chairman of the Board shall be appointed by the President with the approval of the National Assembly. The term of the tenure of the Chairman shall be four years, and he may be reappointed only for one more consecutive term.

(3) In case of vacancy in the office of the Chairman, the tenure of a successor shall be the remaining period of the predecessor.

(4) The members of the Board shall be appointed by the President upon the proposal of the Chairman for a period of four years, and may be reappointed consecutively as determined by law.

Article 94.

The Board of Inspection shall inspect the closing accounts of the revenues and expenditures every year, and report the results to the President and the National Assembly in the following year.

Article 95.

The organization of the Board, the scope of functions, the qualifications of the members of the Board, the range of the public officials subject to inspection, and other necessary matters shall be determined by law.

SECTION III. THE COURTS

Article 96.

(1) The judicial power shall be vested in courts composed of judges.

(2) The courts shall be composed of the Supreme Court, which

is the highest court of the State, and other courts at specific levels.

(3) The qualifications for judges shall be determined by law.

Article 97.

(1) Departments may be established within the Supreme Court.

(2) The number of judges for the Supreme Court shall be less than sixteen.

(3) The organization of the Supreme Court and lower courts shall be determined by law.

Article 98.

The judges shall judge independently according to their conscience and in conformity with the Constitution and law.

Article 99.

(1) The Chief Justice of the Supreme Court shall be appointed by the President with consent of the National Assembly upon the proposal of the Judge Recommendation Council. Upon the proposal of the Council, the President shall request the National Assembly for its consent and shall appoint the Chief Justice after consent of the National Assembly has been obtained.

(2) Justices of Supreme Court shall be appointed by the President upon the proposal of the Chief Justice after he has secured the consent of the Judge Recommendation Council. If such a proposal is submitted, the President shall appoint the proposed person.

(3) Judges other than the Chief Justice and justices of the Supreme Court shall be appointed by the Chief Justice through the decision of the Council of the Supreme Court Justices.

(4) The Judge Recommendation Council shall be composed of four judges, two lawyers, one professor of law nominated by the President, the Minister of Justice and the Prosecutor General.

(5) Matters pertaining to the Judge Recommendation Council shall be determined by law.

Article 100.

(1) The tenure of the Chief Justice shall be six years and he shall not serve a consecutive term.

(2) The tenure of judges shall be ten years and they may be reappointed in accordance with the provisions of law.

(3) The judges shall retire from office at the age of sixty-five.

Article 101.

(1) No judge shall be dismissed from office by impeachment or criminal punishment, nor shall he be suspended from office or his salary reduced, or suffer from other unfavorable measures, except through disciplinary actions.

(2) In event a judge is unable to discharge his duty because of

mental or physical deficiencies, he may be removed from office in accordance with the provisions of law.

Article 102.
(1) The Supreme Court shall have the power to make final review of the constitutionality of a law when its constitutionality is prerequisite to trial.
(2) The Supreme Court shall have the power to make final review of the constitutionality or legality of administrative orders, regulations or dispositions, when their constitutionality or legality is prerequisite to trial.

Article 103.
Any decision to dissolve a political party shall have the concurrence of a three-fifths or more of the duly authorized number of justices of the Supreme Court.

Article 104.
The Supreme Court may establish, within the scope of law, procedures pertaining to judicial proceedings, internal rules and regulations on routine administrative matters of the courts.

Article 105.
Trials and decisions of the courts shall be open to the public; however, trials may be closed to the public by a court's decision when there is a possibility that such trials may disturb the public safety and order or be harmful to decent customs.

Article 106.
(1) Court-martial may be established as special courts to exercise jurisdiction over military trials.
(2) The Supreme Court shall have the final appellate jurisdiction over the courts-martial.
(3) The military trials under an extraordinary state of siege may be limited to the original jurisdiction only in case of crimes of soldiers and civilian employees of the armed forces, in case of espionage on military affairs, and crimes as defined by law in regard to sentinels, sentry-post, provision of harmful food, and prisoners of war.

SECTION IV. ELECTION MANAGEMENT

Article 107.
(1) Election Management Committees shall be established for purpose of fair management of elections.
(2) The Central Election Management Committee shall be composed of two members appointed by the President, two members elected by the National Assembly, and five members elected by the Council of Supreme Court Justices. The Chairman of the Committee shall be elected from among its members.

(3) The terms of office of the committee members shall be five years and it may be renewed by consecutive reappointment.

(4) The members of the Committee shall not join political parties nor shall they participate in political activities.

(5) No members shall be dismissed except through impeachment or criminal punishment.

(6) The Central Election Management Committee may, within the limit of laws and ordinances, establish regulations pertaining to the management of elections.

(7) The organization, the scope of functions and other necessary matters of the Election Management Committees of each level shall be determined by law.

Article 108.

(1) Election campaigns shall be conducted under the management of the Election Management Committees of each level within the limit determined by law. Equal opportunity shall be guaranteed.

(2) The expenditures incident to the elections shall not be borne by political parties or candidates except where otherwise provided for in the law.

SECTION V. LOCAL SELF-GOVERNMENT

Article 109.

(1) Local self-government bodies shall deal with matters pertaining to the welfare of local residents, manage properties, and may establish, within the limit of laws and ordinances, rules and regulations regarding local self-government.

(2) The kinds of local self-government bodies shall be determined by law.

Article 110.

(1) A local self-government body shall have a council.

(2) The organization, powers and the election of the members of the local councils, the methods of election for the heads of local self-government bodies, and other matters pertaining to the organization and operation of such bodies shall be determined by law.

Chapter IV. The Economy

Article 111.

(1) The economic order of the Republic of Korea shall be based on the principle of respect for freedom and creative ideas of the individual in economic affairs.

(2) The State shall regulate and coordinate economic affairs within the limit necessary for the realization of social justice and for the development of a balanced national economy to fulfil the basic living requirements of all citizens.

Article 112.

License to exploit, develop or utilize mines, and all other important underground resources, marine resources, water power, natural powers, available for economic use may be granted for limited periods in accordance with the provisions of law.

Article 113.

Agricultural tenancy shall be prohibited in accordance with the provisions of law.

Article 114.

The State may impose restrictions or obligations necessary for the efficient utilization of the farm and forest land in accordance with the provisions of law.

Article 115.

The State shall encourage the development of cooperatives founded on the self-help spirit of the farmers, fishermen, and the small and medium businessmen, and shall guarantee their political impartiality.

Article 116.

The State shall encourage the foreign trade, and shall regulate and coordinate it.

Article 117.

Private enterprises shall not be transferred to the State or public ownership nor shall their management be controlled or administered by the State except in cases determined by law to meet urgent necessities of national defense or national economy.

Article 118.

(1) An Economic and Scientific Council shall be established to advise the President on the formulation of important policies concerning the development of national economy and promotion of the science for the purpose of such development prior to their deliberation by the State Council.

(2) The President shall preside over the Economic and Scientific Council.

(3) The organization, the scope of functions, and other necessary matters of Economic and Scientific Council shall be determined by law.

Chapter V. Amendments to the Constitution

Article 119.

(1) A motion to amend the Constitution shall be introduced either by one-third or more of the members of the National Assembly

duly elected and seated or by the concurrence of five hundred thousands or more of the voters eligible for the election of the members of the National Assembly.

(2) Proposed amendments to the Constitution shall be announced by the President to the public for more than thirty days.

Article 120.

(1) The National Assembly shall decide upon proposed amendments to the Constitution within sixty days of its public announcement.

(2) The decision on a proposed amendment to the Constitution shall require the concurrence of two-thirds or more of the members of the National Assembly duly elected and seated.

Article 121.

(1) After an amendment to the Constitution has been adopted, it shall be submitted to a national referendum within sixty days and shall receive the affirmative votes of more than one half of votes cast by more than one half of all voters eligible to vote for the election of the members of the National Assembly.

(2) When the proposed amendment to the Constitution has received the affirmative votes referred to in the preceding paragraph, the Constitution shall be thus amended, and the President shall promulgate the amendment immediately.

SUPPLEMENTARY RULES

Article 1.

(1) This Constitution shall come into force on the date of the first convocation of the National Assembly which is constituted pursuant to this Constitution. However, the enactment of the necessary legislation for the enforcement of this Constitution, the elections of the President and the members of the National Assembly pursuant to this Constitution, and other preparations, may be carried out prior to the enforcement of this Constitution.

(2) The Law Regarding the Extraordinary Measures for National Reconstruction shall lose its effect upon the coming into force of this Constitution.

Article 2.

The first general elections for the President and the members of the National Assembly and the first convocation of the National Assembly pursuant to this Constitution shall take place within one year from the date of the promulgation of this Constitution. The term of the President, and the members of the National Assembly thus elected, shall begin from the date of the first convocation of the National Assembly and end on June 30, 1967.

Article 3.
The law, orders and treaties pursuant to the Law Regarding the Extraordinary Measures for National Reconstruction shall remain in force to the extent not incompatible with this Constitution.

Article 4.
(1) The Special Law Regarding the Punishment of Special Crimes, the Law for the Punishment of Those Involved in Fraudulent Elections, the Law Regarding the Purification of Political Activities, and the Law Regarding the Disposition of Illicit Profiteering and other laws related thereto shall remain in force, and no objection thereto shall be raised.
(2) The Law Regarding the Purification of Political Activities, the Law Regarding the Disposition of Illicit Profiteering and other laws related thereto shall not be amended or abolished.

Article 5.
The trials, the budget or disposition pursuant to the Law Regarding the Extraordinary Measures for National Reconstruction, or pursuant to the orders and decrees on the basis of the Law, shall remain in force and shall not be brought to court action on account of this Constitution.

Article 6.
The public officials and the staffs of enterprises appointed by the government at the time of coming into force of this Constitution shall be considered to have been appointed pursuant to this Constitution. However, the public officials, for whom the method of selection has been changed by this Constitution shall perform their functions until the successors are selected in accordance with this Constitution.

Article 7.
(1) The organs which are, at the time of coming into force of this Constitution, performing the functions belonging to the jurisdiction of the organs to be newly established pursuant to this Constitution shall continue to perform their functions until the new organs are established under this Constitution.
(2) The organs to be newly established pursuant to the Constitution shall be organized within one year after the coming into force of this Constitution.
(3) The time of the establishment of the first local councils pursuant to this Constitution shall be determined by law.

Article 8.
The number of the members of the National Assembly after the recovery of the national territory shall be separately determined by law.

Article 9.

The orders of the President, the orders of the State Council, and the cabinet ordinances existing at the time of the coming into force of this Constitution shall be considered to be the Presidential ordinances issued pursuant to this Constitution. Supplementary Rules and this Constitution shall come into force on the date of promulgation.

BIBLIOGRAPHY

Documentary Materials and Government Publications

Bank of Korea. *Bank of Korea Statistics.* Seoul: Bank of Korea, 1961, 1962.

Hanguk Hyŏngmyŏng Chaep'an Sa P'yŏnch'an Wiwonhoe. *Hanguk hyŏngmyŏng chaep'ansa* [*Records of the Korean Revolutionary Tribunal*]. Vols. I, II, III. Seoul: Dong-A Sŏjŏk Co., 1963.

Hanguk Kukka Chaegŏn Ch'oego Hoeui. *Military Revolution in Korea.* Seoul: The Secretariat, Supreme Council for National Reconstruction, 1961.

Hanguk Kunsa Hyŏngmyŏng Sa P'yŏnch'an Wiwonhoe. *Hanguk kunsa hyŏngmyŏngsa* [*Records of the Korean Military Revolution*]. Vols. I and II. Seoul: Dong-A Sŏjŏk Co., 1963.

Korea Exchange Bank. *Monthly Report*, Vols. I, II, III. Seoul: Korea Exchange Bank, 1967, 1968, 1969.

Kunsa Hyŏngmyŏng Sa P'yŏnch'an Wiwonhoe. *May 16 Kunsa hyŏngmyŏng ui chŏnmo* [*A Complete Study of the May 16 Military Revolution*]. Seoul: Moonkwangsa, 1964.

Minju Hanguk Hyŏngmyŏng Ch'ŏngsa P'yŏnch'an Wiwonhoe. *Minju Hanguk hyŏngmyŏng ch'ŏngsa* [*History of the Korean Democratic Revolution*]. Seoul: n. p., 1963.

Republic of Korea. *Haenjŏng paeksŏ* [*Administrative White Paper*]. Seoul: Kwangmyŏng Printing Co., 1962.

Republic of Korea, Department of National Defense. *Kukpangbusa* [*The History of the Department of National Defense*]. Seoul: Sungkwang Printing Co., 1956.

————. *ROK Armed Forces*, Vols. I and II. Seoul: Ministry of National Defense, 1955, 1957.

Republic of Korea, Economic Planning Board. *Cheich'a kyŏngje kaebal ogaenyŏn keihoekan* [*The Second Five-Year Economic Development Plan*]. Seoul: Economic Planning Board, 1966.

————. *Summary of the First Five-Year Economic Plan, 1962–66*. Seoul: Economic Planning Board, 1966.

————, National Assembly. *Taehan minguk kukhoe sipyŏnji* [*The Ten-Year History of the National Assembly*]. Seoul: T'aesong Printing Co., 1959.

————, Office of Planning and Coordination. *Cheilch'a kyŏngje, Kaepal ogenyŏn keihoek chunggan p'yŏngka* [*Interim Evaluation of the First Five-Year Economic Development Plan*]. Seoul: Samwha Printing Co., 1965.

————, Office of Public Information. *Hyŏngmyŏng chŏnpu ch'ilgaewolganui ŏpjŏk* [*Accomplishments of the Revolutionary Government in the First Seven Months*]. Seoul: Samwha Printing Co., 1962.

————. *Hyŏngmyŏng wansurŭl wihan uri kugmin ui nagalgil* [*The People's Path to the Fulfillment of the Revolutionary Task*]. Seoul: Office of Public Information, 1962.

————. *Park Chung-hee deachang chŏnyŏpsik ui yŏnsŏl* [*General Park Chung-hee: His Address at His Retirement Ceremony*]. Seoul: Office of Public Information, 1963.

————. *Uri chŏngbu neun muŏtsŭl ŏttŏkke haewatneunga?* [*How and What our Government Accomplished?*]. Seoul: Office of Public Information, 1964.

————, (ROK Army), Office of Information, Headquarters. *Republic of Korea Army*. Vol. II. Seoul: ROK Army, 1956.

Tewksbury, Donald G., compiler. *Source Materials on Korean Politics and Ideologies*. New York: Institute of Pacific Relations, 1950.

United Nations. *U.N. Economic Bulletin for Asia and the Far East*. Vols. 9,10,14, and 15. New York: United Nations, 1958–1963.

U.S. Department of State. *The Conference at Yalta and Malta: 1945*. Washington, D.C.: Government Printing Office, 1955.

————. *Korea: 1945–1948*. Far Eastern Series 28. Washington, D.C.: Government Printing Office, 1948.

————. *Korea's Independence*. Far Eastern Series 18. Washington, D.C.: Government Printing Office, 1947.

————. *The Record of Korean Unification: 1943–1960*. Far Eastern Series 101. Washington, D.C.: Government Printing Office, 1960.

U.S. Senate. *Asia*. Washington, D. C.: Government Printing Office, 1959.

————. *The United States and the Korean Problem, 1943–54.* Washington, D.C.: Government Printing Office, 1955.

World Peace Foundation. *Documents on American Foreign Relations, 1944–1945.* Norwood, Mass.: World Peace Foundation, 1947.

Biographical and Statistical Yearbooks

Haptong yŏngam, 1961 [*Haptong Almanac*]. Seoul: Haptong News Agency, 1962.

Japan, Foreign Ministry. *Kendai chosen zinmei ziten* [*Biographical Dictionary of Modern Koreans*]. Tokyo: Sekai Janarusha, 1962.

Korea Annual, 1964, 1965, 1966, 1967. Seoul: Haptong News Agency, 1965, 1966, 1967, 1968.

Books

An, Chae-hong. *Hanminjok ui kibon chillo* [*The Basic Course for the Korean People*]. Seoul: Choyang sa, 1947.

An, Tong-il, and Hong Ki-kwon. *Kijŏk kwa hwansang: 4.19 haksaeng undongji* [*Miracle and Illusion: April 19 Student Movement*]. Seoul: Yangshin munwha sa, 1960.

Andrezewski, Stanislaw. *Military Organization and Society.* London: Routledge & Paul, 1954.

Arendt, Hannah. *On Revolution.* New York: The Viking Press, 1963.

Berger, Carl. *The Korea Knot: A Military-Political History.* Philadelphia: University of Pennsylvania Press, 1957.

Black, Cyril E., and Thomas P. Thornton, eds. *Communism and Revolution.* Princeton: Princeton University Press, 1964.

Brinton, Crane. *Anatomy of Revolution.* New York: W. W. Norton & Company, 1938.

Byas, Hugh. *Government by Assassination.* New York: Alfred A. Knopf, 1945.

Ch'ae, Kun-sik. *Mujang toknip undong p'isa* [*A Hidden History of the Military Independence Movements*]. Seoul: Republic of Korea, Office of Public Information, 1956.

Chang, Do-bin. *Hanguk toknipsa wa toknip undong chisa* [*The History of the Korean Independence Movement and Its Patriots*]. Seoul: Kukawon, 1954.

Cho, Dŏk-song, ed. *Sawŏl hyŏngmyŏng* [*The April Revolution*]. Seoul: Changwon sa, 1960.

Chŏnsa P'yŏnch'an Wiwonhoe. *Hanguk Chŏnjaengsa: Haebang kwa Kŏngun* [*History of the Korean War: Liberation and Creation of an Army*]. Seoul: Bochinje, 1967. Vol. 1.

Chorley, Katharine C. *Armies and the Art of Revolution.* London: Faber, 1943.

Clark, Mark W. *From the Danube to the Yalu*. New York: Harper & Brothers, 1954.

Colegrove, Kenneth W. *Militarism in Japan*. New York: World Peace Foundation, 1936.

Conroy, Hilary. *The Japanese Seizure of Korea*. Philadelphia: University of Pennsylvania Press, 1961.

Council on Foreign Relations. *The United States in World Affairs*, *1951, 1953, 1955, 1960, 1961, 1962*. New York: Harper & Brothers, 1952, 1954, 1956, 1960, 1961, 1962, 1963.

Dallet, Charles. *Traditional Korea*. New York: Human Relations Area Files, 1954.

Dean, Vera M., and H. D. Harootunian. *Builders of Emerging Nations*. New York: Rinehart & Winston, 1961.

Dooran, J. V., ed. *Armed Forces and Society*. The Hague: Mouton, 1968.

Deutsch, Carl, and W. J. Foltz, eds. *Nation-building*. New York: Atherton Press, 1966.

Evans, M. Filmer. *The Land and People of Korea*. New York: Macmillan Co., 1963.

Farely, Marian Southwell. *Korea and World Politics*. Toronto: Canadian Association for Adult Education, 1950.

Finer, S. E. *Man on Horseback: The Role of the Military in Politics*. New York: Frederick A. Praeger, 1962.

————, ed. *The Military in the Middle East: Problems in Society and Government*. Columbus: Ohio State University Press, 1962.

Fredericks, Carl J., et al. *American Experience in Military Government in World War II*. New York: Rinehart & Winston, 1948.

Gayn, Mark. *Japan Diary*. New York: Sloan, 1948. Pages 347–443, 490–91, and 505–10 deal with Korea.

Grajdanzev, Andrew Janah. *Korea Looks Ahead*. New York: American Council, Institute of Pacific Relations, 1944.

————. *Modern Korea: Her Economic and Social Development Under the Japanese*. New York: Institute of Pacific Relations, 1944.

Grant, Meade E. *American Military Government in Korea*. New York: King's Crown Press, 1951.

Hagan, Everett E. *On the Theory of Social Change*. Homewood, Ill.: Dorsey Press, 1962.

Ham, Sŏk-hŏn, et al. *Hanguk hyŏngmyŏng ui panghyang* [*Direction of the Korean Revolution*]. Seoul: Chung-ang kongron sa, 1961.

Han, Hong-gŏn. *Kaiho kara konnichi madeno kangogu no chempo* [*Prospects of Korea from the Day of Liberation to Today*]. Tokyo: Tachibana Shobe, 1953.

Han, T'ae-soo. *Hanguk chŏngdangsa* [*A History of Korean Political Parties*]. Seoul: Shint'a yangsa, 1961.

Han, T'ae-yŏn. *Kukka chaegŏn pisang choch'ipŏb* [*The Law Re-*

garding Extraordinary Measures for National Reconstruction].
Seoul: Pŏbmun sa, 1961.

Hanna, Willard A. Eight Nation Makers: Southeast Asia's Charismatic Statesmen. New York: St. Martin's Press, 1964.

Henderson, Gregory. Korea: The Politics of Vortex. Cambridge, Mass.: Harvard University Press, 1968.

Howard, Michael, ed. Soldiers and Government: Nine Studies in Civil-Military Relations. Bloomington: Indiana University Press, 1959.

Huntington, Samuel P. The Soldier and the State: The Theory and Politics of Civil-Military Relations. Cambridge, Mass.: Harvard University Press, 1957.

————, ed. The Changing Patterns of Military Politics. Glencoe, Ill.: Free Press of Glencoe, 1962.

Hurewitz, J. C. Middle East Politics: The Military Dimension. New York: Frederick A. Praeger, 1969.

Janowitz, Morris. The Military in the Political Development of New Nations: An Essay in Comparative Analysis. Chicago: University of Chicago Press, 1964.

Johnson, John J., ed. The Role of the Military in Underdeveloped Countries. Princeton: Princeton University Press, 1962.

Kang, Chin-hwa. Taehan minguk kŏnguk sipyŏnji [A Ten-Year History of Korean Nationhood]. Seoul: Kangmun sa, 1956.

Karpat, Kemal H. Turkey's Politics: The Transition to a Military-Party System. Princeton: Princeton University Press, 1959.

Khan, F. M. The Story of the Pakistan Army. Karachi, Pakistan: Oxford University Press, 1963.

Kim, Chin-hak, and Han Ch'ŏl-yŏng. Chaehŏn kukhoesa [A History of the Constituent National Assembly]. Seoul: Shinjo Publishing Co., 1954.

Kim, Chong-shin. Seven Years with Korea's Park Chung-hee. Seoul: Hollym Corp., 1967.

Kim, C. I. Eugene, ed. The Patterns of Korean Politics. Kalamazoo, Mich.: Western Michigan University, 1964.

Kim, Rin-sŏh. Mangmyŏng noin Rhee Syngman paksa rŭl pyŏnhoham [In Defense of Syngman Rhee]. Pusan, Korea: Samhyup inshaeso, 1960.

Lasswell, Harold D. National Security and Individual Freedom. New York: McGraw-Hill, 1950.

Lattimore, Owen. Manchuria: Cradle of Conflict. New York: The Macmillan Co., 1935.

Lee, Chong-sik. The Politics of Korean Nationalism. Berkeley: University of California Press, 1963.

Lee, Sŏn-kŭn. Hanguk doknip undongsa [The History of the Korean Independence Movement]. Seoul: Sangmum won, 1956.

Lee, Won-soon. *Ingan: Syngman Rhee* [*A Human: Syngman Rhee*]. Seoul: Shintai-yang-sa, 1965.

Lenczowski, George. *The Middle East in World Affairs*. 3rd ed. Ithaca: Cornell University Press, 1962.

Lerner, Daniel. *The Passing of Traditional Society*. New York: Free Press, 1958.

Lieuwen, Edwin. *Arms and Politics in Latin America*. New York: Frederick A. Praeger, 1960.

Lyons, Gene M. *Military Policy and Economic Aid: The Korean Case, 1950–53*. Columbus: Ohio State University Press, 1954.

Ma, Han. *Hanguk chŏngch'i ui ch'ong pip'an* [*A Critique of Korean Politics*]. Seoul: Hanguk chongch'i yŏnguwon, 1959.

McCune, George M. *Korea's Postwar Political Problems*. New York: Institute of Pacific Relations, 1947. Submitted by the International Secretariat as the document for the Tenth Conference of the Institute of Pacific Relations, in England, September 1947.

―――. *Korea Today*. Cambridge, Mass.: Harvard University Press, 1950.

―――, and J. A. Harrison. *Korean-American Relations*. Berkeley: University of California Press, 1951. Vol. I.

McCune, Shannon. "Korea." In *The State of Asia*, edited by Lawrence K. Rosinger. New York: Alfred A. Knopf, 1951.

―――. *Korea: The Land of Broken Calm*. New York: D. Van Nostrand, 1966.

MacIver, Robert M. *The Modern State*. New York: Oxford University Press, 1964.

―――. *The Web of Government*. New York: Macmillan Co., 1947.

McKinley, Silas Bert. *Democracy and Military Powers*. New York: Vanguard Press, 1954.

M.I.T., The Center of International Studies. *United States Foreign Policy: Social and Political Change in the Underdeveloped Countries and Its Implication for United Policy*. Study no. 10. Washington, D.C.: Government Printing Office, 1960.

Moon, In-kyu. *Shinkukka boanpŏb gaeron* [*The New National Security Law and Its Interpretation*]. Seoul: Shinhung Publishing Co., 1959.

Nelson, Melvin Frederick. *Korea and the Old Orders in Eastern Asia*. Baton Rouge: Louisiana State University Press, 1945.

Oh, John K. C. *Democracy on Trial*. Ithaca: Cornell University Press, 1968.

Oliver, Robert T. *Syngman Rhee: The Man Behind the Myth*. New York: Dodd, Mead & Co., 1954.

―――, ed. *Korea's Fight for Freedom*. Seoul: Korea Pacific Press, 1951.

Onish, Seido. *Minami chosen: Assei no aegu minshu* [*South Korea: People Striving Under Misrule*]. Tokyo: Dokushosa, 1959.
Park, Chung-hee. *Kukka wa hyŏngmyŏng kwa na* [*Nation, Revolution and I*]. Seoul: Hangmun sa, 1963.
————. *Our Nation's Path: Ideology of Social Reconstruction.* Seoul: Dong-A Publishing Co., 1962.
Pye, Lucian W. *Aspects of Political Development.* Boston: Little, Brown & Company, 1966.
————. *Politics, Personality, and Nation Building.* New Haven: Yale University Press, 1962.
Reeves, W. David. *The Republic of Korea.* London: Oxford University Press, 1963.
Riggs, Fred W. *Administration in Developing Countries: The Theory of Prismatic Society.* Boston: Houghton Mifflin Co., 1964.
Rustow, Dankwart. *The Military in Middle Eastern Society and Politics.* Washington, D.C.: The Brookings Institution, 1962.
Sawyer, Robert. *Military Advisors in Korea: KMAG in Peace and War.* Washington, D.C.: Office of the Chief of Military History, 1962.
Schurmann, Franz. *Ideology and Organization in Communist China.* Berkeley: University of California Press, 1966.
Shin, Won-shik. *Taehan Kukkun paldalsa* [*The History of the Development of the Republic of Korea Army*]. Seoul: Tongwon munwha sa, 1959.
Stamps, Normal L. *Why Democracies Fail: A Critical Evaluation of the Causes for Modern Dictatorship.* South Bend: Notre Dame University Press, 1957.
Suh, Byŏng-cho. *Jukwonja ui chŭng'ŏn: Hanguk daeui chŏngch'isa* [*A Testimony by a Sovereign: A History of a Representative Government*]. Seoul: Moumsa, 1964.
Torrey, Gordon H. *Syrian Politics and the Military, 1945–1958.* Columbus: Ohio State University Press, 1963.
Vagts, Alfred. *A History of Militarism: Civilian and Military.* London: Oxford University Press, 1959.
Vatikiotis, P. J. *The Egyptian Army in Politics.* Bloomington: Indiana University Press, 1963.
Von der Mehden, Fred R. *Politics of the Developing Nations.* Madison: University of Wisconsin Press, 1964.
Weiker, Walter F. *The Turkish Revolution, 1960–1961: Aspects of Military Politics.* Washington, D.C.: Brookings Institution, 1963.
Whang, Dong-chun. *Minjujuiwa gŭui unyŏng* [*Democracy and Its Operation*]. Seoul: Hanil Munwha sa, 1962.
Yang, U-jong. *Yi daet'ongnyŏng kŏnguk inyŏm* [*Political Philosophy of President Rhee in His Efforts in Founding the Nation*]. Seoul: Yŏnhap shinmun sa, 1949.

Yi, Ki-ha. *Hanguk chŏngdang paldalsa* [*A History of Korean Political Party Development*]. Seoul: Uihoe chongchisa, 1961.
Yu, Cha-choo. *Choson minju sasangsa* [*History of Democratic Ideas in Korea*]. Seoul: Chosen kumyung chohap yonhaphoe, 1949.

Articles

Allen, R. C. "South Korea: The New Regime," *Pacific Affairs*, XXXIV, no. 1 (Spring 1961), 54–57.
"Atlantic Report on Korea," *Atlantic Monthly*, CCVI, no. 2 (August 1960), 14.
Baldwin, Roger N. "Blunder in Korea," *Nation*, CLXV (August 1947), 119–221.
Barr, J. M. "Second Republic of Korea," *Far Eastern Survey*, XXIX, no. 9 (September 1960), 129–32.
Bertsch, Leonard M. "Korea Partition Prevents Economic Recovery," *Foreign Policy Bulletin*, XXVIII, no. 16 (January 28, 1949), 3–4.
Bradner, Stephen. "Korea: Experiment and Instability," *Japan Quarterly*, VIII, no. 4 (October/December 1961), 412–20.
Briggs, Walter. "The Military Revolution in Korea and Its Leader and Achievement," *Koreana Quarterly*, V, no. 2 (Summer 1963), 17–34.
"Chairman Unanimously Nominated Presidential Candidate: General Park Expresses Willingness to Run on DRP Ticket," *Korean Report*, III, no. 4 (June 1963), 3–4.
Chatterjee, B. R. "The Role of the Armed Forces in Politics in Southeast Asia," *International Studies*, II (January 1961), 22–33.
Cho, Ga-kyŏng. "Hyŏngmyŏng chuch'ae ui chŏngsinjŏk honmi" ["Spiritual Confusion of the Main Body of the Revolution"] *Sasangge Monthly*, IX, no. 4 (April 1961), 70–79.
Cho, Ji-hoon. "Tradition of the Korean Thought," *Koreana Quarterly*, II, no. 1 (Spring 1960), 72–84.
Cho, Soon-sung. "The Failure of American Military Government in Korea," *Korean Affairs*, II, nos. 3–4 (1963), 331–47.
Ch'oi, Ho-chin. "Major Problems Involved in the Program," *Korean Affairs*, I, no. 1 (March/April 1962), 1–6.
Ch'oi, Mun-hwan. "The Path to Democracy: A Historical Review of the Korean Economy," *Koreana Quarterly*, III, no. 1 (Summer 1961), 52–71.
Ch'oe, Sok-che. "Daet'ongnyŏng sŏngŏjonui punsŏk" ["An Analysis of the Presidential Elections"], *Sasangge Monthly*, XI, no. 11 (November 1963), 35–45.
———. "Kunsa hyŏngmyŏng chŏkchŏp" ["The Legacy of Military Revolution"], *Sasangge Monthly*, XI, no. 4 (April 1963), 72–77.

Clippinger, Morgan E. "The Development of Modernized Elites in Korea Under Japanese Occupation," *Asiatic Research Bulletin,* VI, no. 6 (September 1963), 1–11.

Douglas, William A. "Korean Students and Politics," *Asian Survey,* III, no. 12 (December 1963), 584–95.

Earle, David M. "Korea: The Meaning of the Second Republic," *Far Eastern Survey,* XXIX, no. 11 (November 1960), 169–75.

Emerson, Rupert. "The Erosion of Democracy," *Journal of Asian Studies,* XX, no. 1 (November 1960), 1–8.

Hahm, Pyŏng-ch'oon. "Korea's 'Mendicant Mentality'?: Critique of United States Policy," *Foreign Affairs,* XLIII, no. 1 (October 1964), 165–74.

Han, Dong-sŏb. "Saehŏnpŏbŭl pip'anhanda" ["A Critique of the New Constitution"], *Sasangge Monthly,* X, no. 12 (December 1962), 56–58.

Han, P'yo-wook. "Trials of Democracy in Korea," *Vital Speeches,* XIX, no. 16 (June 1, 1953), 495–98.

Han, T'ae-soo. "A Review of Political Party Activities in Korea: 1953–1954," *Korean Affairs,* I, no. 4 (1962), 413–27.

———. "A Review of Political Party Activities in Korea: 1955–1960," *Korean Affairs,* II, nos. 3–4 (1963), 318–330.

Hong, I-sŏb. "Revolution and Democracy in Korea," *Koreana Quarterly,* III, no. 1 (Summer 1961), 11–17.

———. "Sawŏl hyŏngmyŏng ui chaep'yongka" ["Reapraisal of the April Revolution"], *Sasangge Monthly,* IX, no. 4 (April 1961), 54–59.

Huang, Sung-mo. "Whither the Revolution in Korea?" *Korean Affairs,* II, no. 1 (1963), 44–50.

Inmulge Sa, "Hyŏngmyŏng chidoja: Park Chung-hee ron" ["On a Revolutionary Leader: Park Chung-hee"], *Inmulge,* Special ed., V, no. 10 (November 1961).

Kahin, George M., Guy J. Pauker, and Lucian W. Pye. "Comparative Politics of Non-Western Countries," *American Political Science Review,* XLIX, no. 4 (December 1955), 1022–41.

Kang, I-sŏp. "Yuksa p'alkisaeng" ["The 8th Class of the Military Academy"], *Shindong-A* (September 1964), pp. 170–98.

Kang, Man-gil. "The Modernization of Korea From the Historical Point of View," *Asiatic Research Bulletin,* VI, no. 1 (March 1963), 1–6.

Kim, C. I. Eugene. "Patterns in the 1967 Korean Election," *Pacific Affairs,* XLI, no. 1 (Spring 1968), 60–70.

———. "Significance of the 1963 Korean Elections," *Asian Survey,* IV, no. 3 (March 1964), 765–73.

———. "South Korean Constitutional Development: The Meaning of the Third Constitution," *Papers of the Michigan Academy of Science, Arts and Letters,* XLIX (1964), 301–12.

Kim, C. I. Eugene, and Kim Ke-soo. "The April 1960 Korean Student Movement," *The Western Political Quarterly*, XVII, no. 1 (March 1964) 83–92.

Kim, Dong-ch'ŏl. "Korean Newspapers: Past and Present," *Korean Report*, II, no. 9 (November/December 1962), 10–12.

Kim, Dong-ki. "The Five-Year Plan and the Problem of Capital Formation," *Koreana Quarterly*, V, no. 2 (Summer 1963), 84–122.

Kim, Ha-ryong. "The Modernization of Korean Politics," *Asiatic Research Bulletin*, VI, no. 8 (November 1963), 1–6.

Kim, Kyu-t'aek. "The Behavior Patterns of the Rulers and the Ruled in Korean Politics," *Korean Affairs*, I, no. 3 (1962), 319–26.

Kim, Myŏng-whoi. "The Presidential Election in Korea, 1963," *Korean Affairs*, II, nos. 3–4 (1963), 372–78.

Kim, Se-Jin. "Korea's Involvement in Vietnam and Its Political and Economic Impact," *Asian Survey*, X, no. 6 (June 1970), 519–33.

———. "Moral Imperative in Political Development: A Caveat to the Park Regime in Korea," *Asian Forum*, I, no. 3 (October 1969), 43–45.

Kim, Sŏng-t'ae. "May 16 ihuui ch'ŏngnyŏn simni" ["The Mental Attitude of the Youth Since May 16"], *Sasangge Monthly*, XI, no. 5 (May 1963), 214–21.

Kim, Yu-t'aek. "The Economic Plan and Foreign Investment," *Korean Affairs*, I (March/April 1962), 39–43.

Lasswell, Harold. "The Garrison State," *American Journal of Sociology*, XLVI, no. 4 (January 1941), 455–68.

Lauterback, Richard E. "Hodge's Korea," *Virginia Quarterly Review*, XXIII, no. 3 (June 1947), 349–68.

Lee, Hyo-chai. "The Korean's Understanding of Democracy," *Korean Affairs*, II, no. 13 (1962), 12–19.

Lee, Chong-sik. "Voting Behavior in Korea," *Korean Affairs*, II, nos. 3–4 (1963), 348–61.

Lee, Pun-sŏk. "Saeroun uihoe minju ch'ŏngch'iui gil" ["The New Path for Representative Democracy"], *Sasangge Monthly*, XI, no. 6 (June 1963), 37–43.

Liem, Channing. "United States Rule in Korea," *Far Eastern Survey*, XVIII, no. 7 (April 6, 1949), 77–80.

Lovell, John P., et al. "Recruitment Patterns in the Republic of Korea: Military Establishment," *Journal of Comparative Administration*, I, no. 4 (February 1970), 428–54.

———. "Professional Orientation and Policy Perspectives of the Military Professional in the Republic of Korea," *Midwest Journal of Political Science*, XIII, no. 3 (August 1969), 415–38.

McCune, George M. "Occupation Politics in Korea," *Far Eastern Survey*, XIII, no. 3 (February 1946), 33–37.

McCune, Shannon. "The Thirty-eighth Parallel in Korea," *World Politics*, I (1949), 223-32.

"Minjujui wa kunsa hyŏngmyŏng" ["Democracy and Military Revolution"] *Sasangge Monthly*, IX, no. 6 (June 1961), 4.

"Nation's First Referendum Approves New Constitution," *Korean Report*, II, no. 10 (November/December 1962), 3.

"New Basic Law Builds Foundation for Stable, Strong Third Republic," *Korean Report*, II, no. 9 (November/December 1962), 4-8.

Oh, Byŏng-hun. "Hanguk minjujui ui chongch'irul wihayo" ["For the Process of Korean Democracy"], *Sasangge Monthly*, V, no. 5 (May 1962), 32-39.

Padover, S. K. "Korean Drama," *Reporter*, XXII, no. 11 (May 26, 1960), 20-21.

Park, Chong-bong. "Ideology of the Korean Peoples' Life," *Korean Affairs*, I, no. 4 (1962), 381-89.

Park, Chung-hee. "What Has Made the Military Revolution Successful?" *Koreana Quarterly*, III, no. 1 (Summer 1961), 18-27.

Park, Yong-ki. "Trade Unionism in Korea," *Free Labor World*, XLI (January 1963), 11-15.

Parr, E. Joan. "Korea: Its Place in History," *Political Quarterly*, XXIII, no. 4 (October/December 1952), 352-67.

Pauker, Guy J. "Southeast Asia As a Problem Area in the Next Decade," *World Politics*, X, no. 2 (January 1959), 325-45.

"Political Prospects in Korea: Symposium," *Nation*, CLXXIV, no. 6 (February 9, 1952), 132-34.

Reischauer, E. O., Kim Choon-yŏp, and Lee Man-gap. "Innae mani minjujuirŭl chik'inda" ["Only Patience Protects Democracy"], *Sasangge Monthly*, VIII, no. 12 (December 1960), 210-17.

Rustow, Dankwart A. "The Army and Founding of the Turkish Republic," *World Politics*, X, no. 4 (July 1959), 513-52.

Scalapino, R. A. "Korea: The Politics of Change," *Asian Survey*, III, no. 1 (January 1963), 31-40.

Scalapino, R. A., and Lee Chong-sik. "The Origin of the Korean Communist Movement, I and II," *Journal of Asian Studies*, XX, no. 1 and no. 2 (November 1960 and February 1961), 9-32 and 149-68.

Shin, Do-sŏng. "Ch'ong bip'an minjudang" ["A Critique of the Democratic Party"], *Sasangge Monthly*, IV, no. 2 (February 1956), 301-12.

Shin, Sang-ch'o. "Hangukŭn mingukida" ["Korea is a Republic"], *Sasangge Monthly*, XI, no. 3 (March 1963), 106-11.

———. "Minjujuinŭn sach'iin'ga ["Is Democracy a Luxury?"], *Sasangee Monthly*, X, no. 5 (June 1962), 40-51.

Sunoo, Harold W. "The Possibility of 'Koreanic Democracy,'" *Korea Journal*, I, no. 1 (September 1961), 5.

Tai, S. Y. "Wither Korea?" *Current History*, XXVII, no. 159 (November 1954), 298–306.

Tak, Hee-jun. "Early Trade Unions in Korea: 1919–1950," *Korean Affairs*, I (March/April, 1962), 75–80.

————. "Minjujui ui chungdanŭn ŏbda" ["Democracy Cannot be Interrupted"], *Sasangge Monthly*, XI, no. 3 (March 1963), 111–23.

Tchah, Kyun-hi. "Through the Periscope: A View of the Korean Economy," *Koreana Quarterly*, VI, no. 2 (Summer, 1963), 123–29.

Wagner, Edward W. "Failure in Korea," *Foreign Affairs*, XL, no. 1 (October 1961), 128–35.

————. "Korean Modernization: Some Historical Considerations," *Korea Journal*, I, no. 3 (January 1963), 22–29.

Warner, Denis. "Korea Without Rhee," *Reporter*, XXIII (September 1960), 23–27.

Weems, Clarence N. "Korea: Dilemma of an Underdeveloped Country," *Foreign Policy Association Headline Series*, no. 1441 (November/December 1960).

————. "South Korea's Continuing Problem," *Foreign Policy Bulletin*, XXXIX, no. 18 (June 1960), 137–38, 143.

Wolf, Charles, Jr. "Economic Planning in Korea," *Asian Studies*, II (December 1962), 22–28.

Yi, Gou-zea. "Some Organizational Characteristics of the DRP of Korea," *Koreana Quarterly*, X, no. 1 (Spring 1969), 75–91.

Yi, Kuk-chan. "Chŏngch'ijŏk mukwansim kwa minjujui ui wiki" ["Political Apathy and the Crisis of Democracy"], *Sasangge Monthly*, IX, no. 4 (April 1961), 60–69.

Yu, Chin-o. "Korean Democracy Under Overlapping Attacks," *Koreana Quarterly*, III, no. 1 (Summer 1961), 1–10.

Yu, Kwang-yul. "Minju kukmindang ui komin" ["The Agony of the Democratic National Party"], *Shinch'unji*, VIII, no. 1 (April 1953), 4–27.

Yu, Tal-yŏung. "The National Reconstruction Movement in Retrospect and Prospect," *Korean Affairs*, I, no. 3 (1962), 291–99.

Unpublished Material

Berger, Morroe. "Military Elite and Social Change: Egypt Since Napoleon." Mimeograph No. 60. Princeton: The Center of International Studies, 1960.

Bradburn, N. M. "The Managerial Role in Turkey: A Psychological Study." Ph.D. dissertation, Harvard University, 1960.

Cravan, John. "Members of ROK's Ruling Junta and Their Associates." SAIS, Johns Hopkins University, 1963.

Johnson, Chalmers A. "Revolution and Social System." Paper presented to the Annual Meeting of the American Political Science Association, September, 1963, in New York, N. Y.

Kim, Han-kyo. "The Demise of the Kingdom of Korea: 1882–1910." Ph.D. dissertation, University of Chicago, 1962.

Rivlin, Benjamin. "Some Observations on the Concept of Political Systems in the Study of Developing States." Paper presented to the Annual Meeting of the American Political Science Association, September, 1964, in New York, N. Y.

INDEX

A

Administrative democracy, 109–10, 124, 133. *See also* Democracy

Agriculture, 90–91, 106, 110, 119

Anticommunism, 11–12, 22–23, 30, 33–35, 93, 100, 108, 120, 176; Anticommunist Act, 145. *See also* Communism

Antirevolutionary movements. *See* Counterrevolutionary cases

Armed forces. *See* Republic of Korea Army; Military, Korean

Asian and Pacific Cooperation (ASPAC), 137

B

Buddhism, 5, 64

Bureaucracy: under Japanese, 6–7, 21; under Rhee, 20–21; under Park, 165–66

C

Capitalism, 119, 122

Central Intelligence Agency (CIA), 102, 129, 156, 175; creation of, 111–12; on counterrevolutionary elements, 102, 112–17; "Four Major Cases of Grave Suspicion" and political fund-raising, 116, 118, 129; on civil liberties, 145–48

Ch'a, Col. Chi-ch'ŏl, 163

Ch'ae, Maj. Gen. Pyŏng-dŏk, 44, 46

Chang, Lt. Gen. Do-young, 46, 58n, 84, 88–89, 93–95; chairman of the Military Revolutionary Council, 93–99, 104n; liquidation of, 112–17

Chang, Hsueh-liang, 53

Chang, John M., 18, 35, 52, 83; as Premier, 27; as party chief and political organizer, 28; failure of, 29; handling of unification issue, 33–34; involvement with the military, 60, 83–85; overthrow of, 98–99, 165. *See also* Chang government

Chang, Tso-lin, 53

Chang government, 19, 27, 91, 96–97; instability of, 27; involvement with military, 80–86; overthrow of, 30, 98–99

Cheju Island incident, 55

China: Imperial, 5; relations with Japan, 54

Cho, Maj. Gen. Si-hyŏng, 163

Ch'oe, Nueng-jin, 16n